THE QUIET HERO

THE QUIET HERO

Figures of Temperance in Spenser,
Donne, Milton, and Joyce

Richard Douglas Jordan

The Catholic University of America Press
Washington, D.C.

Publication of this book has been funded in part by a gift from the
Associates of The Catholic University of America Press.

820.9
J82q

LIBRARY OF CONGRESS CATALOGING-IN-PUBLICATION DATA

Jordan, Richard (Richard Douglas)
    The quiet hero : figures of temperance in Spenser, Donne, Milton,
and Joyce / by Richard Douglas Jordan.
      p.   cm.
    Bibliography: p.
    Includes index.
    1. English literature—History and criticism.   2. Heroes in
literature.   3. Temperance (Virtue) in literature.   4. Spenser,
Edmund, 1552?–1599—Characters—Heroes.   5. Donne, John, 1572–1631—
Criticism and interpretation.   6. Milton, John, 1608–1674—
Characters—Heroes.   7. Joyce, James, 1882–1941—Characters—
Heroes.   I. Title.
PR409.H5J6   1989
820'.9'352—dc19   88-25775
ISBN 0–8132–0671–5

Contents

v

Preface

Literary study has become so politicized in recent years that it is no longer enough for a critic simply to get on with the business of applying his methods to a text; he must first announce his preconceptions and argue for the validity of his practice, and the critical-theoretical camp with which he identifies may well be a determining factor in whether or not his work is taken seriously.

The following studies of literary heroes who are symbolic figures of temperance constitute unrepentant exercises in historical criticism, though they are by no means free of an interest in literary theory—particularly renaissance theory. They examine a phenomenon that has recently been of considerable interest to modern literary theory: non-mimetic characterization. One ignores one's enemy at one's peril, but in this particular study I have come to believe that there are aspects of contemporary literary theory that can be of real use to the literary historian without, as is often the case, appearing to undermine the very principles on which conventional scholarship is based.

The methods and concerns of post-structuralist criticism have at least had the advantage of offering readers new ways of looking at narratives that lie outside the mimetic traditions of the eighteenth- and nineteenth-century novel. They have thus helped to clear the way for better understandings of the symbolic techniques of allegorical romances such as Spenser's *Faerie Queene*.

Post-structuralist criticism developed out of the demands being made upon readers by the post-modernist "new novel" and offered a valuable way of making such texts readable. Recent attempts to apply these theories to earlier narratives, however, have been much less successful. Such approaches could, I believe, be of greater value were they freed from the a-historical and anti-humanist ideological positions that lie behind them. What would be left of post-structuralist criticism in such a case is an open question, but at least one of the things to survive would be an ability to approach characters in narratives and poems from the Middle Ages and the Renaissance without the necessity of employing the language and concepts of realism.

The fullest and most recent statement of contemporary theory about characterization is Thomas Docherty's doctoral thesis, *Reading (Absent) Character,* published as a book by the Clarendon Press.[1] Docherty draws together and synthesizes much recent thought on characterization and then attempts to generalize these theories in order to apply them not only to post-modernist fiction, but also to the mimetic novel. He reads characters in earlier fiction almost as if they too were part of the *nouveau roman.* In making this attempt to re-read older novels in a post-structuralist way, Docherty must necessarily destroy the binary opposition between mimetic and post-modern narratives that other critics have used as a foundation for their theories. He then must find a new bogey to stand in opposition to what he sees as of value in fiction. He identifies this new antithesis and enemy as pre-eighteenth-century allegory. However, in order to accomplish this change, he trivializes allegory in his theoretical statements, and reads actual allegories in the most simplistic ways possible.

According to Docherty, allegory produces single, stable meanings in characters who have signpost-like names such as Obstinate or Pliable, names that tell all the reader needs to know about them. Against this, and with an implied evolutionary view of the history and development of characterization in fiction, Docherty offers what he describes as "a theory which will not translate characters into their unproblematical essences" (p. xii).

As those of us who spend a good deal of time reading allegorical works know, simplistic readings of Bunyan do not provide a basis for understanding what a writer like the Gawain Poet intends in his multiple and complex presentation of the Green Knight, what Chaucer means to indicate about the moral and spiritual significance of Griselda in the *Clerk's Tale,* or what Spenser is signifying in his Red Crosse Knight, Guyon, or any other of his heroes and heroines. The notion of a single, stable significance in an allegorical character is in fact inappropriate for almost any major figure in these allegorical narratives. Only those briefly mentioned personifications who occupy the background of some allegories might be seen to fit such a description, though even they seldom have the kind of separate individuality attributed to allegorical figures by Docherty. Rather, they establish their meanings and their place in a narrative by means of thematic, psychological, or other links to the major characters. Indeed, these minor personifications are often simply aspects of the larger, more complex allegorical figures, without any individual existence at all beyond that of the narrative technique that created them as figures with names.

Rather than being opposed to the methods of allegorical characterization, much of what Docherty says about the multiple and shifting natures of post-modernist characters, about their freedom from the conventions of psychological realism, about their positional importance in narrative, and about their changing relationships to the reader, could be found to apply much more readily to allegorical romances than to eighteenth- and nineteenth-century novels. In these elements of its treatment of characterization, the *nouveau roman* is very old indeed.

In his study, Docherty argues for a theory that will be able to take into account "the possibility of change or mobility in the meaning of character (and equally of the writer and reader) as the text is reproduced in the reading" (p. xiv). The character, in recent fiction, rather than being a discrete entity to which we as readers discover a relationship, is instead a fragmentary, unstable "subject," often anonymous. Instead of a fixed selfhood, such a character is "a series of subjectivities."

The meaning of such characters is determined solely by what they do. There is no attempt in these novels to create a sense of depth through a narrator's analysis or initial description. Rather than being anything stable or static, meaning, according to Docherty, here becomes "a dynamic process, the configurations produced through the series of positional interrelations between character and reader" (p. 11). Such description of characters as does exist within the work is metaphorical. Docherty agrees with Robbe-Grillet that "characters must exist only at the level of the symbol, of the discourse itself" (p. 28), though the world in which the symbol exists does not extend beyond the novel itself. Docherty repeatedly stresses the ways in which the new fiction manipulates the responses and perspectives of the reader rather than offering stability, the ways in which the reader is actively involved in the creation of meaning. In such fiction, characters may have multiple identities, names cannot be taken as reliable indices, and the voice of the narrator has no authority. Instead, narration is impersonal and de-centered, and the time in which characters live ceases to be historical time and becomes instead an eternal present.

Many of the possible connections to renaissance allegory are no doubt already clear from this summary of Docherty's theory. Nevertheless, one cannot import a theory based on the fiction of one age holus-bolus to a period four centuries earlier (though the a-historical basis of post-structuralism would justify just such an action). The intellectual positions that lie behind Docherty's theory are not hidden, and they are distinctly modern ones: they include a reaction against the Cartesian split between mind and body, a hostility to Protestant bourgeois individualism, and a celebration of the notion of man as a collective noun—a notion that Docherty calls Catholic, but to which more politically minded modern critics might attach another name.

But the phenomenon that Docherty describes can, nevertheless, be seen in purely technical terms with some degree of independence from the ideological positions with which Docherty explains and justifies it. It can then help to provide a way of discussing characterization in the allegorical romances. Characterization in the works from the Renaissance discussed in the following chapters is, I suggest, quite similar to characterization in twentieth-century non-realistic fiction, even though a vastly different ideology lies behind it. However, these characters differ essentially from modernist characters in the way in which they point as symbols beyond the literary work—to a universe of analogical forms held together by a Christian, Neoplatonic world order. One cannot ignore this larger universe, this greater discourse. It is possible to treat a medieval or renaissance text as a self-referential discourse only so long as one acknowledges that the "discourse" of such a text is not confined to the words on the page, that is, that the book being read is the world itself. Foucault has accurately described this essential difference in *The Order of Things*. Until the triumph of the age of science, says Foucault,

resemblance played a constructive role in the knowledge of Western culture. It was resemblance that largely guided exegesis and the interpretation
of texts; it was resemblance that organized the play of symbols, made
possible knowledge of things visible and invisible, and controlled the art
of representing them. The universe was folded in upon itself.[2]

Language and literature in such a world are very much integral parts
of this system of analogous realities and not simply artificial reflections
of it. The world is a book; and a book, a little world. Language, he
writes,

has been set down in the world and forms part of it, both because things
themselves hide and manifest their own enigma like a language and because words offer themselves as things to be deciphered. . . . Knowledge
therefore consisted in relating one form of language to another form of
language; in restoring the great, unbroken plain of words and things; in
making everything speak. (pp. 35, 40)

One post-structuralist critic of Spenser who has misread Foucault's
opposition between the past and the present as an equation is Jonathan
Goldberg. His book *Endlesse Worke: Spenser and the Structures of
Discourse*[3] is the first major attempt to apply post-structuralist theoretical principles to Spenser's poem. Goldberg focuses on the least self-
contained book of *The Faerie Queene*, Book IV, "The Legend of Cam-
bel and Telemond or of Friendship." Goldberg's starting point is the
change of the original ending of Book III, a change that permitted
Spenser to continue the story of that book into a new one. To this he
adds the fact that no character named "Telemond" appears in Book
IV; he then goes on to accumulate a very long list of ambiguities,
contradictions, loose ends, and failures to achieve narrative closure
within the text. Many of these, it should be noted, are problems within
the text that have never bothered anyone before. It should not perhaps
be surprising that a critic with a conception of literature as important
for the fragments and shards it contains should find them wherever
he looks. Goldberg takes pleasure in being unable to resolve the problems he raises, frustration being a reader response he values very
highly. Nevertheless, Goldberg's approach is valuable because of its
very refusal to jump to easy conclusions or syntheses of apparent

oppositions. Because of his inability to perceive organic principles of unity or meaning operating, Goldberg can examine the threads of the narrative—where they begin, where they break off, how they appear when set next to each other—without immediately moving to those higher levels of abstraction where other critics operate most of the time. He sees the trees very well, while denying the existence of the forest. He seeks problems rather than solutions because (and here again ideology conditions everything) he believes there are only problems, that texts consist of words in freeplay (using Derrida's term) around a void. Therefore he sees as the chief pleasures of Spenser's text its "continuous disequilibrium, frequent disruptions in narration, and characters who exist to disappear" (p. xi). If the world is a book for Goldberg, it must be a *nouveau roman,* void at the centre, not the Word of God sent forth in a creative act.

In addition to "problematizing" the text, Goldberg achieves his ends by employing a naive concept of closure, which appears to demand absolute ends to narrative lines. He then triumphantly points out that there are no such endings in Spenser. But, one might ask, in what narratives are there any absolute endings, either internally or even on the last page. Stories reach points beyond which they would cease to be interesting, or at least interesting for the same reasons; but even "They lived happily ever after" is not an absolute ending; it is simply the plot of an unnarrated, uninteresting story. Perhaps the Bible does not permit a sequel, but every other narration does.

The Faerie Queene is for Goldberg, however, an example of Barthes's writerly text—endless and reversible, "infinite, replete, broken, empty, arbitrary, structured and deconstructed" (p. 11). Nevertheless, much of what Goldberg has to say about characterization in *The Faerie Queene* anticipates and even goes beyond Docherty's theory.

Goldberg sees Spenser's characters as defined not in mimetic terms but by their functions in the poem, which itself is "a grid on which different positions and relationships define an actor from moment to moment" (p. 8). The knights and ladies of the poem are all faceless and capable of being duplicated endlessly; they are only "names, words written on a page, signifiers without any signifieds." In these terms, Spenser's characters are neither people nor ideas, since they cannot exist, says Goldberg, "other than in the textual space they are allotted" (p. 75). There is no "outside" to the text.

In so far as this reductivist view of Spenser's characterization is supported by a nihilist world view, it cannot be opposed in its own terms, but only on the basis of an alternative ideology. That it is historically unsound is obvious to the literary historian and unimportant to the post-structuralist. But in so far as it is a theory of characterization based on theories of language, it can be opposed from within. I have little space in which to do that here, but I can at least point to the work of Tzvetan Todorov on the nature of the symbol, particularly in his book *Symbolism and Interpretation,* first published in 1973 and translated into English in 1982.[4] This study seems to me to undercut the whole linguistic basis of post-structuralist deconstruction by its acknowledgment of the dual nature of symbols: its demonstration that, on the one hand, symbols are merely signifiers within a lexicon, but that, on the other hand, they may simultaneously point to indirect meanings within and outside the text in which they are embodied. Though this referential quality in a symbol may not be strictly a linguistic function, it is still a real function, and only by ignoring it can literature be read as the freeplay of words around a void. The idea of words as symbols with indirect meanings extending beyond the limits of the text guarantees the possibility of interpretation.

Todorov goes on to point out those elements in a text that indicate the need for symbolic interpretation. His account of this is particularly telling in that he points to those very fragments and shards that other theorists employ to undercut the notions of interpretation and coherence. Looking at the history of both Eastern and Western hermeneutics, he finds that ambiguities, incompleteness, contradictions, and fragments have always provided the justification for symbolic or allegorical interpretations of texts. All self-deconstructions of the organic text are signs that a secondary meaning is operating.

Spenser and his readers would have been familiar with the historical version of Todorov's theory of the symbol from St. Augustine's *On Christian Doctrine,* where Augustine discusses at length the dual nature of the sign and argues for the necessity of symbolic reading whenever a biblical text seems not to conform to reason, truth, and charity. Todorov cites Philo of Alexandria's extensive index of textual features that indicate the need for symbolic exegesis, including among them contradiction, discontinuity, superfluity, implausibility, inappropriateness—indeed, all the de-stabilizing elements for which Goldberg searches in *The Faerie Queene.*

If such characteristics were conventionally regarded as signs of the need for a symbolic reading, it is hardly surprising that Spenser would have included them in a poem he called a continued allegory. But he would have done so with the assumption that they would generate not frustration but interpretation. Post-structuralist deconstructions have enabled us to perceive more clearly the fragments and shards of earlier narratives; but they have stopped short of the kind of interpretation that would have been the next step within the older hermeneutics: interpretations that would have involved seeking within the texts for coherent meanings to which the apparent incoherency could be accommodated, and beyond the text for the inherited meanings of the symbol.

Thus, in spite of the similarity of the surface between Spenserian narration and characterization and the techniques of the new novel, these similar techniques support far different ends. The renaissance symbol opens outward to a world of multiple meanings rather than playing around a void. It opens up a world that can be expressed only in symbols—in words, objects, people, and events that are themselves part of the system but that also, because of the ways in which they are perceived and presented, point toward other parts of the system and toward a general Truth about things. Modern discontinuous perception of the world has turned this plurality of significance into something that we cannot share except through the efforts of historical reconstruction. The conceptions operating behind mimetic methods of presenting literary characters in particular have transformed the reading methods of un-theoretical readers so much that many of the central characters of the older literature now look as though they are little more than cartoon personifications. On the other hand, this deflation of significance in such characters has inspired many critics to try to find "realistic" aspects, to discover unique and discontinuous natures in characters who were intended primarily to be symbolic complexes of allusions and ideas—that is, parts of intricate allegorical structures.

Avoiding both post-structuralist and realist extremes, the following studies attempt to define the multiple nature of the symbolic life (which was, for the period, the *real* life) of three major figures in English renaissance literature, each of whom represents the virtue of heroic temperance. Also included is a study of James Joyce's Leopold Bloom, a temperate Ulysses whose characterization is a result both of modern realism and of a revival by Joyce of the systematic symbolic methods of the earlier period. I have chosen such heroes because I see their development in the Renaissance as an important stage in the evolution of literature and ideas. In addition, their dominant virtue of temperance is one that lends itself far less than other heroic characteristics to presentation in large-scale, dramatic action. The symbolic aspects of these characters can thus be seen all the more clearly.

Much of the research and the writing of this book is the product of a nine-month period of study leave from the University of Melbourne. I wish to thank the Humanities Research Centre of the Australian National University for a subsequent three-month Visiting Fellowship, which gave me time for writing. I also wish to thank those critics and scholars who read the manuscript of my work in whole or part and who offered valuable suggestions: John Spencer Hill, John Carey, Joseph H. Summers, Vincent Buckley, Howard Felperin, Robert R. Wilson, and Tom Gibbons.

Part of the chapter on *Paradise Regained* has appeared in *Milton Studies*. The appendix has been published previously in *Milton Quarterly*.

R. D. J.

Symbolic Characters and the Character of Symbols

The gods take pleasure in the multiform representation of multiform things.

(Giordano Bruno)[1]

One name stands for one thing, and another for another thing, and they are connected together. And so the whole, like a living picture, presents the atomic fact.

(Ludwig Wittgenstein)[2]

Of heroes in literature, as of nearly everything else in our world, there are two very different main types with an infinite number of combinations and gradations possible within and between them. The primary and most easily recognizable type is the active hero, the one who slays the dragon and saves the maiden, the one who redeems his people by defeating their enemies. He is the literary character one normally thinks of as central to epics, romances, and even realistic novels. His opposite, who is not so easily recognized, is what I will call here "the quiet hero." He (or she) is not what is normally called an anti-hero, a figure that generally represents the failure of modern culture; rather, he is a hero who achieves important successes, but achieves them for the most part by not acting, by merely waiting, or by undertaking (at the end of a period of restrained or thwarted action) a climactic action that has a symbolic relationship to the outcome rather than being a major cause of it.

Even though the Christian religion might seem to be something that would naturally inspire such heroism in literature, quiet heroes did not in fact come into their own until the Renaissance.

Quiet heroism was certainly not a major characteristic of the classical hero. Helen North has traced in detail the development of the Greek concept of *sophrosyne* (self-restraint, self-knowledge, quietness, temperance) in classical literature.[3] What her study shows is a slow development indeed; she mentions no important classical hero, except perhaps Aeneas, who has the quiet virtue of *sophrosyne* as a major characteristic. Homer's Odysseus was allegorized, long after Homer's time, as an exemplum of prudence; and such a misreading of him lies behind Spenser's characterization of Guyon and Joyce's characterization of Leopold Bloom—which I discuss in later chapters. But to Homer and to those earliest readers of Homer who published their own views of Odysseus, he was anything but a quiet hero. The epithets with which Homer describes him stress his martial ability, his endurance, and his intelligence. Though intelligence, at least, might seem a quiet virtue, this characteristic of Odysseus was seen as reprehensible craftiness, and throughout both the classical and medieval periods Odysseus was subjected to attacks by those who read his guilefulness as immoral or even criminal.[4] "What saved the Homeric Odysseus," according to M. I. Finley, "was the fact that his guile was employed in the pursuit of heroic goals" (p. 70). Outward actions, not inward stability, identify the classical hero. *Sophrosyne,* however, was attributed to characters of other types in classical literature. North points to Nestor, Menelaus, Diomedes, and even Ulysses himself as representatives of this virtue in works by Sophocles, Isocrates, and Plato, but in contexts where it is "clear that *sophrosyne* is not a 'heroic' virtue" (p. 2). It came to be valued in Greece only with the growth of the *polis* and the socially necessary de-emphasis on individual heroism that followed. Even then it was a virtue associated mainly with the young (including Homer's Telemachus) and with women. In classical literature it most often belongs to secondary characters who serve as foils to the hero or who are in fact unheroic and hypocritical in their apparent self-restraint; and Greek tragedy always illustrates the failure of the hero's *sophrosyne,* never its success. (This is true even in the case of Euripides's Hippolytus, in whom the virtue becomes a fatal excess.)

If *sophrosyne* was a Greek virtue that found little positive expression in the characterization of Greek heroes, it was even less at home in the literary world of Rome. While it is common today to stress, as North does, the *pietas* and *humanitas* of Aeneas—a welcome relief from those older attacks on his heartless infidelity—it could still be argued that these virtues would not have been accepted as virtues by Virgil's audience had they not been coupled with Aeneas's skill as a fighter and as a leader of fighters. We tend sometimes to allegorize classical heroes almost as much as the Renaissance did; and when a scholar like Ernst Curtius admits Aeneas's ability as a soldier but qualifies this by saying: "Aeneas never *wants* war, in which the poet too sees something terrible,"[5] he is reflecting a twentieth-century sentiment and distorting a Virgilian one. Virgil's Aeneas is almost a non-satiric version of Auden's "Unknown Citizen": "When there was peace, he was for peace; when there was war, he went."[6] However restrained and prudent the hero, "the heroic act," as Thomas Greene has noted, "must be visible, external, objective" in classical literature.[7]

The Christianization of *sophrosyne* was as difficult as the Romanization of it, and it required a major shift of emphasis that established a connection between it and the Christian idea of chastity. It remained throughout the Middle Ages primarily a feminine virtue and in literature characterized martyrs rather than victorious representatives of the dominant culture, who succeeded here on earth. Ulysses went out of favor in the Middle Ages and was most often seen as a trickster rather than as a prudent man; and Christ himself, when he was presented in heroic literary modes, was generally characterized as a military hero, battling the old dragon and harrowing hell, not as a quiet hero winning victories through self-restraint.

The quiet hero as a major literary figure and a symbolic savior had to wait for the stoic strain inherent in Christianity to come to the forefront and combine itself with the introspective, individualistic spirit of the Renaissance;[8] it had particularly to wait for Christianity to absorb the methods of symbolic, analogical thinking of renaissance Neoplatonism. The virtue of *sophrosyne* entered the Renaissance in its medieval form as Temperance, bearing with it all the theological and symbolic equipment it had acquired during the Middle Ages, but also reasserting its classical meanings of self-knowledge and soundness of mind; it found its literary embodiment in Heroic Temperance, the chief virtue of the quiet hero.

Quiet heroism, even in an age that values it as a characteristic of real men, is a quality very difficult to give to a literary hero, because inaction is a highly undramatic mode of behavior. Even in lyric poetry the passive virtues have been problematic, with Yeats declaring (after Matthew Arnold) that "passive suffering is not a theme for poetry."[9] A quiet, restrained hero complicates immensely the difficulty of getting from the beginning of a story to the end, and it makes holding the reader's interest even more difficult. In fact, for the work to succeed as a narrative at all, the lack of dramatic, external action must be compensated for by something else. One possible alternative is the substitution of psychological "action" for the missing physical heroics, a concentration on the forces in conflict and development within the hero's mind. This is a modern alternative that, with certain notable exceptions, was not used as a way to structure narratives in earlier ages. Medieval and renaissance narratives do include excursions into the minds of their characters—often as exercises in the "complaint" genre—but in those few cases where the story itself is a psychological conflict, such conflict is *externalized* and is allegorically represented in dramatic, normally military, action. The mind in which such a psychomachia is meant to be taking place is seldom that of a unique character; rather, it is the mind of everyman.

Modern readers, bred in the cultural climate that produced the modern psychological novel, often try to read older literature as if it too was concerned primarily with the psychological condition and development of the main characters; but such reading is an anachronistic error. The first question one should ask of a "quiet hero" in renaissance literature is not, "What is he thinking?" but "What does he symbolize?" The question applies to the whole field of quiet heroes, who might be diverse in other ways—heroes ranging from Spenser's Guyon to such characters in Shakespeare as the Duke in *Measure For Measure*. The alternative to dramatic, mimetic characterization that the Renaissance employed for its quiet heroes was symbolic characterization.

By symbolic characterization, I do not mean the relatively simple kind of one-to-one, A equals B, symbolic representation that is sometimes used in medieval allegories and that still survived in some of the minor characters of renaissance narrative and in the works of

Bunyan. What identifies symbolic characterization in renaissance literature is the multiplicity of meanings that are associated with a single character. A symbolic hero is a complex harmony of ideas and allusions in which one may perhaps be dominant (holiness in Spenser's Red Crosse, temperance in Guyon, etc.) but in which no one symbolic meaning is ever exclusive. Because of this, the proper reading of such a character is not an attempt to interpret what he thinks or to trace his moral growth so much as it is an attempt to identify the ideas he symbolizes and to recognize the literary/historical types of which he is an antitype, and then to trace the relationships of these meanings to each other and to the actions and other characters of the narrative. This applies not only to narratives that are obviously allegories, but to "realistic" works from the period as well. Just as Botticelli combined fidelity to human and natural forms with Neoplatonic symbolism, so Shakespeare's truth to life exists in joint service with his "symbolized" precedents and ideas. Realism and symbolism are not hostile literary categories (as this book will in part demonstrate); nor does the claim that a writer like Shakespeare is symbolic imply that he is didactic (as many "realists" think): writers of all ages have embodied ideas and precedents in symbolic forms without attempting to teach their readers lessons in philosophy or history, for the important ideas and literary/historical sources of any culture have an existential reality at least as important to the artist as the pots on the shelf of Romeo's apothecary. Symbolic allegory is a way of giving such ideas dramatic life, not merely a way of teaching them.

It is appalling how much ink has been wasted analyzing the psychological causes of Hamlet's delay as if he were a real man with mental operations not directly revealed in his words. When a modern writer, attempting to trace the cultural achievement of the Renaissance, speaks of "the astonishing way in which, quite naturally, Shakespeare searches out and explores the unconscious,"[10] he is being astonished by his own culture and the kind of criticism it has produced. No renaissance literary critic that I know of ever interpreted narratives in any genre as explorations of either the conscious or the unconscious mind of the hero; there is overwhelming evidence, however, supporting the notion that readers in the period read the most "realistic" works as allegories and moral exempla. One is not necessarily required to accept the judgments of a renaissance critic as any more authoritative than those of a modern critic, but one must at least accept the *methods* of the critics of an age as representative of how people of the period read. *Hamlet* could not have been seen as built around one man's subconscious mental condition. It could, on the other hand, have been seen as founded on the idea of revenge, with the conflicts of the play that delay the crisis existing in that concept, rather than in hidden peculiarities of Hamlet's psychology.

However, *Hamlet* and its main character are involved in something more than simply an exploration of the theme of revenge; and, like symbolic characters in general, Hamlet never becomes the kind of two-dimensional figure one could call Revenger. Hamlet is a complex character, even though that complexity is only in part a function of his individual personality. All of the themes of *Hamlet*—the problem of revenge, the nature of melancholy, the reality of the supernatural, Hamlet's moral and spiritual doubts about suicide, the conflict of the life of action versus the life of contemplation (which are presented in the play as complex, unresolved issues, not as moral lessons)—these are what determine the character of Hamlet. All of the revengers and matricides of past history and literature are behind him, calling him toward a symbolic union with them. Had these themes and precedents not existed and been important to Shakespeare and his audience, Hamlet could not have existed as he is, for he is their symbolic embodiment—which in no way alters the fact that they also are part of his personal problems as a literary character. And more goes into his characterization than even this. There is Hamlet's language, for instance, which, since it is poetry, is only partially realistic; it is partially something that never could take place in real human discourse. The visual imagery of the poetry, as well, helps to characterize Hamlet. Yet all of these diverse things are harmonized within the play; the visual and the philosophical, for example, do not exist as separate categories, for, as Rosemond Tuve so conclusively demonstrated, visual imagery in the Renaissance takes its character from contemporary philosophy, from a "definition of the real" that is "not precisely ours."[11] And the harmony of these themes, precedents, poetic language, imagery, and personal traits ultimately *is* Hamlet, a figure important both in himself and for what he represents—that is, a symbol.

It is my contention here that the culture of the Renaissance, and particularly its analogical, Neoplatonic world view, made possible the development of this kind of characterization as a major form, and that some of the same patterns and assumptions reappeared in the culture of the early twentieth century (after a retreat of nearly two centuries into "common sense" mimesis), giving quiet heroism a rebirth in the fiction of James Joyce. I intend to consider what the primary assumptions are that make the use of quiet heroes possible and important, and to examine the literary techniques that have been employed in their development. My examples are from works by four of the most significant writers in English since the dawn of the Renaissance: Spenser, Donne, Milton, and Joyce, each of whom has presented an important "passive" hero whose relatively undramatic character is nevertheless heroic and victorious, and whose victories are far more than simply personal ones. These are Spenser's Guyon, Donne's Elizabeth Drury, Milton's Christ in *Paradise Regained,* and Joyce's Leopold Bloom.

The suggestion that Neoplatonism lies behind this kind of symbolic heroic literature requires some explanations and qualifications. Neoplatonism, particularly as it existed in renaissance England, was an amorphous, synthetic creature with many different heads, any one of which can be the dominant one for a given writer or for a modern critic with an interest in the subject. Though there were no major figures who identified themselves as Platonists in England until the late seventeenth century, there were a number of identifiable ideas in circulation throughout the Renaissance that were commonly thought of as Platonic and yet were not incompatible with, or always distinguishable from, the philosophical commonplaces of the remainder of what has become known as the renaissance world picture.

The well-known danger in dealing with "world views" and in applying such views to literature is that even within the most homogeneous of periods different men have somewhat different views of their world. Beyond that, what is most interesting and significant in writers like Spenser, Donne, Milton, and Joyce very often lies in those areas where they go beyond the accepted beliefs of their periods. Nevertheless, one's caution must not take one too far in the opposite direction. The romantic period's notion of originality has no important relationship to the Renaissance or, for that matter, to Joyce, whose later works depend heavily on creative pastiche. The most "original" authors of the Renaissance were, as every student of the period knows, engaged in the art of imitation. This was not an art of repetition or of reproduction but of re-creation, of the artist converting what he had inherited into something of his own. (All good artists work this way, though not every period recognizes the fact.) As Ben Jonson said,

The third requisite in our *Poet,* or Maker, is *Imitation,* to bee able to convert the substance, or Riches of an other *Poet,* to his owne use. . . . Not, as a Creature, that swallowes, what it takes in, crude, raw, or indigested; but, that feedes with an Appetite, and hath a Stomacke to concoct, divide, and turne all into nourishment. Not to imitate servilely, as *Horace* saith, and catch at vices, for vertue: but, to draw forth out of the best, and choicest flowers, with the Bee, and turne all into Honey.[12]

Such an art could surpass its originals when practiced by the best writers of the period; it in no way hindered those writers from producing work that was distinctive and enduring.

An art like that of the Renaissance, which always keeps one eye on its sources and precedents, is, as a result, not bound to its particular moment in history except in so far as all historical moments include the past within them. This exploitation of the past is undertaken, however, not simply for its own sake but as a way of commenting on the contemporary cultural milieu; the historical inclusiveness of such art makes judgments on its own time through constant comparison and contrast. And the world that is eternally present in renaissance literature includes not only previous and contemporary history and literature, but also the cosmologies, metaphysics, and other systems of ideas that were available to the period. These "world views" do not need to be reconstructed today from literary or other sources, which were doing something more important than simply describing the world through renaissance eyes; the period itself produced comprehensive "anatomies" of the world which, in encyclopedic fashion, attempted to summarize and organize man's knowledge of the universe. These renaissance encyclopedias tend to share common assumptions and sources. To set any one of the more popular of them beside a major work of renaissance literature is not to imply that Spenser, Donne, or Milton were retailers of commonplace ideas; rather, it is to suggest that these writers would have been consciously aware of the relationship of their own ideas to the most widely circulated ideas of their period and that they would have expected their readers to recognize both the connections and the differences.

But whatever differences may have existed within renaissance world views, there is one major assumption that ties them all together: the shared belief that the universe was created as a rationally organized construction and that its main method of organization was by means of analogy. It is this assumption of an analogical, symmetrical organization to the world that we are sometimes told came under threat from Copernican cosmology, Machiavellian politics, and other new intellectual developments, and finally broke down. But in fact, it never really went under. Men of the period, faced with evidence of disorder in the universe, did not try to construct new systems on nonanalogous bases or to embrace the idea of a fragmented universe. The renaissance idea of order was in a constant process of transformation of content but never of structure as it attempted to incorporate more and more of the multiplicity of material and metaphysical reality. If the structure had to give up some of its older content and make major rearrangements, it always did so—often slowly and reluctantly, yet with an unchanging faith that all the patterns that existed in the universe were analogous to each other.

It is this analogical structuring of being and thought, taken together with certain specific areas of content within that structuring, that can be described as Neoplatonic. One must understand that the term refers to a synthesis of ideas that was perceived in the Renaissance as a unitary philosophy found in Plato, the Bible, Hermetic literature, and the classical and Florentine Neoplatonists—a synthesis that had actually had its first flowering in the renaissance of the twelfth century.[13] Historians of ideas attempt to trace the origin of different elements

in this synthesis and to identify different types of Neoplatonism, and
there are times when the literary scholar needs to do the same thing;
but in the Renaissance itself the emphasis was placed on the unitary
coherence, the analogical coherence, of Neoplatonic philosophy, and
especially upon its analogy with Christian theology. Since A. O. Lovejoy's *The Great Chain of Being* and E. M. W. Tillyard's *The Elizabethan World Picture,* a large number of scholarly works have attempted
to describe this synthesis and various aspects of it. The present intro-
ductory chapter can do little more than add a footnote pointing the
reader to some of the important recent works on which this study
depends, and then go on to describe briefly one major renaissance
presentation of the synthesis.[14]

A very comprehensive survey of the Neoplatonic aspects of the
renaissance world view, and perhaps the most important for the popular diffusion of these ideas in the period, is Cornelius Agrippa's
Three Books of Occult Philosophy, which had a major influence in
England at least through the time of Thomas Vaughan.[15] The type
and extent of the synthesis that was possible between Platonic doctrines (of the world of Ideas, the One, the relationship of the One to
the many) and other aspects of renaissance thought about the structure and operation of the world are nowhere better exemplified than
in Agrippa's encyclopedic work. It was itself a source for other encyclopedic harmonies of the world, including the popular *Batman uppon Bartholome, his Booke De Proprietatibus Rerum* (London, 1582). In
dealing with the Neoplatonic world view, renaissance writers, like
modern scholars, had their own individual points of emphasis. The
emphasis of Agrippa's book is magic; but, though magic was a somewhat dangerous area for the renaissance mind, it was not an isolated
one. Its principles were essentially the same as those of the more
respectable fields of philosophy and science; its study was almost a
necessary adjunct for any renaissance thinker with an interest in Platonism.

Agrippa covers most of the areas of renaissance thought that have
been identified by historians of ideas from Lovejoy on: the four elements and humors, the microcosm and the macrocosm, the golden

chain of being, the harmony of the world as a musical structure. There is little need to go into detail here about what is so well known from other sources. Agrippa's work also covers what might be called the trivia of magic: lists of good and evil omens, catalogues of the supposedly occult mathematical relationships between parts of the body, tables of astrological characteristics, a discussion of the occult nature of hieroglyphics. But of more importance for the purposes of the present study is the conscious sense Agrippa displays of the unity and of the analogical relationships of everything that he is including. The universe Agrippa describes is not only a totally organized one, it is also a totally symbolic one; everything is significant in itself, but points beyond itself by analogy.

Agrippa combines the notion of a hierarchical chain of being— linked by analogical similarities and ordered by essential differ- ences—with the concept of a threefold universe containing three worlds of elementary, celestial, and intellectual being. Each world is analogically harmonious with, and exerts real influence upon, the oth- ers "because there is one operative vertue that is diffused through all kinds of things" (p. 76; sig. F6, v). This "vertue" is the World Soul, the *anima mundi,* which makes one of the many without destroying their multiplicity.

The soul of the world therefore is a certain only thing, filling all things, ... that it might make one frame of the world, and that it might be as it were one instrument making of many strings, but one sound, sounding from three kinds of creatures, intellectuall, Celestiall, and incorruptible, with only one breath and life. (p. 331; sig. Y6, r.)

This World Soul will be discussed at length in the chapter on Donne below.

The triple unity of the three worlds is reflected in the three persons of God and in the three souls of man. This reflection makes man analogously (and hence really) the image of God—a key concept in Agrippa's system.

God also created man after his Image; for as the world is the Image of God, so man is the Image of the world.... The world is a Rationall creature, Immortall; man in like manner is rationall but mortal.... as God comprehendeth this whole world, and whatsoever is in it in his minde alone; so man's minde comprehendeth it even in thought. (p. 458; sig. Gg5, v.)

This Neoplatonic belief in the comprehensiveness of man's mind as a result of its analogy with the Divine Mind provides a theoretical justification for the complex and comprehensive symbolism of Edmund Spenser or for the visionary inclusiveness of the poetry of Thomas Traherne,[16] and in general for the plenitude that characterizes the imagery and ideas of renaissance literature. Limited modern minds may need comprehensive footnotes or critical essays to perceive this multiple unity, but to miss seeing it is to misread the literature itself.

Other areas of the Neoplatonic synthesis that are important to Agrippa and to the four authors considered in the present book are the symbolism of numbers, the connections between the movements of the spheres and the actions of men, the significance and power of names—which are far more than simply signs to designate objects— and the relationship between the soul and the body, particularly when the soul leaves the body through death, metamorphosis, or the experience of rapture. I discuss these things when they occur in the works considered below, but of interest here are their featured roles in the parallel systems that form the metasystem of renaissance Neoplatonism. Agrippa's subjects encompass the range of this metasystem, the true unity of which is to be found not so much in the historical processes that brought these diverse ideas together as in the nature of the system itself, with its governing principle of analogy.

"Symbol" and "analogy" in their ordinary senses are inadequate words to describe the kinds of thinking that characterize Agrippa's work, in that these words seem to imply only positive relationships. But such thinking not only sees positive connections within and between symbols; it is alert for contrasts as well. Consequently such symbolic thinking always seems paradoxical; Cornelius Agrippa, we are told,

contemneth, knows, is ignorant, weeps, laughs, is angry, carps at all things, being himself a Philosopher, a Demon, an Heroes, a god, and all things.[17]

This may sound mad, but it is a rational claim in a world where all things are interrelated and each thing implies, by similarity and contrast, all other things. This is the world as Agrippa viewed it, and he himself regarded this philosophy as Platonic: "It is the unanimous consent of all Platonists, that as in the originall, and exemplary world, all things are in all; so also in this corporeal world, all things are in all" (p. 32; sig. C2v).

Allegory, in the Western tradition, is itself largely Platonic in origin and nature.[18] Further, the philosophy of the involvement of all in all is the necessary abstract basis for any adequate definition of renaissance symbolism or for any definition of the symbolism employed by Joyce. Definitions that ignore this unitive principle, and particularly those definitions that postulate meanings or other elements that can be detached and isolated from the symbolic embodiment itself, will always be found in contradiction to actual literary practice. C. S. Lewis's Coleridge-like distinction, in *The Allegory of Love,* between symbolism and allegory has been found wanting so often by previous writers that it is not necessary to mount a lengthy criticism of it here. Lewis's fundamental error, however, was to credit separation and temporal priorities to what are unified and simultaneous aspects of symbolic images. In allegory, said Lewis, you "start with an immaterial fact, such as the passions which you actually experience, and can then invent *visibilia* to express them"; symbolism, on the other hand, is "the attempt to read [a form in the invisible world] through its sensible imitations, to see the archetype in the copy."[19]

Not only do these definitions ignore the basic principle of the unity and simultaneity of symbolic meanings, they take no account of the multiple and hierarchical aspects of symbols. Yet in both renaissance and Joycean symbolism there is seldom if ever a simple two-level correspondence between an image and a detachable meaning. While an image may indeed point to its archetype, it will normally do so because in the narrative it functions both as itself and as its archetype, while doing other things as well. (Una in *The Faerie Queene* is, *inter alia,* both Truth and truth; she is also a Maiden in Distress and an individualized young girl named Una.) In addition, such a symbol usually functions as an allusion to a number of other "copies." (Una is, symbolically, Langland's Unitas, a daughter of Adam and Eve, the scriptures, the English Church, and the Bride of Christ.) "Allegory," according to Isabel MacCaffrey, "refers 'upward' to the final truths of God, as well as outward to the multiple truths of human life in the middest, and forward to figurally anticipated futures."[20] However, the relative importance of any aspect of a symbol can be determined by no set rule and no simple distinction between the "material" and the "invisible." Indeed, distinctions between material and invisible mean very little when applied to works from what MacCaffrey has described as "the centuries which sustained belief in both the objective reality of an invisible realm, and a required relation between that realm and the realities perceived by sense" (p. 28). What aspects of a symbol are of the most importance at any one time in a work is determined solely by the literary context in which the symbol is placed.

Even the "highest" meaning is not necessarily the most important one. In the Renaissance the multiple aspects of a symbol carried the same possibility of hierarchical arrangement on the chain of being as all other things. But, while it may be important for a reader to recognize a hierarchy among a symbol's meanings, it is a mistake to assume that the archetypal idea in the Divine Mind is always the main significance. As Susanne Langer demonstrated in *Philosophy in a New Key,* symbolic art and idealistic interpretations of reality are not inseparable companions.[21] The focus of significant attention may move up and down the hierarchy during the course of a symbolic narrative. A Christ-figure in an allegory, for example, may be used in an episode that has little to do with Christ beyond being the actions of a good man. An immortal golden bird on a golden bough may still sing songs about mortality, and those songs may be the most significant thing in the image.

But though the emphasis may change, a true symbol never completely drops any of its intended aspects—a fact not recognized by those critics who have claimed that Spenser sometimes forgets his allegory and allows his "realistic" narrative to carry on alone.[22] Meanings of a symbolic figure that are not dominant in a particular episode—even those meanings established *after* the episode—condition in important ways the meanings that are stressed there. When a symbolic aspect has been established for a figure, only the reader can forget it: it is forever present in the literary work itself, defining the figure and all associated figures; there is no way to hide or forget it. As Rosemond Tuve has said of renaissance imagery in general: "Reading on the figurative level has to be sustained rather than intermittent."[23] Spenser deserves credit for understanding his own work when he described it as a "continued Allegory" in his letter to Raleigh. Meanings are not forgotten but become functionally more or less important in relationship to each other, creating their own hierarchies in individual episodes, hierarchies that are not necessarily identical with the chain of being, though they share the same type of unity within a coherent, analogically organized whole.

Most interpretations of allegories seem so different from the allegories themselves, and so inadequate to them, because the interpreter normally chooses a "level," one area within the total range of symbolic meanings, and then follows its path through the narrative. Since, unless he has made a mistake, the critic will no doubt find that the particular meaning he has chosen is a ubiquitous one, he may become convinced that he has found the True Meaning of the allegory. Yet such a single-level reading, or even a series of parallel separate readings on the order of medieval biblical exegesis, will always be found reductive by other readers, who will feel that important ideas or events have been distorted,[24] or that the interpretation offered is important to some episodes but not to others. Some distortion of this kind is inevitable in any interpretation of an allegory. The present book will be found guilty of it as well, because the true reading of allegorical/ symbolic literature is a polyphonic experience comparable to listening to an orchestra. To talk about the music of a symphony, one must isolate elements of it; listening to the music, however, is a unified experience of multiplicity in which certain elements (themes, instruments, harmonies) command the consciousness of the listener, while others enter only the periphery of the mind or sink in unnoticed. Yet all of these elements are simultaneously present in the experience itself and are necessary to making it what it is.

A complete analysis of any allegory or symbolic poem (*allegory* from here on meaning any narrative structured around symbolic figures) would have to be written like an orchestral score in order to demonstrate the several different things that take place simultaneously and the nature of a development in which elements submerge and reappear or move from one level to another. Even then, one would need some further system of annotation to account for one of the most remarkable elements of allegory—especially as it was practiced by Spenser and Joyce—the element of metamorphosis, through which a trumpet becomes a violin while still remaining in some ways a trumpet. After writing out this "score," one would still be obliged to write a discursive account of the effects of the performance.

Thus, though an interpreter must abstract elements from the whole in order to get on with his job, the separation is a purely artificial process which, to be of any value, requires a constant awareness of an interpretation's part in the total context. The word "symbol" seems originally to have been connected with the tessera broken between two men as a device for future recognition. The idea of a symbol as the putting together of the parts of a whole is still relevant. No part by itself is the whole, and yet all parts are individually important and share the characteristics of the whole. Etymologically as well as actually, the symbol centers on a process of analogy for its significance. In a world where analogy is the basic structural principle, the symbol comes into its own; and it is interesting to note that the first example in English in the *Oxford English Dictionary* of the use of "symbol" to describe something other than a formal summary of religious beliefs is from Edmund Spenser's *Faerie Queene,* where the stain on Ruddymane's hands is described in Book II as "a sacred Symbole" (ii, 10).

When analogy is not simply an effective rhetorical device but the fundamental organizing principle of the universe (as it was actually in the Renaissance, and aesthetically and perhaps even actually for Joyce) no element in a symbol's complex of meanings can be detached without producing a split in reality itself. Symbolic images, whether presented as characters, objects, or events, are the embodiments of such analogies. All the meanings of such images are "literal" meanings. The function of the critic, and of the reader who is not content simply to listen to the music, is not only to discover the different meanings but to analyze their relationships to each other and to their context in the literary work.

William York Tindall, whose study of *The Literary Symbol* recognizes this inseparability of a symbol and "what it stands for" within a context,[25] still errs in the direction of Lewis's distinctions in assuming a simple dual relationship between symbol and meaning. And Tindall exceeds Lewis in his desire to find the meaning of a symbol in an invisible or at least "indeterminate" world hidden behind the image, "a residual mystery that escapes our intellects" (ibid.). Both his definitions and his tastes are conditioned, as also were Lewis's, by early twentieth-century Symbolist poetry and poetic theory. This is part of a tradition—of valuing the indefinite in a symbol—that is Romantic in origin and found its theoretical expression in English first in Coleridge and Carlyle. In following this tradition, Tindall devalues the different nature of the medieval and renaissance symbol as he understands it. Describing the allegory of Dante, Tindall says: "What he calls his 'polysemous' method, unlike the ambiguity and paradox dear to romantics, offers many meanings without contradiction or uncertainty" (p. 30). Tindall concludes that we, as modern men, "lacking certainty . . . prefer indefinite analogies. Definite analogies, such as the allegory and metaphor of the Middle Ages and the Renaissance, were designed to present not abstractions alone but the nature of things" (p. 33). Whether or not "we" prefer indefinite abstractions, this falsifies the nature of renaissance symbolism. If recent studies of Spenser have demonstrated anything, they have shown that Spenser does not deal, as Tindall claims, with "cool equations" (p. 34). The mathematics of a Spenserian symbol is a form of symbolic logic that has left the simple equation far behind. The renaissance symbol, with its multiplicity of analogous meanings, does indeed describe "the nature of things," but "things" in the Renaissance also had their ambiguities and paradoxes and contradictions; and these as well as more definite meanings are elements in most symbolic images of any importance in the period.

Renaissance literary theory is replete with definitions of allegory as a veiling of hidden truths; but the essential difference between this and the type of modern Symbolism that Tindall prefers is that the Symbolist is often content to marvel at the trembling of the veil, while the renaissance writer expected his reader to try to see through it. It was not absolutely essential that the reader succeed in this: renaissance allegories were written simultaneously for those who would be able to see and enjoy only the surface and for those who were, or would make the effort to become, initiates. However, because the veil of renaissance allegory was translucent, even the uninitiated might be illuminated, though they might not understand the source of the light. Stress on the Hermetic nature of renaissance and also of Joycean symbolism is not mistaken so long as it is realized that, as Gay Clifford has remarked, this method has been chosen because it is the *simplest* way to represent truths that are "too complex to be rendered in baldly prescriptive or descriptive language. The allegorical action is not paraphrase of something capable of alternative expression."[26] The apparent simplicity of the method (in spite of the complexity of its significance) means that, even in a world where the symbolic significances have been forgotten or supplanted by new structures, an allegory may still be enjoyed on aesthetic grounds by an unprejudiced reader. Most nineteenth-century readers turned to Spenser for his pictorial and musical qualities alone. But the function of literary scholarship as it deals with symbolic imagery should nevertheless be to reconstruct for the reader the structures of meaning, the complexity that the figure embodies.

Twentieth-century readers have not only sought the invisible world of ideas and the indefinite world of ambiguities in symbols, they have also regarded them as expressions of mystical experience. This kind of reading had its basis in theories similar to those that lay behind the definitions offered by Lewis and Tindall; but it is an even vaguer critical procedure, in that mystical experience is, by definition, incommunicable. Those critics who attempted to define the symbols of renaissance poetry as mystical found few grounds on which to do so except their own faith. There are still books written about the "mystical" poetry of such writers as Henry Vaughan and Thomas Traherne, but the later twentieth century has generally preferred different perspectives.

Yet the renaissance notion of "all in all" might perhaps justify the leap from an image to a mystical vision. In a unitary world view structured by a universal system of analogies, every image is potentially a mystical symbol—all symbols are God symbols (though sometimes with a negative valence). But a writer, whether a mystic or not, whose purpose is communication rather than self-expression (that is, all important writers of the Renaissance) cannot afford the economy of writing nothing but the names of God. When Henry Vaughan began a poem with the line, "I saw eternity the other night," he quickly discovered that there was little more he could say directly on this theme, and he devoted the rest of *The World* to a satire on the vanities of human ambitions. Nevertheless, that poem is held together and succeeds because of a structure of analogies—generally negative—between the world and eternity, though the specific characteristics of the latter are largely implied rather than stated. The renaissance writer will almost invariably choose to present his symbolic image so that the dominant aspects are well down the chain of being from Divine Unity. This is particularly true in Protestant countries like England, where hostility to symbolizing God in images merely displaced somewhat the eternal human need to discover symbols. But the One, the All, still forms a possible extension of the secular symbol's meaning. Nevertheless, reading a renaissance allegory or symbolic poem is a process of perceiving the most immediate and relevant connections first. The ultimate "true" reading *is* perhaps a mystical experience—but so, no doubt, would be the "true" perception of anything. Lacking mystical revelation, we must content ourselves with understanding as much as we can of what is given in the work itself. Otherwise, we must forgo that attempt and confine our reading to surfaces and the forever indefinite. This book chooses the former course.

The realization of such plurality in a literary text need not lead to mysticism, idealism, vagueness, or even to the "vast dissolve" perceived by Roland Barthes and his followers.[27] Barthes, who in his own practical criticism identified and interpreted symbols constantly, made theoretical claims that would free symbols from the necessity of any connection with the denotative surface of the text. Yet such connections clearly did exist for him, however strained they may seem to his reader; and the nature of his own specific comments about literary texts unintentionally reveals that the alternative to a unitary text is not "the fragment, the shards, the broken or obliterated network" (p. 20) that he valued so highly, but an interconnected system of networks without which he himself could have communicated nothing. When Barthes says that we read "to multiply the signifiers, not to reach some ultimate signified" (p. 165) he is merely revealing himself as yet another, and a rather belated, modernist with a taste for the indefinite, not a pluralist. His theory does make an advance on earlier realist and dichotomous (surface-plus-meaning) theories and also, obviously, avoids the mystical leap to Divine Unity. But the split he emphasized between denotation and connotation, the latter of which he regarded as more important, is still intellectually bound to the older systems of reading, in spite of the shift of priorities; and it is one of the things that kept him from seeing the unity of the multiplicity that he identified. His work indicates the dangers of leaping too soon into any kind of indefinite—be it All or Nothing—and of making simple divisions between surface and background.

The fullest reading of symbolic imagery requires the exercise and interplay both of analytical, empirical thinking and of what Ernst Cassirer has called "mythical consciousness."[28] While attempting to understand meanings, relationships, and causes of changes and of shifts in priority among these, the reader must avoid establishing "any fixed dividing line between mere 'representation' and 'real' perception . . . between image and thing" (ibid.).

The "image" does not represent the "thing"; it *is* the thing; it does not merely stand for the object, but has the same actuality, so that it replaces the thing's immediate presence. (p. 38.)

For myth similarity of contents is not a mere relation between them but a real bond which attaches them to one another. (p. 142.)

Over and over again we thus find confirmation of the fact that man can apprehend and know his own being insofar as he can make it visible in the image of his gods. (p. 218.)

Mircea Eliade, also, has emphasized the "realistic" as well as the multiple nature of the products of mythical thinking, claiming that "myths reveal the structure of reality, and the multiple modalities of being in the world."[29] And in another work Eliade has applied this idea to symbols and images generally:

Images by their very structure are *multivalent*. If the mind makes use of images to grasp the ultimate reality of things, it is just because reality manifests itself in contradictory ways and therefore cannot be expressed in concepts.[30]

As applied to symbolic imagery in poetry, mythical consciousness is identical with poetic consciousness, and no reader can afford to do without it.

Renaissance symbolic imagery and allegory is not, then, definable either as a rigidly closed form or as "an open form which sets up and dramatizes certain ideal patterns."[31] It is a hierarchical system of significances "closed" in the case of each individual manifestation since specific points of analogical connection link specific aspects of meaning together, but open in so far as each manifestation is analogous with others and part of the All. The verbal image itself has equal reality with any aspect of its significance that one may choose to isolate for analysis, but it remains incomplete in itself.[32]

The nature of the "reality" of a symbolic image is still, however, of a distinctive type. One oversimplified antithesis, which the present study will maintain for the sake of economy, is that between mimesis and symbolism, between Aristotelian and Platonic methods of representation. This is, in fact, more a distinction of degree than of kind. Both methods of representation are imitations of reality; they differ in the range of the reality they choose to imitate and in the emphasis given by each to horizontal or vertical structural principles. Writers and critics made peace between them long before the Renaissance, though modern criticism has had to fight the battle over again.

Theoretically, mimesis confines the major elements of its imagery to a limited area on the chain of being, centered heavily on the phenomenal world as perceived by the senses; it presents these images (characters, objects, events) as existentially distinct from each other through the use of specific, unshared details; and the structure that encloses these images assumes a basically non-repetitive, ongoing chronology and psychology. On the other hand, symbolism also uses physical images; but the vertical structural principle of analogy and the freedom that symbolic meaning has to center anywhere on the analogical chain of being means that symbolic images do not have the same stability as mimetic images—they are not bound to time or to psychology. They are not even bound to maintain the same physical appearance; they metamorphose. But neither of these literary methods exists alone in any important piece of literature. A totally symbolic, non-mimetic work would not communicate anything, at least to creatures in this fallen world; there would be no point of reference, nothing to take hold of. It would be like an algebraic equation with no known equivalents for the symbolic notations. On the other hand, a totally non-symbolic, ungeneralized slice of life, if such a thing were possible, would be equally empty of any recognizable meaning or significance; a reader would be free to impose on it any meaning he liked, but the work itself would be simply a massive pile of details. Meaning in literature depends on the interaction between mimesis and symbolism.

And even if the modernist view that a meaningless world can best be reflected in a meaningless literature were valid, the realization of that theory in practice would be impossible as long as words themselves exist as symbols and not either as actual representations of existential objects or as purely connotative counters. Very few words are even aurally mimetic; like symbolic images, most have several related definitions, any one of which can be dominant depending on the context in which the word is placed. A purely mimetic literature would have to be written in a language with words devoid of secondary denotations. The words of this inhuman language would also have to be free of historical, philosophical, rhetorical, and even personal associations, all of which directly condition a reader's response to language. Of the parallel between words-as-symbols and symbols in general, Susanne Langer has said:

Many symbols—not only words, but other forms—may be said to be "charged" with meanings. They have many symbolic and significant functions, and these functions have been integrated into a complex so that they are all apt to be sympathetically invoked with any chosen one.[33]

Critics such as Barthes, placing themselves at the other extreme from a theoretically pure mimesis by giving absolute priority to the connotative aspects of language, reveal themselves as supporters of symbolism (and, often, of Symbolism); but in dismissing the denotative they unjustifiably separate themselves from meaning.

The realization that every important image in literature exists centered somewhere on a scale ranged between the moment atomized and the All mystically comprehended makes new demands upon the interpreter; among the first of these is that he suspend value judgments based on preferences for either the "life-like" or the "indefinite," judgments that have, particularly in the criticism of Spenser and of Joyce, led to the application to their works of what can only be called incorrect standards. As the following chapters will attempt to show, in-depth analysis of the psychology "behind" the actions of Spenser's Guyon or of Milton's Christ, criticism of the "unrealistic" presentation of Donne's Elizabeth Drury, attempts to find mimetic characters and events masked by the symbolic aspects of Joyce's *Ulysses,* are all approaches to these texts made from the wrong end of the scale, as mistaken in their way as, for example, those older allegorizings of Spenser's poem that neglected all other aspects in order to read *The Faerie Queene* as a masked pageant of English history during Elizabeth's reign.

Allegorical narrative and symbolic poetry are realistic modes that omit many of the particularizing details of strongly mimetic literature in order to emphasize the multiple aspects of analogical relationships. All of the works considered in this book are founded, as John Bender says of Spenser's allegory, "in careful observation of human action in the phenomenal world";[34] but reading them is not a process of filling in unstated phenomenal details. The characters, objects, and events never lose whatever mimetic reality the text gives them; allegory, Rosemond Tuve has said, "does not need to turn some personage into Christ or into God the Father."[35] But allegory may none the less stress analogical (i.e., real) connections with these Beings wherever the context demands.

Even though symbolic images have their basis in past usage and in the world view of the writer and of his period, they are creative as well as representational devices.

Like words themselves, symbolic images are seldom simply coined for the occasion by a writer. They have pre-established significances and histories of usage.[36] But it is their function in the literary text itself that determines their value. Claude Lévi-Strauss's discoveries about the transformations of myths can be applied to the kinds of transformations that take place when an inherited symbolic image is employed creatively by a writer. Lévi-Strauss finds that transformations affect "sometimes the framework, sometimes the code, sometimes the message of the myth, but preserving always the myth as such."[37] When historically established meanings become attenuated by the process of cultural change, myths tend to be revived either by "romantic elaboration" or by "redeployment for the purposes of historical legitimation" (p. 280). Lévi-Strauss gives the credit for such changes and redeployments to an apparently unconscious social process rather than to the creative powers of the human mind. However, the writers of the Renaissance and of the early Modern period were fully conscious both of the essential permanence of ancient myths and symbols and their multiple possibilities; they consciously set out to redeploy them.

To describe the history and inherited meanings of an image is an important task, but it is comparable to the work of the lexicographer. The meaning and creative value of an allegory or symbolic poem is determinable only by a further study of the permutations and combinations of these images and of their multiple meanings within the work. The critical reader must therefore be both lexicographer and rhetorician, because meaning exists both within the images and in their creative extensions and unions. Paul Ricoeur, speaking of metaphors and the plural unity they contain, says:

Metaphorical meaning does not consist of a semantic clash but of the *new* predictive meaning which emerges from the collapse of the . . . meaning which obtains if we rely only on the common or usual lexical values of our words. The metaphor is not the enigma but the solution of the enigma.[38]

This provides a concise account of the way symbolic imagery (which includes metaphor) creatively generates rather than conceals or merely transmits meanings. "The mythical image," according to Cassirer, "does not merely reproduce existing distinctions but in the strict sense of the word *evokes* distinctions" (op. cit., p. 203).

The present study concentrates on one particular use of symbolic imagery: the creation of a literary character, a symbolic human figure. As all literature exists somewhere on a scale between absolute mimesis and pure symbolism, so all literary characters are both mimetic and symbolic. A character presented only in terms of specific details not analogous to known human types (again, all but impossible) would be little more than a meaningless face seen briefly in a crowd. A true Everyman, identical at all points with the entire taxonomy of mankind, would be Noman. Twentieth-century readers perhaps required a Roland Barthes to remind them of the fact that literary characters are not real people but artificial constructions. The rise of mimetic literature, which culminated in the realistic/naturalistic novels of the late nineteenth and early twentieth centuries, generated a criticism more strict in its assumption that mimesis was the true imitation of reality than were most of the modern novelists themselves. Literary characters were, and still are, subjected to moral and psychological analyses that seem to suggest that these verbal images are human beings with complete biographies and psychologies only implied by the details included in the novels. But, as Barthes emphasized, a literary character is a combination of selected characteristics centered on a name:

When identical semes traverse the same proper name several times and appear to settle upon it, a character is created. Thus, the character is a product of combinations: the combination is relatively stable (denoted by the recurrence of the semes) and more or less complex (involving more or less congruent, more or less contradictory figures).[39]

Such "semes" can also include implications about non-specified bio-graphical and psychological details—as every reader of Henry James knows. But confidence in the validity of any interpretation drops away quickly as one moves from the implications, which are present in the work, to unspecified details, which are not. That one should even be making such moves must be justified by the nature of the work itself. A plethora of mimetic details suggests the validity of assuming even more such detail as possible and relevant. A work whose structures and meanings are primarily symbolic justifies the exploration of wider symbolic aspects; it does not permit much expansion of the mimetic details about the minds and lives of the characters.

To approach Spenser's *Faerie Queene* by attempting to reconstruct the unstated mental operations of his heroes or to interpret their ac-tions without reference to the analogical links within the work and within the symbolic hierarchy—as has so often been attempted in this century—is to mistake a symbolic poem for a mimetic novel. For a critic then to *judge* the morality of a character's imagined motives approaches absurdity. When a character's psychology matters in the context of a Spenserian narrative, we are taken inside his mind; when we are denied psychological explanations, it is because some other explanation is more important to the context. One is always free, of course, to play author and imagine what might be happening in a character's "mind" at such points, but it is a rather pointless game. And when one's imaginings are at variance with the symbolic impli-cations actually present in episode, they are only irrelevant distractions.

All of the characters studied in the following chapters—whether they are based on "real" people, as in the cases of Elizabeth Drury and Christ, or are purely literary creations like Guyon and Bloom—are strongly symbolic characters. Their nature as symbols is estab-lished by a de-emphasis on dramatized action of the sort that mimetic literature leads one to expect from literary heroes. They are quiet heroes, not only because there is heroic nobility in some kinds of suffering, but also because the quiet hero in some measure sacrifices his mimetic identity in order to gain his symbolic multiplicity. Gu-yon's actions can appear shamefully unheroic if read in purely mi-metic terms, but significantly heroic when he is seen as a symbol. The reality of Elizabeth Drury's individual life is only one, and a much-subdued, element of her presence in Donne's poems. Christ's failure to act, in *Paradise Regained,* is a proper symbolic response to Satan's temptations, though it tends to disturb both Satan and his modern realistic heirs. The partial exception to this pattern is Joyce's Leopold Bloom, who is *both* a symbolic hero and a strongly individual mimetic creation. Joyce was able to exploit opposite ends of the scale at once, but then he had the whole history of literature's movements between mimesis and symbolism to teach him. I suggest in my last chapter, however, that, like Milton, the reader of Joyce will find Spenser a better teacher than Aquinas.

[2]

Spenser's Image of Temperance: Guyon in the Cave and the Bower

Do not prevent the noblest souls which dwell
In Heaven as Ideas eternally
From taking form on earth, and visible,
As your descendants, their true destiny
Achieving.

(*Orlando Furioso*, VII, 61)[1]

The epic is the first flower . . . of a new symbolic mode, the
mode of art. It is not merely a receptacle of old symbols,
namely those of myth, but is itself a new symbolic form, great
with possibilities, ready to take meanings and express ideas
that have had no vehicle before.

(Susanne Langer)[2]

The hero of Book II of *The Faerie Queene* is a signal example of a character in renaissance literature who cannot be successfully interpreted in terms that emphasize either mimetic actions or psychological reactions (though the history of the criticism of this book is full of attempts to grasp Guyon's significance by just such means). Certainly Guyon acts in believable ways, and we are at times given glimpses of the workings of his mind; but the structure, the development, and the meaning of this book do not depend upon these things, but upon a symbolic complex centered on the concept of Temperance. Guyon's thoughts and actions form only a part of this complex. Guyon is a symbolic hero and is not presented as a markedly individualized human being, to whom we can impute motives not specifically mentioned in the text.

Harry Berger, Jr.'s claim, for example, that Guyon, in entering the Cave of Mammon, falls victim to the sin of curiosity,[3] must be judged as arbitrary and mistaken, given that it has no explicit support in the text of the poem itself: had it been so, our author would have told us. Spenser's allegory may veil many things, but it never conceals for long the motives of the characters, when these matter. Certainly Spenser often gives his reader an opportunity to judge a character's motives before they are revealed, but they are always finally revealed. He does not ask us to intuit secret motivations.

Guyon's reasons for entering the Cave of Mammon are far different from and far more important than mere curiosity. Surely Milton interpreted the motivation of this episode correctly, even if he made a mistake about the plot,[4] when he wrote in *Areopagitica*:

That which purifies us is triall, and triall is by what is contrary. That vertue therefore which is but a youngling in the contemplation of evill, and knows not the utmost that vice promises to her followers, and rejects it, is but a blank vertue, not a pure; her whitenesse is but an excrementall whitenesse; Which was the reason why our sage and serious Poet *Spenser*, whom I dare be known to think a better teacher than *Scotus* or *Aquinas*, describing true temperance under the person of *Guion*, brings him in with his palmer through the cave of Mammon, and the bowr of earthly blisse that he might see and know, and yet abstain.[5]

The motive for Guyon entering the Cave is the poem's, much more than it is Guyon's; he is as fated to enter that cave as is any epic hero who ever made a journey to the underworld. The kind of knowledge that Guyon and, more importantly, the reader gain here is not the fruit of idle curiosity, nor is it dangerous to the soul of one who rightly understands his own ability to abstain when confronted with temptations of this kind. Guyon's self-confidence in this episode is not the pride that some critics perceived; if it were, he would have fallen victim to Mammon. (This is the unerringly logical way in which Spenser's narrative inevitably works, not by punishing a hero who has just escaped from temptation and a representative of evil.) His immunity to Mammon's assault proves Guyon right both in his actions and in his understanding of himself.

In a narrative such as this, one must generally take the author at his word. The narrator of *The Faerie Queene* may speak with a voice that belies its claims to antique rusticity, he may utter dark symbolic mysteries and, like Ariosto, he may hold back for a time the names and natures of some of his characters; but he is no modern "unreliable" narrator. The judgments he utters and those that he puts in the

mouths of his heroes are to be taken at face value unless later modified or reversed within the poem. Spenser begins Canto vii, the Cave
of Mammon episode, with an epic simile that must be allowed to
govern interpretation of that episode:

> As Pilot well expert in perilous wave,
>   That to a stedfast starre his course hath bent,
>   When foggy mistes, or cloudy tempests have
>   The faithfull light of that faire lampe yblent,
>   And cover'd heaven with hideous dreriment,
>   Upon his card and compas firmes his eye,
>   The maisters of his long experiment,
>   And to them does the steddy helme apply,
> Bidding his winged vessell fairely forward fly:
>
> So *Guyon* having lost his trusty guide,
>   Late left beyond that *Ydle lake,* proceedes
>   Yet on his way, of none accompanide;
>   And evermore himselfe with comfort feedes,
>   Of his owne vertues, and prayse-worthy deedes.[6]

Only the most one-eyed ironist would find anything but praise in
this epic comparison of Guyon's virtues and deeds to the map and
compass of a master mariner. The simile indicates that it is Guyon's
self-sufficiency, not his weakness, that is being illustrated by his separation from the Palmer in this episode. This initial figure is the
narrator's own agreement with his hero's self-analysis, and neither
pride nor undue curiosity has anything to do with the matter.[7] The
episode also contains a direct statement of what would have happened
had Guyon been morally weak:

> All which he [Mammon] did, to doe him deadly fall
>   In frayle intemperance through sinfull bayt;
>   To which if he inclined had at all,
>   That dreadfull feend, which did behind him wayt,
>   Would him have rent in thousand peeces strayt:
>   But he was warie wise in all his way. . . .
>   (64)

Any leaning toward intemperance would have resulted in Guyon's
destruction within the cave.

If, as an alternative view, one is prepared to accept the claim made by Patrick Cullen that Guyon's decision to enter the Cave of Mammon is an "unknowing demonstration ... of his fallen nature,"[8] it must be in the face of the fact that it is also unknown to all the other characters in the episode, as well as to the narrator himself, who is seldom reluctant to mention the effects of the Fall elsewhere. That the inclination toward intemperance alone would have destroyed Guyon also throws out of court the claims of William Nelson and of Maurice Evans that Guyon sins in the direction of excessive virtue, through what Nelson calls "the ascetic froward"—equally a form of intemperance.[9] In fact, as soon as Guyon's "vitall powres gan wexe both weake and wan" (65), he asks to be returned to the outer world, a retreat from suffering that is difficult to read as the behavior of an extreme ascetic.[10]

The Sibyl in Book VI of the *Aeneid* tells Aeneas that it is very easy to make a journey into hell; coming back is the difficult part. Guyon's swoon on returning to the air is not a sign that he has weakened morally; nor should it be said, as J. E. Hankins says without any justification, that "it is his virtue of temperance that fails, unable to endure any longer after prolonged exposure to temptation."[11] Virtues of the type Spenser deals with are strengthened rather than weakened by testing, and Guyon encounters nothing outside the cave that could cause his temperance to fail. The direct cause of the faint that is given in the poem is not even Guyon's hunger or lack of sleep; rather, Guyon's faint is described simply as the natural result of too quick an exposure to fresh air after three days in underground fumes, an explanation that has proven too concrete for even the most realistic critics.

Of course, physical causes in Spenser often point toward moral causes, but this is not inevitably the case, and especially not always in Book II, which is very much concerned with man's physical health. Guyon's faint carries none of the usual accompaniments of a physical event in *The Faerie Queene* meant to point in an important way to the morality of the characters: there is no mythological parallel to it given, the immediate physical cause is not charged with anything supernatural—it is not a charmed cup or symbolically named fountain—it is merely "this vitall aire" (66). The faint is metaphorically likened to death, but such sleep-death metaphors are commonplace in the period, and this one tells us nothing in particular about Guyon. Though much of importance happens around him during the swoon, Guyon awakens from it unchanged, except perhaps a bit rested, and no other explanation is offered.

That Guyon's divine and human protection during his faint has a spiritual significance has long been recognized, and such a reading is justified by the actual presence in the poem of an angel. But the fact that the operation of Grace in this book is directed toward saving an unconscious hero makes such supernatural intervention even less relevant to the hero's characterization than it would normally be; Grace is something that by its very nature always comes unsought and undeserved; that a character is saved while completely unaware of it can tell us very little about him.

If one refuses to treat Guyon as though he were a character in a modern novel (intuiting his unstated psychological and moral characteristics on the basis of one's reactions to his behavior), the spiritual aspects of the allegory inevitably become more prominent. Those critics who have rejected the view of Guyon as guilty of much more than original sin have nearly all gone on to argue for the primacy of the parallel between Christ's Temptation in the wilderness and Guyon's temptation in the Cave. (Perhaps Milton was the first writer to develop this link at length, in turning the Temptation itself into an epic poem with a quiet hero, though modern detailed critical explication of the parallel originates with the essay by Frank Kermode cited in note 7 above.) The difficulty of stepping even this far from novelistic approaches, to what is, after all, simply an analogue with another narrative, is evidenced by many hostile responses to this interpretation, all asserting strongly that Guyon is not Christ. But of course Guyon is not Christ. He is a man (or, more accurately, an elf) doing what every Christian must do, imitating Christ in his life.

The Christian doctrine of the imitation of Christ had no more important biblical text than the Temptation, because in this episode of his life Christ was more purely human than in any other. Indeed, the most common theological interpretation of the event asserted that

Christ had here divested himself of his divinity in order to act solely as a man, so that his resistance to temptation could serve as an example for all men facing similar situations.[12] What Guyon goes through in the Cave would have been recognized in the Renaissance as the replication of an archetypal pattern, and his behavior would have been seen as modelled on, among other things, that of the Divine Archetype. But in so far as Christ acted as a man during the Temptation, this parallel imputes no especially elevated spiritual nature to Guyon who, like Christ, does nothing humanly impossible. In so far as Christ's actions in the wilderness made it easier for his followers to meet temptation—according to commentators on this text—imitations of Christ in this event have a major difference from the original: Grace has already been established in the world. Grace operates on Guyon's behalf even while he is in the Cave and is not delayed until the following canto. That supernatural laws superior to Mammon are in effect here is demonstrated, in one way, by the fact that Mammon is "constraind t'obay" Guyon's request for an end to the ordeal in spite of his own desires. (66)

But there is more to this episode than an allegorical ritual imitating the Temptation. The dramatic action of the book as a whole is not really advanced by the episode: Guyon is no closer to Acrasia's Bower at the end of Canto vii than he was at the beginning (a fact that is true of many of the cantos of this book). In addition, the episode has little psychological effect on Guyon: he goes into the Cave confident in his ability to resist the temptations of Mammon, and he awakens from his swoon still impervious to the lure of earthly wealth and vainglory, and still subject to the temptations of wrath and of lust. The episode develops the idea of temperance—not so much in Guyon's character as in the book itself and thus in the reader. Since the idea of temperance (i.e., the symbolic structure in all of its manifestations, not simply the abstract idea) is primary, rather than the characters or events, the relationship between that idea and the events, and between the idea and the characters, is always a symbolic one of the type discussed in the previous chapter.

Guyon may learn something of the nature of temperance in some events; he may simply demonstrate temperance in others. In either case, the choice is determined not by a novelistic need for character development but by the needs of those aspects of the idea that are in focus at any given time. Some events may take the hero closer to his journey's end, some may not; the demands of narrative movement are secondary to the demands of symbolic development. We know early on that Guyon will reach his goal in Canto xii, however many seeming digressions he and his author may make along the way; and in the development of the idea of Temperance, the digressions are not digressive.

This does not leave us with a character who is a simple personification or a mere counter in a game of symbolic relationships. Guyon is a very complex character, but his complexity is determined by the meanings he carries with him and (often the same thing) the materials Spenser draws upon in order to create him, not by his psychology or mimetic actions.

In one aspect of his characterization Guyon is a typical young man; in fact, his name is an anagram of the word "young."[13] No book of *The Faerie Queene* is more obviously concerned with the education of a young renaissance nobleman, with what the "Letter to Raleigh" described as the poet's intention "to fashion a gentleman or noble person in vertuous and gentle discipline" (for it is ultimately the reader rather than Guyon toward whom this education is directed). *The Faerie Queene* is not, however, a guide to "how to succeed at court," and the education Book II offers is a radical rather than a conservative one by renaissance standards.

The education in temperance that the book provides is, in spite of Spenser's indebtedness to Aristotle's *Nichomachean Ethics,* a radically Christian one, though it is a Christianity that finds itself in harmony with both Aristotle and Plato. The radical nature of the Christian temperance of Book II springs from no hostility to classical ethics, but rather, from opposition to some aspects of the gentlemanly, chivalric ethos that provides the book's very milieu. Spenser repeatedly places his young hero in situations that would appear, from an external point of view, to be unheroic, even shameful, according to renaissance standards of honor. And yet Guyon is a typical young man in having consciousness of shame (*verecundia,* an aspect of temperance) as one of the important aspects of his character—as he is reminded by Alma at his encounter with Shamefastnesse (ix: 43). Guyon, however, is not dishonored by the seemingly unchivalrous actions he is obliged to take, because the honor with which he is concerned has little to do with simply appearing to be honorable. Guyon can violate some of the accepted codes of behavior of the Renaissance because the virtue he represents exists in independence of such codes.

The relationship between Book I and Book II has often been described as one between the active life and the contemplative life, though there is no agreement among critics about which book represents which type of life. But in fact, both books present heroes who combine the two modes. The difference is one of emphasis. It has always been the function of the epic hero *agere et pati,* both to do *and* to suffer (or to experience). Red Crosse, though he is the Knight of Holinesse and at one point has a vision on the Mount of Contemplation, is nevertheless a true warfaring, very active Christian, for whom any pause can prove destructive; in the narrative action he is repeatedly engaged in chivalric duels with representatives of evil. Guyon is introduced in his book as though he were the same sort of martial hero as Book I's St. George. His countenance is described as paradoxically temperate and terrible, and he is known for his skill in "tourney and in lists" (i: 6). Archimago confidently addresses him as "Faire sonne of *Mars,* that seeks with warlike spoile, / And great atchiev'ments great your selfe to make" (8). But if Guyon is a son of Mars, he takes after his father very little in this book; most of his combats are interrupted or aborted, and, far from being caught with Venus in a net, he is one of her captors.

Yet ironic comparison with Mars is apt in a book that sets its virtue against the two themes of Ariosto's *Orlando Furioso*: wrath and erotic love, Mars and Venus. Spenser's Book II is, like Ariosto's epic, "Of ladies, cavaliers, of love and war, / Of courtesies and of brave deeds,"[14] but with an interpretation of these themes at marked odds with Ariosto's, all the more so because in other ways Ariosto is one of Spenser's main models.

When Guyon's deeds of arms appear on the surface to be heroic,

the reader is likely to find Guyon criticized by the narrator or by a
trustworthy character; it is when he looks dishonorable that we learn
he has achieved honor. Since he knew well in advance whom he was
attacking and what device he bore, Guyon's swerving from his charge
at Red Crosse in Canto i is not justified by the law of arms and
within that system would have been taken as a sign of cowardice;
once entered into, fortune should have been allowed to decide the
issue. But the law of temperance here overrules the law of arms. In a
later episode Guyon fights with apparent heroism against Huddibras
and Sans-loy in the Castle of Medina, but he shares with them the
condemnation of the narrator, who finds it a "Straunge sort of fight
. . . A triple warre with triple enmitee, / All for their Ladies froward
love to gaine" (ii: 26). He also earns the criticism of Medina, who
includes Guyon in her attack on those who seek to right wrongs with
bloodshed:

> Ah puissaunt Lords, what cursed evill Spright,
>   Or fell *Erinnys,* in your noble harts
>   Her hellish brond hath kindled with despight,
>   And stird you up to worke your wilfull smarts?
>   Is this the joy of armes? be these the parts
>   Of glorious knighthood, after bloud to thrust,
>   And not regard dew right and just desarts?
>   Vaine is the vaunt, and victory unjust,
> That more to mighty hands, then rightfull cause doth trust.
>
> And were there rightfull cause of difference,
>   Yet were not better, faire it to accord,
>   Then with bloud guiltinesse to heape offence,
>   And mortall vengeaunce joyne to crime abhord?
>   O fly from wrath, fly, O my liefest Lord:
>   Sad be the sights, and bitter fruits of warre,
>   And thousand furies wait on wrathfull sword;
>   Ne ought the prayse of prowesse more doth marre,
> Then fowle revenging rage, and base contentious jarre.
>
> (ii: 29–30)

After his defeat of Furor and the old hag Occasion, Guyon is
accused of base behavior by two literalistic critics, Atin and Pyrochles,
who cannot see beyond the mimetic surface. "Vile knight," says Atin,

That knights and knighthood doest with shame upbray,
And shewst th'ensample of they childish might,
With silly weake old woman thus to fight.
Great glory and gay spoils sure hast thou got,
And stoutly prov'd thy puissaunce here in sight.

(iv: 45)

Guyon commits another breach of the rules of combat when he beheads Pyrochle's horse in v: 4–5 and is called a coward for it by his opponent; and when Pyrochles is asked why he attacked Guyon, he gives an answer that would have more than justified his actions within the renaissance code of honor:

It was complaind, that thou hadst done great tort
Unto an aged woman, poore and bare,
And thralled her in chaines with strong effort,
Voide of all succour and needfull comfort;
That ill beseemes thee, such as I thee see,
To worke such shame.

(17)

Guyon smiles at this, and that is perhaps the proper response to those who read symbols mimetically; but there is more here than simply a joke at Pyrochles's short-sightedness. It is yet another indication that the chivalric code of honor may misjudge the truly heroic act.

In Canto vi the fight between Guyon and Cymochles is interrupted by Phaedria who describes such combat as self-destructive (32). "Debatefull strife," she goes on to say, "and cruell enmitie / The famous name of knighthood fowly shend" (35). She has, of course, her own reasons for opposing combat, being herself a representative of the concupiscent humors, always opposed to the irascible. But, like other figures of excess in Book II, Phaedria is capable of producing beneficial results when she is used to temper her opposite—a technique that makes Spenser's allegory no simple battle between good and evil. Again in this episode Guyon is accused of cowardice because of his temperate behavior (39).

The combats of Canto viii are undertaken for Guyon by Arthur while Guyon lies unconscious on the ground; and in Cantos xi and xii, it is Arthur who does battle while Guyon faces no opposition of the martial variety at all in his invasion of the Bower of Bliss. Even the battle that Arthur and Guyon share against the rabble outside Alma's castle in Canto ix is of reduced heroic proportions, the enemy being "idle shades" without substance, compared in an epic simile to a swarm of Irish gnats (15–16).

Yet the book does not really devalue military heroism nor suggest that Guyon's reputation for it is undeserved. We are repeatedly reminded of Guyon's reputation and of the unspecified "hard assayes" (i: 35) that are said to intervene between events in Book II. Belphoebe, whose voice must be taken as an absolutely reliable one, is given lines describing "deedes of armes and prowesse martiall" as deserving praise "most of all" (iii: 37). Guyon in the Cave of Mammon expresses his desire to spend the "flitting houres" of his life "in armes, and in atchievements brave" (vii: 33). But for symbolic reasons this aspect of Guyon's character is played down and thwarted in the narrative action. That he has this aspect to his character at all serves mainly to prevent the reader from judging him as do his opponents. Spenser's main point is that the true warfaring knight is willing to appear wrong for the right reasons. It is not, therefore, the reader's task to find what is at fault in Guyon's actions—when he goes wrong, we are told—but to find the errors in the ethic that would judge him cowardly or weak when he is instead being temperate.

The distinction being made in Book II between right and wrong uses of combat is essentially between what is appropriate in war and what is suitable in "domestic" conflicts—when these do not involve civil war. The action and symbolism of the book deal almost exclusively with "internal" disputes, including conflicts between persons and between psychological states. They are conflicts that cannot be resolved by violence. The book is about hostilities at home rather than abroad, and Guyon as an elf is more literally "at home" in Fairyland than any of Spenser's other heroes. The true enemy in his encounter with Red Crosse is Guyon's faulty initial judgment, which he corrects by ending the fight.

This point about the uses of combat is stressed through the relationships between Guyon and his avatars. Guyon is linked by the narrative with Huddibras and Sans-loy. He is also linked with Pyrochles and Cymochles, who are knights like Guyon, but victims of the excess of qualities that in proper control are valuable, qualities that exist in better balance in Guyon himself. The poet's descriptions of Pyrochles and Cymochles, in fact, sound very much like the opening description of Guyon:

> *Pyrochles* is his name, renowmed farre
> For his bold feats and hardy confidence,
> Full oft approv'd in many a cruell warre.
>
> (iv: 41)

> He [Cymochles] was a man of rare redoubted might,
> Famous throughout the world for warlike prayse,
> And glorious spoiles, purchast in perilous fight.
>
> (v: 26)

This apparent closeness of Guyon to his enemies has led to readings of this book as a kind of psychomachia, but to see Guyon's opponents as merely aspects of himself or of the reader is to ignore the important public purpose of the book: its presentation of an ethic for use in times of peace at home. Belphoebe, after her praise of military heroism in Canto iii, adds: "Abroad in armes, at home in studious kind / Who seekes with painfull toile, shall honor soonest find" (40). Book II is interested in both types of honor, to be sure, but its main interest is overwhelmingly in the home-bred variety. Guyon in the action of the book is primarily a student rather than a warrior, the Palmer is his tutor, and one entire canto (x) is devoted to the reading of books. Reason and rule, not arms, are held up in this book as the proper judges of conflict. Consequently, the gentlemanly code of defending one's honor by duelling and the conventional justifications for taking personal revenge are subjected here to severe questioning.

In holding Guyon up as a model for his contemporaries to imitate, Spenser was asking a good deal of them. He was advocating that quarrels once entered into and slights to one's honor be resolved by temperate mediation rather than by combat, even when such a resolution would appear to the world as dishonorable. This was, of course, the position adopted by Elizabeth herself; but it remained at odds with the gentleman's private code throughout her reign, and violent private quarrels became a major social problem in the next reign. Public interest in the subject of personal revenge found its literary outlet in the revenge tragedy, though it is perhaps because Spenser's poem pre-dates *Hamlet* that the influence of that genre upon Book II of *The Faerie Queene* has not been recognized. Nevertheless, though the book shares few of the stock characteristics that identify the seventeenth-century variety of the genre as it descended from *Hamlet,* some of its roots are the same as those of Shakespeare's play, and its subject involves the same ethical conflict. Guyon's behavior can also be examined from some of the same historical and ethical bases as Hamlet's has been.

Guyon's quest against Acrasia is described throughout the book as a quest for vengeance, and revenge serves as a motivation for much of the minor action as well. Guyon vows his services to the disguised Duessa in Canto i in order "That short revenge the man may overtake" who had supposedly dishonored her (18). The encounter with Amavia and the dead Mordant in the same canto is full of the rhetoric and imagery of vengeance and of allusions to other tragedies involving revenge. Amavia's first words, uttered with "a ruefull voice, that dearnly cride / With percing shriekes" (35) include a plea for revenge, in which she echoes the lament of Dido before her own self-immolation in Book IV of the *Aeneid.*

> But if that carelesse heavens (quoth she) despise
>   The doome of just revenge, and take delight
>   To see sad pagents of mens miseries,
>   As bound by them to live in lives despight,
>   Yet can they not warne death from wretched wight.
>   Come then, come soone, come sweetest death to mee.
>   (36)

Guyon suspects the cause before he is told that "revenging fate" brought about Amavia's condition (44). The cup poisoned with a charm, which Acrasia gave to Mordant, is a standard revenge device, the charm itself implying that some kind of revenging justice is accomplished by the gift: *"Give death to him that death does give, / And loss of love, to her that loves to live"* (55). This is reminiscent of, among other things, the robe and chaplet Medea sent to Jason's wife; and it is thus no surprise to come upon the story of Jason and Medea worked in ivory on the gate of the Bower of Bliss.

The episode of Mordant and Amavia ends as it began, with a call for vengeance, though this time from the lips of Guyon:

> Sir *Guyon* more affection to increase,
> Bynempt a sacred vow, which none should aye releace.

> The dead knights sword out of his sheath he drew,
> With which he cut a locke of all their heare,
> Which medling with their bloud and earth, he threw
> Into the grave, and gan devoutly sweare;
> Such and such evill God on Guyon reare,
> And worse and worse young Orphane be thy paine,
> If I or thou dew vengeance doe forbeare,
> Till guiltie bloud her guerdon doe obtaine:
> So shedding many teares, they closd the earth againe.

> (60–61)

Several writers have commented on the pagan nature of the burial scene that includes this vow, and more recently Carol V. Kaske has found Christian and classical precedents for the burial in four of the Seven Corporal Works of Mercy (as listed by Spenser in Book I) and in Sophocles's *Antigone,* though she concludes that the episode's paganism is "more conspicuous than its Christianity."[15]

But more surprising than either the unusual concern Spenser shows for the treatment of corpses or Guyon's willingness to judge Amavia's suicide as legal is the archaic nature of this vow, which ends the canto. God does indeed get a mention in it, but He is here a God whose vengeance can extend even to a negligent revenger. Spenser's main source for the vow, I Sam. 3:17, comes nowhere near the violence of this passage. The cutting of the hair in Spenser may remind the reader of the death of Dido in the *Aeneid,* but mingling of the hair with blood and earth and casting it into the grave is a *magical* rite through and through. It is an act of sympathetic magic, which creates a simulacrum of a man out of the essential elements of creation, the hair carrying the very souls of the participants into the effigy. This magical ritual makes Guyon one with Mordant and Amavia. He is sympathetically and symbolically buried with them (an idea that is anticipated by the death-like physical reaction he experiences when he sees Mordant, Amavia, and the Babe in stanza 42).[16] Their cause is now his.

The rite is, as it turns out, white magic; though one needs to be a careful reader to recognize this in the first instance. The pagan and Old Testament overtones of the burial make it sound as though Guyon wishes to turn himself into a personification of Revenge rather than into Mordant's ritual brother, and there remains a possibility that he intends both. Under the pagan revenge code, which still survived in Spenser's day, particularly in Ireland, the revenger needed to be related to the dead victim by blood or by adoption, and Guyon's ritual union would thus symbolically qualify him to be Mordant's and Amavia's blood revenger. The end of Canto i leaves open some of the same questions about revenge that plague Hamlet: what type of vengeance is demanded, and who is justified in seeking it; but the renaissance reader would no doubt have imagined at this point that Guyon meant to kill Acrasia, not merely to arrest her for prostitution and break up her brothel.

However, the important questions about revenge that this episode raises exist in the mind of the reader, not, apparently, in the mind of the main character. Hamlet may concern himself with the ethics of being a revenger, but so far as we know Guyon from the very beginning intended the kind of temperate vengeance he exacts. Guyon's thinking on the matter is closed to the reader. The development of the idea is realized instead in symbolic action, as various aspects of wrath, love, and temperance are given imaginative life in episodes that each add their contribution to the whole.

The reader's psychology is skillfully manipulated by Spenser. If we expect Guyon, after Canto i, to become a blood revenger, there is much to support and keep alive that expectation—though there is much more to keep it ambiguous. The blood on the hands of the baby Ruddymane may, as has been suggested, represent original sin or the Irish O'Neils. The text itself, however, offers its own definition from the Palmer: "a sacred Symbole it may dwell / In her sonnes flesh, to minde revengement, / And be for all chast Dames an endlesse moniment" (ii: 10). The Palmer's interpretation of the symbol is as reductive as any single definition of a symbol can be, but it brings to the surface of the narrative the meaning necessary at that point to keep alive the idea and the question of revenge. Attitudes toward revenge in the Castle of Medina are also ambiguous, but suggestive of the direction in which the idea is developing. Even though Medina speaks out, in the lines quoted earlier, against increasing a crime with "bloud guiltinesse" through "mortall vengeaunce" (30), Guyon later instructs Medina to name the child Ruddymane in order that he might be "taught / T'avenge his Parents death on them, that had it wrought" (iii: 2).

But as blood revenge begins to seem less and less of a likely motive to attribute to Guyon, the name of revenge itself becomes contaminated by association. The villain Archimago is also characterized in this book by a desire for revenge, in his case against Red Cross and Guyon; and in Canto iii the deceiver is deceived when he foolishly chooses Braggadocchio as "a person meet, / Of his revenge" (11). Occasion, in Canto iv, urges Furor "to heape more vengeance on that wretched wight" Phedon (5); and when Furor himself is captured, he gnashes his iron teeth "threatning revenge in vaine" (15). Atin seeks out Cymochles in Canto v in order that he might revenge his brother Pyrochles, and Cymochles, at the end of that canto, utters a vow of vengeance which, though briefer than Guyon's vow, is certainly intended to remind us of it. When we finally meet the personification of Cruel Revenge beside the road to hell in Canto vii: 22, we can have no doubt that what Guyon is seeking is something other than this.

In Canto viii vengeance is qualified with the adjectives "hot" (11), "vile" (13, 16), and "greedy" (15); and when Arthur in that canto has defeated Cymochles, he has no real wish to kill him, "But casting wrongs and all revenge behind, / More glory thought to give life, then decay" (51). Yet earlier in the canto Arthur had expresesed his belief that guilt is inherited and may be wiped out only by vengeance:

> Indeed (then said the Prince) the evill donne
> Dyes not, when breath the bodie first doth leave,

> But from the grandsyre to the Nephewes sonne,
> And all his seed the curse doth often cleave,
> Till vengeance utterly the guilt bereave:
> So streightly God doth judge.
>
> (29)

The solution to this apparent contradiction is included in the last line above: vengeance belongs to God, not to man. The civil struggles that fill the book of *Briton moniments,* which Arthur reads in Alma's castle, illustrate graphically what happens in history when men seek to usurp this divine right. Yet Guyon continues to describe his quest as one "to avenge" the wicked deeds of Acrasia (ix: 9); thus, when his revenge takes the form of capturing her in a net, dismantling her garden, and sending her off to Gloriana, our final understanding of "vengeance" in its proper human form is of a preventative rather than a retributive force.

For a direct statement of the ethics of revenge that motivate Guyon's actions, one need look no further than the *Discourse of Civill Life* by Spenser's friend Lodowick Bryskett.[17] Though not published until 1606, this book purports to be a record of a series of conversations in which Spenser himself was a participant. Bryskett acknowledges *The Faerie Queene* as a work with a parallel purpose to his own; and, though much of the *Discourse* is not original to Bryskett, a good deal of it reads as though it were a commentary on Book II.

The aim of the *Discourse* is to demonstrate "practicke felicite," the only type possible in a world that has no true felicity; and it finds that condition to consist "in vertuous actions, and reducing of a man's passions under the rule of reason" (p. 22).

Bryskett offers a Platonic rather than an Aristotelian definition of temperance. Like the temperance of Spenser's book, it is grounded upon knowledge: "For Temperance being the rule and measure of Vertue, upon which dependeth mans felicitie; the opinion of this divine Philosopher [Plato] was, that he that was ignorant could not know temperance" (pp. 62–63).

The book includes a long discussion of revenge, duelling, giving and taking the lie, in which Bryskett suggests that justice through personal combat is a modern rather than a primitive code, and that private duelling was not permitted in ancient times, when one-to-one combats took place only between national enemies (pp. 64–67). Fredson Bowers, in his study of revenge tragedy, has said that part of the problem of the ethics of revenge in Elizabeth's times lay in the fact that "the Elizabethans were conscious of the earlier periods of lawlessness when revenge was a right."[18] The primitivism of Bryskett, however, looks back to an earlier time that reverses the possibilities of justifying revenge by historical precedent. I would suggest that Spenser does the same thing in Book II—that the primitiveness of Guyon's behavior in the burial scene is not only a mask for modern Christian attitudes but also a much more primitive behavior than it at first appears. While seeming to be the actions of a pagan living in a world of dark rites and blood revenge, Guyon's actions turn out to be those of a hero living close to the golden age.

Bryskett states the common argument against revenge: it usurps God's right and the rights of the magistrate (p. 77). He invokes the example of Aristotle's magnanimous man, who despises injuries done to him. His conclusions about the available alternative to blood revenge are the same as those reached by Spenser in his presentation of Guyon's vengeance:

And what more glorious revenge can a man desire, or what more notable testimonie of his vertue, then to have him [the offender] corrected, and rest infamous by the punishment which law shall inflict upon him who hath done him injury? Or what else do these furious minded men seeke in fine by their combat? (pp. 78–79)

Guyons quest is not, therefore, inconclusive, as Berger suggests (p. 240); nor is there any need to argue, as Fowler does, that the vengeance Guyon seeks is an impossible reestablishment of prelapsarian justice and that "Acrasia [i.e., concupiscence] cannot in this life be put to death."[19] As this and subsequent books of *The Faerie Queene* make clear, Spenser has no desire to put concupiscence to death; he seeks to control it with temperance and chastity.

In developing the idea of just revenge in this way, Spenser is consciously manipulating reader response, inviting the reader to suspect the wrong definition of revenge, while the poem is developing the right one. In seeming to set up the plot of a revenge tragedy, he manipulates reader expectations of genre; and epic, as the genre that includes all others, gave him free reign to do this. Tragedy and Seneca are very much in the air throughout this book. The story of the deaths of Mordant and Amavia is described by the narrator as "their sad Tragedie" (ii: 1). Phedon, in Canto iv, speaks of his experience as "my Tragedie" (27), and it too is a story of jealousy and revenge.

Senecan tragedy offers an ideal foil for Spenser's temperate reevaluation of passion and revenge, which are Seneca's two main themes. The story of Jason and Medea, alluded to in the first canto and recalled elaborately in the last, would probably have been known to the widest section of Spenser's audience through the translation of Seneca's *Medea* made by John Studley in 1566, which had been included in 1581 in *Seneca his Tenne Tragedies*. Spenser's choice of the name Phaedria for one of his seductresses was perhaps also intended to bring the shadow of Seneca into the poem, reminding the reader of the vicious enticer Phaedra in Seneca's version of the *Hippolytus,* the allusion suggesting the deeper evil that lies behind the laughter of Spenser's light-hearted advocate of the pleasure principle.[20] The false accusation of rape in Seneca's play is also a motif that appears in Spenser's poem, in Duessa's accusation against Red Cross; and Hippolytus himself, in his devotion to Diana and rejection of womankind, may have been one of the models for Guyon. The ghost of Tantalus, who appears in the Cave of Mammon, had previously materialized in Seneca's *Thyestes,* where he introduced the theme of inherited guilt.

In addition to such allusions, there is a direct link in Spenser's poem to one of the first English Senecan tragedies, Sackville's and Norton's *Gorboduc.* Spenser borrowed from it his account of the Gorboduc story in *Briton moniments,* which as a whole parallels Sackville and Norton in its theme of British national unity, in its derivation from Geoffrey of Monmouth, and in the importance of revenge.

But the Senecan themes and any possible allusions to Seneca are, as I have suggested, subversive and subverted. Though Guyon is apparently passive throughout most of the book, he is not Prince Hamlet, nor meant to be. His failure to move forward decisively to his goal, his refusal to act when circumstances seem to demand it, are not due to the melancholy of a man harboring an unfulfilled desire for revenge, or to the stoic brooding of a Senecan hero. Nor is this the result of any indecisiveness about the rightness of his actions.[21] Guyon is passive throughout so much of his book because he is a "quiet hero," whose primary function is to "see and know, and yet abstain." This does not make him a negative creation, because the emphasis of the poem is not on his abstention but on what he sees and knows, and it is this that determines what he "is" as a character.

To return at last to the Mammon episode, Guyon sees the glories of the world as Christ saw them, from their diabolic perspective; he knows that the proper response to these powerful but, to him, un-tempting sights is a quiet sufferance and a final turning away (in which Guyon proves to be even milder than Christ). To have avoided the experience would have transformed Guyon's temperance into one of those cloistered virtues of which Milton was so contemptuous; true temperance must arise from knowledge and abstention.

If Guyon actually were the revenger that the poem ironically sug-gests he might be, then the Cave of Mammon would in fact be a diversion from his goal, and a most appropriate one in terms of the code of revenge that the poem opposes, since under that code, wealth could serve as a substitute for vengeance. Even under Brehon law, as Spenser records in his *View of the State of Ireland,* money could be accepted as a compensation for murder.[22] From this point of view, Mammon may be seen acting as though he were Acrasia's second, offering *éric,* blood money, as an alternative to vengeance; but Guyon is a Golden Age figure, though he lives simultaneously in the modern world, and he will not accept Mammon's claim that "Thou that doest live in later times, must wage / Thy workes for wealth" (vii: 18). The money Mammon pours out on the ground is associated with "the guiltlesse bloud pourd oft on ground" (13); and while Guyon has no objections to accepting honorable rewards, even of money, he cannot accept gifts when "bloud guiltinesse or guile them blot" (19).

Thus, though Mammon may appear to be offering temptations to Guyon (at least he appears to himself to be doing this), they are no more real temptations than Guyon is a real blood revenger; and the episode does not function as a diversion from the quest. Rather, it is like a dumb-show in a tragedy, or the vision that the witches present to Macbeth. It is, in other words, a ritualistic performance in which heavily stylized characters demonstrate to the hero and the audience the essence of the action in which he is involved. Avarice is a discordant form of love, and the temptations of Mammon, culminating in the black Garden of Proserpina, point symbolically to the Bower of Bliss and show Guyon in an undisguised way the true nature of that garden and the results, not so much of giving in to Acrasia's erotic temptations, as of being the wrong kind of revenger or, more importantly, of being a revenger for the wrong reasons—for love of wealth and position.

I have spent so long on this particular aspect of Guyon's characterization because it is such an excellent illustration of how an author may use in dramatic, imaginative ways what a character *is not,* in order to illustrate what he *is.* It is a particularly effective means of presenting a quiet hero. Guyon is not presented as simply non-vengeful—a fairly negative characteristic in a narrative. He is an anti-revenger. We see him in that character as he reveals himself in the action and symbolic imagery, however, not by any exploration of what he personally thinks about revenge. Spenser makes his temperate point by ironic use of one of the most violent genres he had available to him.

Even within the overt genre of Spenser's poem, the epic, conventional expectations are manipulated as they affect the characterization of Guyon, though here the ambiguities were built into the history of the genre itself. Guyon may give hints of being a wrathful Achilles at the beginning of Book II, but it is clear long before the Homeric voyage of Canto xii that his true epic progenitor is the cautious and wise Ulysses.

An association of a character with Ulysses, as was noted in the first chapter above, is no guarantee that he is meant to appear unambiguously heroic. The history of the criticism of Homer's hero reads like an expanded version of the history of critical responses to Guyon. Qualities of Ulysses that one generation finds praiseworthy are attacked by later generations as signs of his weakness. The Renaissance largely inherited the Stoic tradition of praising Ulysses as a model of patience, prudence, and fortitude, following Horace, Cicero, and Seneca; this was the same view that had influenced Plutarch, Apuleius, Marcus Aurelius, and some Fathers of the Church.[23] In sixteenth-century England, Sir Thomas Elyot suggested Ulysses to Henry VIII as a model to be imitated, describing him as a man "wise, witty, courteous, resourceful, and richly virtuous" (ibid.). But, as Stanford notes, there was also a survival of the old antipathy toward Ulysses. A Ulysses figure could have been developed in either direction.

Historically, negative views of Ulysses have centered on two main points: his craftiness and his tears, the latter of which were judged to be unmanly. Spenser's Guyon ironically attracts to himself some of this negative reputation. Pyrochles, in his first encounter with Guyon, has heard of his opponent before, and attributes to him a reputation for guile: "So hast though oft with guile thine honour blent" (v: 5). Again in Canto viii Pyrochles claims that Guyon has made himself "famous through false trechery, / And crownd his coward crest with knightly stile" (12). The source of this accusation indicates how it is to be taken, as does the presence in the book of yet another foil to Guyon, a character who deserves the charge of having earned honor through guile: Braggadocchio. Spenser guards against the historically possible negative view of his Ulysses figure by displacing it onto a braggart. As for Ulysses's tears, Guyon too has "lamenting eyes" (ii: 45), but in such a context that there can be no doubt that Spenser regards sympathy of this sort as an essential part of virtuous manhood rather than as a fault.

Spenser handles the negative potentials of his analogue in this way in order to direct his reader clear of false interpretations of Guyon, making it quite certain that the "good" Ulysses is being recalled. The misleading early hints that the author plants, suggesting that Guyon might be an Achilles of wrath, are meant to initiate a process of character analysis, which through necessary revisions along the way leads to a true understanding of the hero. Not that the reader is meant to simply forget the misleading suggestions, any more than he is meant to forget the false notion that Guyon is a blood revenger;

wrath, guile, unmanliness are all, according to the ethics of this poem, excesses of passions and qualities that in proper balance and control are positive virtues: i.e., righteous anger, intelligence, temperance. The relationship between the good Ulysses and the deceitful and cowardly Ulysses, between Guyon and Braggadocchio, is not so much one of opposition as of perversion of the true through excess or underdevelopment. To see Guyon's self-esteem before his entrance into the Cave of Mammon as vainglorious is to mistake Guyon for his foils and so to mistake Spenser's method. When Guyon is wrathful, it is sometimes a just anger; it is at other times a tendency toward excess that will very shortly be corrected; but there always remains a vast gulf between the anger of Guyon and that of wrathful Pyrochles. Guyon is never punished for his deviations as the other characters are for their excesses; he is merely corrected—at times, self-corrected.[24]

Guyon must go "below the earth" (vii: 66) to the Cave of Mammon, for one reason among the many, because Ulysses and all of his epic heirs had made journeys to the underworld. The Cave is a part of the symbolic furnishings of the poem and indicates, simply by the fact that Guyon is present in it, what Guyon is. Its epic archetype is the Homeric land of the dead, located by one writer, as Spenser would have learned from Holinshed's *Irish Chroncile,* at the northern edge of Ulster. But the Cave is, I believe, also modelled on the Cave of the Nymphs in the thirteenth book of the *Odyssey,* as that cave had been interpreted by Porphyry; and Guyon, in a dead sleep before the mouth of Mammon's underground home while the action goes on around him, creates a tableau related to that of Ulysses sleeping before the cave in his own homeland. (The *Odyssey,* it should be added, imputes no blame to Ulysses for this sleep.)

The Cave of the Nymphs is, according to Porphyry, a symbol of the world, at least so far as the world has been generated from matter. Like Spenser's cave, it is structured so that one encounters levels of increasingly profound symbolic darkness as one descends, "and its very bottom is darkness itself"[25] like the black Garden of Proserpina. (Porphyry says that Proserpine received her education from nymphs in a cave such as the one in Homer.) The Cave of the Nymphs is therefore a Platonic symbolic structure, each deeper region representing a further removal from Divine Light. In Homer, the Cave is a storehouse for objects of value; it contains the bowls and jars of the nymphs and the honey of the bees, and it also houses the looms on which the nymphs weave their webs. (Arachne is found weaving "her cunning web" in Mammon's Cave [28].) In it Ulysses hides his treasures.

A non-Platonic reading based on the parallels between the caves in Homer and in Spenser might lead the reader to assume that Ulyssean Guyon would discover that the riches of the Cave actually belonged to him, that he had a right to them; Guyon himself makes the suggestion that he could accept offered riches if he were convinced of their guiltless origins. But, according to the Neoplatonic Porphyry, Homer's Cave of the Nymphs is not somewhere to store one's treasures; it is instead a place to divest oneself of them, a place to learn sacrifice, humility, and temperance:

In this cave, therefore, says Homer, all external possessions must be deposited. Here, naked, and assuming a suppliant habit, afflicted in body, casting aside everything superfluous, and being averse to the energies of sense, it is requisite to sit at the foot of the olive and consult with Minerva by what means we may most effectively destroy that hostile rout of passions which insidiously lurk in the secret recesses of the soul. (pp. 38–39)

This is the way Spenser too reads Homer and presents his Ulysses. In the Cave of Mammon episode, the interpretation of Ulysses-Guyon that Spenser does *not* wish to be adopted—that of Guyon as a covetous man—is not merely avoided but displaced to other characters: Mammon, Tantalus, Pilate.[26] The true Ulysses, Porphyry's temperate worshipper of wisdom, then stands forth all the more strongly.[27]

Ultimately, however, an ironic distance separates Guyon even from his model in the good Ulysses, since as a Christian knight Guyon is capable of virtue far exceeding that of his literary ancestor. When Ulysses sails past the sirens, he is bound to a mast and cries to be released; but, as Kitchin noted, when Guyon goes through the same experience in his voyage in Canto xii, his only restraints are verbal, and his self-control produces a victory "far nobler than that of Ulysses."[28] Though the Cave of Mammon alludes simultaneously to the epic Hades, the Cave of the Nymphs, and the wilderness of Christ's

Temptation, the last of these has priority in determining how Guyon behaves in the narrative.

But the book's total image of temperance takes control over all analogues, determines their relationships to each other, and accounts for the differences of Spenser's poem from them. When Guyon faints after his experience in the cave and is guarded by an angel, the event is partially explained by its analogies with Ulysses before the Cave of the Nymphs and its links with Christ's rest and angelic visitation after the Temptation, but it is only fully explained by its relationship to the rest of Book II. The immediate cause of the faint given in the poem is, as I have stressed before, a physical one, and one must trust the teller in a narrative like this. In Book II temperance is presented in both its mental and physical aspects. The relationship between Canto ix, the Castle of Alma, and Canto x, *Briton moniments* and the *Antiquitie of Faerie,* is primarily one between the physical nature of man and the mental. The allegory of the human body that occupies Canto ix includes the mind, but the concern there is with the mind's operation; Canto x is offered as an account of the mind's actual content—its memory. That the same sort of pairing exists, though with a reversal of the physical/mental pattern, between the Cave of Mammon and Guyon's faint is suggested not only by the obvious parallels between Guyon's tours of the two allegorical "houses" of Mammon and Alma, but also by the division of the Cave and the faint between two cantos.

Because of Grace, Guyon can sleep; forced to it by physical necessity, he can relax his wakeful vigilance against the enemies of temperance. The need for sleep may be a human weakness, but it is not a moral one. It is an aspect of human limitations that leads the good man not into sin but into a confident trust in angelic protection: "They for us fight, they watch and dewly ward / And their bright Squadrons round about us plant, / And all for love, and nothing for reward" (viii: 2). Far from being a moral fall, Guyon's faint is an escape from the monster he had seen sitting before the gates of hell: "selfe-consuming Care, / Day and night keeping wary watch and ward ... Ne would he suffer Sleepe once thither-ward" (vii: 25).

Guyon's faint is also an illustration of the concept of Fortune that pervades Book II. Fortune, like her secondary personification in the old hag, Occasion, of Canto iv, is a force hostile to both the virtuous and the vicious. As Guyon tells Arthur:

> Fortune, the foe of famous chevisaunce
> Seldome (said *Guyon*) yields to vertue aide,
> But in her way throwes mischiefe and mischaunce,
> Whereby her course is stopt, and passage staid.
>
> (ix: 8)

The only effective counter to Fortune is Grace (cf. xi: 30). Though an honorable man is as likely to be overthrown by Fortune as an intemperate one, the difference is that the honorable man receives no guilt from his fall; and he has God's Grace to protect him while he is down. The hostility of Fortune is one of the factors that justifies the internalizing of the concept of honor that takes place during Book II. Because the fall of a good man looks very much like the fall of an evil one, distinctions based on something other than appearances have to be made; and the truly honorable man has to accept the necessity of appearing at times as if he were dishonorable.

Readers who insist on the qualities that determine characterization in realistic novels—dramatic action and psychological penetration—have floundered in dealing with Guyon's faint. Yet Spenser himself seems to have been aware of the potential Pyrochleses among his readers and to have deliberately subverted and frustrated their expectations. Nothing could be less dramatic and less revealing psychologically than a hero in a dead faint for fifty-two Spenserian stanzas (a symbolic year). This is a much different device than that of taking a hero off stage for a time; Guyon is present, and the narrative action of Canto viii does not permit us to forget him. Guyon at this point is the quiet hero par excellence, and one is forced to revise one's conventional expectations completely.

Something of the same is true of Canto x. As Hughes long ago pointed out, "Homer or Virgil would not have suffered the Action of the Poem to stand still whilst the Hero had been reading a Book."[29] Hughes concluded that it was a mistake to judge Spenser strictly by the rules of epic poetry. It is equally a mistake today to judge him through the conventions of the novel. *The Faerie Queene* is one of the most inclusive, yet one of the most subversive, narratives ever written. For all of its precedents, it has no real precedent, but demands that the reader learn how to read it by its own rules. Learning these rules opens up a world of richness and complexity that is, in fact, an image of reality itself.

Yet another genre that provides precedents for Spenser's methods of characterization is the morality play; in Book II Spenser seems to draw particularly on that sub-genre of morality plays that dealt with the education of youth. The conventions of this genre determine both character types and the relationships between characters.[30] Guyon, as a young man gaining an education and meeting temptations that threaten his temperance, is in these aspects identical to the Youth figure of the education plays. In nearly all of these moralities, which were performed both on the Continent and in England during Spenser's lifetime, the chief antagonist of the Youth figure is a version of Aphrodite Pandemos at her most seductive. In George Gascoigne's *Glass of Government* (1575) she is the harlot Lamia, named for the female monster that sucks the blood of youth; in Spenser, she is both Phaedria and Acrasia, the latter also metaphorically a lamia (xii: 73). Between Youth and Venus in the moralities stands a figure of Wisdom or Nature, who is generally a teacher, priest, or aged counsellor; in the *Glass of Government* he is Gnomaticus the schoolmaster; in an older play, *Lusty Juventus,* he is Good Counsel, addressed in the play as "father." In Spenser he is the Palmer, a character who is normally seen as an allegorical figure of reason, but who is, less reductively, an embodiment of the wisdom of age.[31]

But though Guyon and the "sage and sober" Palmer (i: 7) are clearly pupil and tutor,[32] Youth being led by Age, the normal plot tracing Youth's seduction and subsequent reformation is subverted. The medieval mistrust of Youth's ability to resist temptation (along with the medieval relish in stories of his failure) did not die out in the Renaissance. When Guyon is carried away from the Palmer by Phaedria, expectations based on genre, as well as on one's knowledge of the young, point toward a fall. Even the argument before the Canto

(vi) seems to predict it: "Guyon is of immodest Merth / led into loose desire." But "loose desire" turns out to be a definition of Phaedria's island rather than of Guyon's emotions. The role of seduced Youth, like that of violent revenger, is displaced to other characters, who then serve as foils for Guyon's virtues. Cymochles, won over by Phaedria, is more than enough like Guyon to indicate what he might have become. Verdant, who is discovered sleeping beside Acrasia in her bed of roses, is Guyon's *alter ego,* another, much simpler, figure of Youth:

> The young man sleeping by her, seemd to bee
>   Some goodly swayne of honorable place,
>   That certes it great pittie was to see
>   Him his nobilitie so foul deface;
>   A sweet regard, and amiable grace,
>   Mixed with manly sternnesse did appeare
>   Yet sleeping, in his well proportiond face,
>   And on his tender lips the downy heare
> Did now but freshly spring, and silken blossomes beare.
>
> His warlike armes, the idle instruments
>   Of sleeping praise, were hong upon a tree,
>   And his brave shield, full of old moniments,
>   Was fowly ra'st, that none the signes might see;
>   Ne for them, ne for honor cared hee,
>   Ne ought, that did to his advauncement tend,
>   But in leewd loves, and wastfull luxuree,
>   His dayes, his goods, his bodie he did spend:
> O horrible enchantment, that him so did blend.
>
>   (xii: 79–80)

Rather than being a medieval Lusty Juventus, Guyon is an exemplary Youth, comparable to that in Giorgio Vasari's now-vanished Florentine fresco, which showed "a young man with books and instruments of music, while other young men were occupied with games, banquets, or love-making";[33] surrounding figures in the fresco included Temperance with her bridle, Venus and Cupid, Self-knowledge and Fraud.

How all of this prepares the way for Guyon's destruction of the

Bower of Bliss does not perhaps require a lengthy exposition. Because of all that has gone before—in the book and in literary history—it is clear that Guyon's deflowering of the Bower is not an intemperate act but, instead, a symbolic one, and the correct one in the circumstances. None the less, the response of the reader is also manipulated subversively; the delights of the garden are presented ambiguously, but with enough true sensuality to produce passions, in both the reader and in Guyon, of the very sort he has come to the Bower to put down.[34] The regret many readers feel over the destruction of the garden is not, however, a false response—it is merely an incomplete one. Because human passion for Spenser is not evil in itself but is a positive good unless carried to excess (at which point it turns on itself), the sensuous beauties of the garden—including the female beauties—have their basis both in Nature and in Nature's handmaiden Art. The art of the garden is in no way hidden, nor is nature here unnatural because of it; the golden grapes could fool no one into tasting them, and we hear of no Marvellian hybridizations. But nature and art, like all the other good things of our world, are subject to excesses and misuse, and are so subjected in this garden.

Guyon's defenders among the critics have called attention to the several direct statements in the poem that indicate that the garden is overdone, that it is too much of a good thing. But these authorial statements are clearly not enough to cancel out the Bower's imaginative appeal to the senses, nor are they meant to do so. Spenser was not of Acrasia's party without knowing it. Instead, he plays the Palmer to the reader's Guyon, taking him into the garden of earthly delights, correcting him when he is liable to go too far wrong, but for the most part allowing him to see and know—both of which are equally important. The appeals to the senses in this canto exist to be tempered by the reader's knowledge of what he is seeing; and one knows the true significance of these temptations because one has read the rest of the book. Only if Canto xii existed by itself would there be grounds for complaint against Guyon.[35] In spite of its multiplicity, the poem is organic and it demands, not only that the reader learn its methods and meanings, but that he remember them.

We know full well before we enter the Bower what kind of a trap the garden is and who it is that inhabits it. We have seen her victims. We have learned that appearances may be deceptive and that "Worse is the daunger hidden, then descride" (xii: 35). We have both seen and been instructed in the subtlety of concupiscent appeals:

> A Harder lesson, to learne Continence
> In joyous pleasure, then in grievous paine:
> For sweetnesse doth allure the weaker sence
> So strongly, that uneathes it can refraine
> From that, which feeble nature covets faine.
>
> (vi: 1)

Spenser has saved the harder fight for last, not because Guyon could not have won it earlier, but because the reader had not yet been fully prepared for it. On the relatively simple level of the recognition of parallels, the golden apples in the Cave of Mammon have prepared us to entertain what are at best mixed feelings about the golden fruit of the Bower; the story of Jason and Medea on the gates reminds us why we are here; the Rose Song reminds us of Phaedria's beautiful and blasphemous parody of the Sermon on the Mount, and Phaedria herself has served as a pre-Acrasia to prepare us for the Bower. The Italianate design of the garden not only alludes to Spenser's sources in Tasso and Ariosto, but also reminds the reader of less-appealing references to things Italian in earlier cantos, including Phaedria's "Gondelay" (vi: 2) with its possible sexual connotations,[36] and the allusions to revenge tragedy, a form associated in the English mind with Italian decadence.

We have also learned to look twice at such things as the golden hair of the Wanton Maids (xii: 65) since such hair has also graced such different characters as Duessa (i: 15), Medina (ii: 15), Belphoebe (iii: 30), the Angel (viii: 5) and Alma (ix: 19), and hair has generally been a frequent image in the book, with no single significance that would encompass all usages. The birds of the Bower too, though they make beautiful music there (xii: 71),[37] must share the reader's mind with the "innumerable flight / Of harmefull fowles" he has just encountered on the voyage (35), as well as with all the other birds of the book and perhaps also with the extensive playing on the word "foul" that occurs throughout. It is not that all the fowl are foul, but rather, that Spenser's usage has made stock responses to images untrustworthy and has established the necessity of discrimination, of analysis, in cases like these. And such analysis, such use of the intellect, inevitably tempers and controls the emotional response.

We have also been given Arthur's fight in Canto xi to set beside this final episode. The relationship of the two events is that between an overt attack on man's mental and physical health and, in the Bower, a covert one. At the beginning of Canto xi Guyon leaves the Castle of Alma, where Arthur remains behind to lead the defense alone—an action that, like nearly all of Guyon's actions, has brought criticism down upon him, even though he departs accompanied by the Palmer and "in bright armour clad" (3). Nevertheless, the first canto of Book III begins as though the two had never parted company:

> The famous Briton Prince and Faerie knight,
>> After long wayes and perilous paines endured,
>> Having their wearie limbes to perfect plight
>> Restord, and sory wounds right well recured,
>> Of the faire *Alma* greatly were procured,
>> To make there lenger sojourne and abode;
>> But when thereto they might not be allured,
>> From seeking praise, and deeds of armes abrode,
> They courteous conge tooke, and forth together yode.

One can rationalize this by imagining Guyon to have returned to Alma after his destruction of the Bower, but the fact that Spenser does not offer such an explanation could also suggest that in Cantos xi and xii Guyon and Arthur were in some sense fighting the same fight, that Malegar and Acrasia are parallel but different threats to the Castle of Alma, that is, to man, and that Arthur and Guyon have responded in parallel yet different ways. In Cantos xi and xii both Arthur and Guyon must face attacks on the human senses; both have moments of weakness when their companions must step in to save them. Arthur's enemy is a creature of wrath whose passion can be cooled only by "tempering" him in water as one would a sword; Guyon seeks a figure of concupiscence who can be chained only with "adamant" (xii: 82). But though both events mean essentially the same thing, though together they eliminate the threats to man's well-being that have been the enemies throughout Book II, they appear very different on their narrative surfaces: the Bower has nothing but a weak fence to protect it (43); Guyon meets no physical resistance in capturing his fowl in his net; and his destruction of the garden— unlike Arthur's violent acts—appears to be without dramatic justification:

> But all those pleasant bowres and Pallace brave,
>   *Guyon* broke down, with rigour pittilesse;
> Ne ought their goodly workmanship might save
> Them from the tempest of his wrathfulnesse,
> But that their blisse he turn'd to balefulnesse:
> Their groves he feld, their gardins did deface,
> Their arbers spoyle, their Cabinets suppresse,
> Their banket houses burne, their buldings race,
> And of the fairest late, now made the fowlest place.
>
>   (83)

Such verse creates a feeling of loss, a sense of regret occasioned by the end of beauty through violence. Yet while one is experiencing these emotional responses, one also wishes to avoid associating himself too closely with the pig-man, Grille, who "repined greatly" at the changes wrought by Guyon and the Palmer (86). Grille exists in the poem as another figure whose function is to deflect an incorrect response; wanting to remain in Acrasia's enchanted garden is a natural desire, but it is subverted, after having been established in the reader, by its final equation with the nature of a beast that has "forgot the excellence / Of his creation" and lives without "intelligence" (87). What we see and what we know in observing Guyon's destruction of the garden are intentionally out of harmony; the tone of the verse— established by its loaded diction and repeated rhetorical falls—creates an emotional response that must be corrected by reason, just as the deliberate erotic stimulation by the two girls in the fountain had earlier demanded correction. By this point the reader is able to recognize the "wrathfulnesse" of Guyon as yet another manifestation of the irascible passions that are naturally and properly opposed to the products of concupiscence. He is also able to see the confusion between appearance and reality, which has plagued hero and reader throughout the Book, now being resolved to an identity. Guyon makes the Bower "the fowlest place" because that is exactly what it is. This is Spenser's realism, and it is intended to carry all the pain of a shattered illusion.

Whether Guyon's wrath, though a proper symbolic response to concupiscence, is still an imbalance in his own character is neither stated nor important, though there exists a sufficient Aristotelian precedent for calling a man who is angry for the right reasons "gentle-tempered." But Guyon has fulfilled his function: that is all one can ask of an epic hero. There is little indication that the experience has changed him personally, even in giving him maturity; his behavior at the beginning of Book III evidences more than anything in Book II his character as an immature young man. In Spenser's interwoven structure, no book or character is complete in itself. Just as the Red Crosse knight was denied a fairy-tale ending to his quest—a happy marriage to Una—so Guyon's voyage has carried him only as far as Circe, who is a false Penelope. It may be rather disturbing to modern readers to see how some of Spenser's heroes, when they reappear in books or episodes after those in which they bear heavy symbolic weight, are of such diminished magnitude; but this is an inevitable result of a system of characterization that makes the individual subordinate to the idea. It is not a weakness but a strength, because it throws the weight of reader response and interpretation onto those very elements that help make *The Faerie Queene* a poem rather than a novel: symbolic images and relationships, significant allusions, and philosophical ideas. And Guyon, in Book II, is by no means a negative or insignificant figure, because these very things are an explicit part of his essence. But, as in a work of modernist architecture, so in Spenserian characterization, form follows function.[38]

The kind of reader participation that Spenser expects is described by his contemporary poet Torquato Tasso in his *Discourses on the Heroic Poem*. In those readers who respond correctly to an epic poem, says Tasso, the

intellect itself becomes a painter who, following its pattern, paints in their souls forms of courage, temperance, prudence, justice, faith, piety, religion, and every other virtue that may be acquired by long practice or infused by divine grace.[39]

According to Tasso, the mind painting ideas of virtue in the soul, from the pattern of images in the poem before it, is engaged in a creative act that is parallel to that of the poet himself and is an inverse reflection of the divine act of creation, in which the idea preceded the image. Though Tasso advocates that epic poetry be based on historical fact rather than the marvellous or fantastic, he regards poetry and philosophy as two aspects of a single substance, and allegory as a proper element in a heroic poem, the icastic realism of which is a visible reflection of the true reality of the intelligible world. Thus, in spite of Spenser's rejection of historical verisimilitude, Tasso's ideal reader would also be the ideal reader of Book II of *The Faerie Queene,* creating the total "form" of temperance within himself by following with his intellect the pattern of images, allusions, events, and characters, in the poem, and discovering their relationship to the symbolized idea, an idea that does not finally exist in any single aspect of the poem alone, but in the work as a whole, and in reality. As Rosemond Tuve has said, "Allegory does not equate a concretion with an abstraction, but shadows or mirrors essences."[40] Spenser's allegory is, in fact, a Platonic version of mimesis.

"Now let any man judge," says Sir John Harington, speaking of allegory, "if it be a matter of meane art or wit to containe in one historicall narration, either true or fained, so many, so diverse, and so deepe conceits."[41] Let him also judge whether it is an impoverished art or intellect that can create a character who *means* as much as Guyon means, and who yet is not an airy abstraction. Guyon, showing himself to be the heir and the anti-heir of heroes from the epic, the Bible, the revenge tragedy, and the morality play, carries through the book to the reader the idea of temperance in ethical, theological, psychological, physical, and dramatic forms. With him we see and know the realities from which temperance is made and which require its existence.

"Harmony Was She": Donne's *Anniversaries* and the Neoplatonic Elizabeth Drury

God proceeds by example, by pattern: Even in this first great act presented in our Text, in the Creation he did so. God had no external pattern in the Creation, for there was nothing extant; but God had from all Eternity an internal pattern, an Idæa, a pre-conception, a form in himself, according to which he produc'd every Creature.

John Donne[1]

The presentation of Elizabeth Drury in John Donne's *Anniversaries* may appear to be a different case from the others discussed in this book, since she is not a fictional or mythic character but, instead, a contemporary person whom Donne chose to memorialize in a pair of mixed-genre poems. But in spite of that she is, in these poems, a symbolic figure of heroic proportions, with little of the dramatically mimetic in her presentation. Free of the minimal requirements of narrative, Donne created in his Elizabeth Drury what is perhaps the most elaborately realized symbolic hero in English literature—a heroic figure who did little more than die. The circumstances of these poems' occasion, as well as the renaissance conventions of characterization that were available to Donne, made it possible for him to create a richly symbolic presentation of his real-life heroine, a presentation of her as a representative, like Guyon, of heroic virtue manifested in essence rather than in action. Indeed, since Donne had not known or even seen the girl in her lifetime, and since her life had been too short to accumulate many of the events that the Renaissance would have regarded as significant in the biography of a particular individual, any presentation other than a symbolic one could have been at least hypocritical on Donne's part, if not artistically fatal. These poems have been misread both in Donne's time and in our own by those readers who have attempted to see a "real" girl being presented in imagery and ideas that would probably have appeared excessive even if applied to Queen Elizabeth or (as Ben Jonson suggested) to the Virgin Mary. On the other hand, those critics who have wished to see her as purely symbolic have limited themselves by defending particular single meanings or small sets of meanings and failing to account for the relationships of what are in fact multiple symbolic meanings to each other and to the poems' occasion.

Donne's *Anniversaries,* however, are fuller than such simplistic methods of reading can account for. Donne took the chief "real" thing he knew about this death—that it was the death of an innocent young girl—and created an entire world picture on the basis of that one fact.[2] The *Anniversaries* are renaissance analogical thinking at its finest.

As in all such thinking, the single "real" object is never forgotten in an effort to present the multiple essence; but in these particular poems the central reality is not something that is any longer in this world. It is, rather, a soul that has left the human body behind, and this fact accounts for the difference between Donne's symbolism and more conventional examples. The poet may look back occasionally to the time when this soul still existed in the body, just as he may look forward to this particular soul's resurrection; but his concern is never simply with this girl and this one soul alone. It is with all souls and their universal history. His point of departure, the "moment" that is anatomized for its eternal truths, is a moment when the soul of an innocent human being has left its body and the world behind. The "subject" of the *Anniversaries* is not, then, the mortal that was Elizabeth Drury, nor is Donne's subject a symbolic abstraction such as Wisdom or Astraea. The subject of the poems is a soul separated from its body by death.

The meanings this subject has are almost inexhaustible, and it deserves glorification far greater than might have been appropriate while the soul was still in the body, for its nature is now far greater. As Donne's friend, Edward, Lord Herbert, said: "Once freed of the body the human soul is greater than anything which can be perceived in this world. . . . It is true that a small urn holds our ashes, but the

whole visible world cannot afterwards comprehend the soul."[3] As the
occasion of Donne's poems was the departure of the soul of Elizabeth
Drury, specific reference to the girl does provide one way of developing this subject. But since that soul's experience after death in no
way differs, so far as we know, from the experience of all virtuous
souls, a universalized symbolic development of this single soul is also
possible to the poet. The problem for the reader is not so much to
isolate some single equivalent for the chief symbol of the poems as to
see how the many stated and suggested meanings of that symbol are
developed and related to each other by the poet, to see how the one
becomes the many and in doing so returns to the one.

The Soul of the World

The soul of Elizabeth Drury is presented, in one major analogy,
as the Soul of the World, the *anima mundi,* a symbolic meaning so
obviously present that it is normally simply mentioned by critics of
the poem and then passed over for less obvious identifications. Yet
presenting this soul as the World Soul is more than simply a conve-
nient device for introducing the microcosm-macrocosm analogy that
is central to this as to most symbolic presentations of human beings.
The departure of the soul from the body of Elizabeth Drury is not
said by Donne to be *like* the departure of the World Soul from the
world, but actually to have been that departure. This is not, I intend
to argue, merely a hyperbolic metaphor. It serves to identify and reinforce the symbolic complex that will be the basis of the entire development of the *Anniversaries,* a complex of ideas and images that
have their basis and unity in Christian Neoplatonism.

Every order has its beginning in a monad and proceeds to a manifold co-
ordinate therewith; and the manifold in any order may be carried back
to a single monad.... The soul-order, originating from one primal Soul,
descends to a manifold of souls and again carries back the manifold to
the one. (Proclus, *The Elements of Theology*)[4]

The entire structure of the world consists of multiplicity and unity....
All bodies fall under the world's one body, all natures under one nature,
all souls under one soul. (Ficino, *The Philebus Commentary*)[5]

The Platonic notion of a World Soul related in some manner to individual human souls was an attractive yet a dangerous idea in the Renaissance. Philemon Holland's summary, prefaced to Plutarch's "Commentarie of the Creation of the Soule," in Holland's translation of the *Moralia* (1603), warns against a blind following of Platonic doctrines about the soul and considers the idea of the World Soul to be "an absurd and fantasticall opinion, if it be not handled and expounded aright."[6] The right way of handling it seems to have been that adopted by Ficino, who carefully kept separate but parallel his conceptions of God, the World Soul, and the human soul. God, according to Ficino, "created first the Angelic Mind, then the Soul of this World as Plato would have it, and last, the Body of the World."[7] But He also gave individual souls to the spheres, the stars, daemons, and men; and these different souls are all related, not because some are contained in others, but because "all souls in the natural order are referred to that first soul" (p. 192), and they all proceed from the Ideas of the one God. The world, in Ficino's version of Plato's creation myth, was generated from the loving union of the World Soul and the formless chaos of matter (p. 129). This World Soul is therefore a generative force in so far as the world of nature is concerned; but, as it forms a link between the world of matter and the world of Mind, it is also characterized by reason and intelligence. Its own unique characteristic, however, is motion, for the angelic Mind exists in unmoved completeness and matter cannot move without a soul. Man shares the World Soul's medial position between Mind and matter, not because his soul is part of the World Soul, but because God creates the souls of men and unites them with bodies in the same manner in which He created the World Soul and united it with the world. "Doubtless, God infuses [His] gifts into the souls as soon as they are born from Him; the souls, slipping down out of the milky way through Cancer into a body, are draped in a certain heavenly and clear wrap, clothed in which, they are then enclosed in earthly bodies" (p. 186). This wrapper is the spirit, a necessary medium in the union of the pure soul with the impure body.

Needless to say, Ficino's view of the soul, however near it might have been to "orthodox" Christianity, was not universally accepted in the Renaissance. Indeed, what was characteristic about contemporary ideas of the soul, as of most areas within the Renaissance world view, was the great diversity of opinion available to those who wished to consider the matter. Cornelius Agrippa, in the book that he wrote to recant his previous works, *Of the Vanitie and Uncertaintie of Artes and Sciences,* includes a long catalogue of philosophers' opinions concerning the soul.[8] "Xenocrates," he says, "called it a number mooving it selfe" (sig. S ii,r). "Zoroastes, Hermes Trismegistus, Orpheus, Aglaophemus, Pythagoras, Eumenius, Hammonius, Plutarch, Porphyrius, Timeus, Locrus" all believed in the divine nature, creation, and unity of the soul and its independence of matter (sig. S ii,v). He catalogues various disputes concerning the actual moment at which the soul of an individual is created and about what happens to the soul after death. "Pythagoras and Plato affirme that it is immortall, and going out of the body, fleeth to the nature of his kinde" (sig. S iii,r). Like Ficino, Agrippa recognizes the presence of both universal and particular souls in Plato's thinking, but he credits the position that "there was but one soule of all or universall things dispersed into all bodies as well living as not living" to the Manichean heretics (sig. S iv,r). Other renaissance writers regarded this last as a Stoic doctrine or as a heresy attributable to Averroes. On the other hand, the influential Philip de Mornay regarded both the derivation of the soul from God and the idea of a Soul of the World as Platonic doctrines; and he cites both theories as being in agreement with the Christian belief in the immortality of the soul.[9]

Certain basic positions were, none the less, shared by nearly all who wrote about the soul in the Renaissance: that it was immortal, that it was created by God (how and when were more vexing questions), and that it was subject to rewards and punishments in the next life. Beyond these positions, and occasionally within these positions, there was considerable room for differences. One reaction possible to the multiplicity of explanations available is that contained in the title of Agrippa's book and in his judgment, also arrived at by many others, that "although Philosophie disputeth and judgeth of all thinges, yet shee is certaine of nothing" (sig. R iv,r). This sort of skepticism about human knowledge, which was perfectly compatible with a belief in Divine Truth, characterizes Donne's position in the *Anniversaries*—and not only in his famous passage about the new science calling knowledge into doubt.[10] Such philosophical doubt brought forth, from both Agrippa and Donne, absolute declarations of faith in God, a faith that was independent of the logic and works of this world. But it also opened up in each writer a valuable vein of indifference. Far from forgetting this rotten world—the advice Donne gives his reader in the *Anniversaries*—each writer turned the renaissance system of universal analogy into a source of satire, and into a source of intellectual nostalgia that "saved" the old stable ontological structure by placing it in older and higher worlds.

As Frank Kermode and others have noted, Donne expresses no personal belief in the discoveries of the new philosophy. All that interests him in contemporary science are the doubts it has cast upon older beliefs about the nature of man and the world. He uses the new philosophy in the same way he uses Neoplatonism and nearly everything else in the *Anniversaries*: as an indication of the limits of human knowledge, as a reason for turning to God, as a source for satire, and as one element only in the poetic play of ideas that creates Elizabeth Drury as a symbol of the redeemed soul.

> Poore soul in this thy flesh what do'st thou know.
> Thou know'st thy selfe so little, as thou know'st not,
> How thou did'st die, nor how thou wast begot.
> Thou neither knowst, how thou at first camest in,
> Nor how thou took'st the poyson of mans sin.
> Nor dost thou, (though thou knowst, that thou are so)
> By what way thou art made immortall, know.
>
> (*Second Anniversary*, 254–260)[11]

If one knows so little about the world and about the soul, the options are either to be very brief (or even silent) about such things, or—Donne's choice—to use what men have thought about these subjects in indifferent, poetic ways in order to illustrate a faith that is not finally open to philosophical demonstration.

Thus the soul of Elizabeth Drury is equated by Donne with the Soul of the World. As to the possibility of any philosophical truth in that equation, Donne is, as he is with all philosophical truths in these poems, unconcerned. What matters is the poetic truth, that is, the manner in which this equation gives an individual soul symbolic values through which it can embody the poet's faith in immortality. What one critic refers to as "the strained metaphor of Elizabeth Drury's soul as the *anima mundi*"[12] is in fact the very center of the poems, though if we expect to be convinced of its literal truth we are seriously misreading Donne and poetry. Like all metaphors, it is a comparison that, if taken literally, is absurd. But, like all symbols, it points through itself toward truth.

Nevertheless, though the metaphor is not strained, it does have the theoretical danger of exploding. To adopt an identification such as this, for the presentation of a symbolic hero who is the embodiment in essence of all good, is to break free of the conventional restraints in the presentation of human characters. Mimesis does not matter here except as one among the large number of possible ways of presenting the soul of Elizabeth Drury. To see her soul as the Soul of the World potentially involves the entire microcosm and macrocosm in the poems.

In order to employ such a symbol, Donne clearly could not have limited himself by the conventions of any single genre. What Rosalie Colie once described as the "rigorous inclusiveness" of the *genera mixta* of the *Anniversaries* has now been thoroughly demonstrated by Barbara Lewalski in *Donne's Anniversaries and the Poetry of Praise,* where she relates them particularly to sixteenth- and seventeenth-century epideixis, Protestant meditations, biblical hermeneutics, and funeral sermons. From each of these Donne draws elements in his presentation of the soul of Elizabeth Drury, and yet these genres in no way define his limits, since theoretically there are no limits whatever for this kind of symbolism. To take the relationship between the microcosm and the macrocosm as your basis of presentation is to set out to write an encyclopedia, and one of infinite possible length. But actual encyclopedias do have limits, other than size, to what they include; and Donne's presentation of his subject is also carefully limited and ordered, though not by mimetic conventions or the decorum of any particular poetic genera. Donne limits, orders, and develops his poems by concentrating on the most significant of the analogical parallels

that had been identified in the Christian Platonism that is his basis
(as did several renaissance encyclopedias, and Agrippa in his *Occult
Philosophy*). He also orders them by considering these Neoplatonic
parallels within a broadly sketched chronological structure based, in
the *First Anniversary,* on the Old Testament and, in the *Second Anniversary,* on time and the soul's movement toward the apocalypse.

The First Anniversary: An Anatomy of The World

The first of the two *Anniversaries* begins with a rich medley from
the various symbolic fields of reference that will be drawn upon at
length afterwards:

> When that rich soule which to her Heaven is gone,
> Whom all they celebrate, who know they have one,
> (For who is sure he hath a soule, unlesse
> It see, and Judge, and follow worthinesse,
> And by Deedes praise it? He who doth not this,
> May lodge an In-mate soule, but tis not his.)
> When that Queene ended here her progresse time,
> And, as t'her standing house, to heaven did clymbe,
> Where, loth to make the Saints attend her long,
> Shee's now a part both of the Quire, and Song,
> This world, in that great earth-quake languished;
> For in a common Bath of teares it bled,
> Which drew the strongest vitall spirits out:
> But succour'd then with a perplexed doubt,
> Whether the world did loose or gaine in this,
> (Because since now no other way there is
> But goodnes, to see her, whom all would see,
> All must endeavour to be as good as shee,)
> This great consumption to a fever turn'd,
> And so the world had fits; it joy'd, it mournd.
>
> (lines 1–20)

The soul described here is the soul of Elizabeth Drury; but it is
equated, either directly or by implications developed later in the
poems, to the *anima mundi,* to Astraea and/or Queen Elizabeth advanced to the heavens, to Christ crucified, to an archetypal soul of

man, to the principle of harmony, to the perfection of Eden now lost, and to the source of the world's order, health, and stability. The following forty lines go on to add to this symbolic complex, primarily by equating the soul with the world's "sense and memory" (line 28), with the world's "name" (line 31), with the source of time (lines 39–40), with an example "equall to law" (line 48), and with the quintessence ("Thy'ntrinsique Balme, and thy preservative" [line 57]). But "equating" begins to be the wrong word for the kind of links Donne is making, because, as with the identification of a single soul with the World Soul, Donne is drawing on pre-established theories of *identity* rather than of mere equality. The World Soul, for instance, does not simply symbolize the quintessence in Neoplatonic thought, it *is* the quintessence.[13] For the Christian Platonist, Christ's position as intermediary between God and man is not simply analogous to the World Soul's position between the Angelic Mind and matter (though there was some disagreement about whether the World Soul was related to the second or the third member of the Trinity); the parallel implies a process of mediation and union begun at the creation and repeated in the incarnation of Christ and in the union of every human soul with a body.

This process of mediation, through which order is established in chaos, has any number of manifestations; but it is the process itself that interests Donne, or rather the process and its end, when the soul returns to God. Donne's poem is as much concerned with disorder as with order; indeed, counting the lines dealing with the world's corruption would give evidence of a far greater concern with disorder. But Donne from the first recognizes this disorder as itself part of order, part of the structure of descent and return, and of creation from chaos and return to chaos, that he elaborates through the use of multiple, parallel symbolic identifications of the soul of Elizabeth Drury. The surfaces, the stated symbolic equivalents, are in themselves relatively unimportant except as they point to their common structure, a universal and eternal structure, which itself is proof of the immortality of the soul—the one thing about his subject that Donne actually claims to know. And it is recognizing this structuralism, the hieratic superiority of the unifying pattern to the individual objects within the pattern, that makes such symbolic poetry some-thing more than simply hyperbolic and witty or (depending on the aesthetics of the reader) grotesque and absurd.

Donne is thus able to exploit the full range of imaginative possi-bilities for his stated meanings. They are presented in the poem with all the impact of metaphors; yet viewed within the Neoplatonic sys-tem, they function not as metaphors but as definitions. Being simul-taneously metaphors and definitions, they open outward to become symbols pointing toward a single abstract form—the pattern, the idea behind and within the poem.

Donne's *Anniversaries* present a variation of Ficino's creation myth, but for the most part they do so in reverse. Or rather, they present the conclusion of that cyclical relationship between the one and the many, between harmony and chaos, which began with the creation. The Soul of the World has left the world, says Donne. Certainly the world continues to exist for a time, but that continued life is only a process of half-life, a gradual winding down of a creation that is still held together by the "Cyment" of spirit (*First Anniversary*, line 49). What now remains is a world that can no longer be called a world, with the soul that "defin'd" it (line 37) now gone. And "defin'd" is clearly a pun here, pointing to the manner in which the *anima mundi* gives limit and order and harmony to the chaotic matter of which the world is made, but indicating also that meaning itself is, for this world, dependent on its relationship to the *anima mundi*:

> Thou has forgot thy name, thou hadst; thou wast
> Nothing but she, and her thou hast o'repast.
> For as a child kept from the Font, untill
> A Prince, expected long, come to fulfill
> The Ceremonies, thou unnam'd hadst laid,
> Had not her comming, thee her Palace made:
> Her name defin'd thee, gave thee forme and frame,
> And thou forgetst to celebrate thy name.
>
> (lines 31–38)

This "name" can be read within a Christian frame of reference as an allusion to the creative Word (the *logos*), suggesting a sort of Joy-cean "word-world" punning. The comparison to the naming of a child at his baptism reinforces this. But there is simultaneously and more directly a reference here to the *anima mundi* as giving both being and name (*mundus*) to what could not, without this creative union, be called a world. As Ficino said, "This composite of all the Forms and Ideas we call in Latin a *mundus,* and in Greek, a *cosmos,* that is, *Orderliness*" (p. 128). Without order, the name no longer applies.

Names are of great significance in Neoplatonic thought, being not simply arbitrary signs but symbolic equivalents with a sympathetic relationship to the object named. One learns about an object by the study of its name—a theory that accounts not only for the great popularity of speculative etymology in the period, but also for the appeal of Cabalistic numerological magic based on the number equivalents of the Hebrew letters of a name. To change the name of an object, in such thinking, is to change the object itself. The world denied its name ceases, in Donne's poem, to be the world. One of the things the *Anniversaries* are attempting is the discovery and recovery of a lost name. Of course, the poems are also attempting to memorialize a name, that of Elizabeth Drury. But that name, as Marjorie Nicolson pointed out, is never mentioned in the poems. Statements in the *First Anniversary* such as: "none / Offers to tell us who it is that's gone" (lines 41–42) may perhaps direct the reader back to the name given on the title page where the poem is described as being called forth "by occasion of the untimely death of Mistris Elizabeth Drury"; but these statements also direct the reader a good way beyond this girl whose death is the occasion, but not the subject, of the poem and whose soul has, before ever being treated in an individualized manner, been symbolically equated with the Soul of the World and its manifestations.[14]

Donne, however, claims that he is going to name names, that he will "define" the world as it now is, offering a definition that will also reveal what that departed soul was, "who it is that's gone." Given the condition of the world he describes, his definition must be largely a negative one, a fact that justifies the satire that occupies so much of the *First Anniversary.* But it is not only by negatives that we come to know the nature of the departed soul. With the Christian-Platonic

concept of creation as an emanation of light from the Son-sun providing a major context, Donne is willing to admit the continued beneficial existence of reflected and refracted light, if not of the direct
rays of the world-and-soul-creating Sun.

> For there's a kind of world remaining still,
> Though shee which did inanimate and fill
> The world, be gone, yet in this last long night,
> Her Ghost doth walke; that is, a glimmering light,
> A faint weake love of vertue and of good
> Reflects from her, on them which understood
> Her worth; And though she have shut in all day,
> The twi-light of her memory doth stay;
> Which, from the carcasse of the old world, free,
> Creates a new world. . . .
>
> (lines 67–76)

But this new world that the *anima mundi* is creating in the midst
of the return to chaos of the old differs significantly from that old
world, since it is not material. The new world exists only *within* men.
"The matter and the stuffe of this [new world is] Her vertue, and the
forme our practice is" (lines 77–78). Our relationships as readers to
the departed soul of the poem are thus identical to those existing
between the *anima mundi* and the world of matter at the creation:
emanation (of light/virtue), reflection, and union. This new world is
the "paradise within," a paradise in which man is safe so long as he
admits no "forraine Serpent" (line 84) from the external world; and
the "Anatomy of the World" is an object lesson in the need to protect
this inner paradise:

> Yet, because outward stormes the strongest breake,
> And strength it selfe by confidence growes weake,
> This new world may be safer, being told
> The dangers and diseases of the old.
>
> (lines 85–88)

The image of mankind continuing to endure in a world of dimin-
ishing light is repeated at later stages in the poem's development. In
speaking of the shortness of modern life compared with the great

ages recorded for the patriarchs, Donne symbolically links original, unfallen man with the sun: "There is not now that mankinde, which was then / When the Sunne, and man, did seeme to strive / (Joynt tenants of the world) who should survive" (lines 112–114).[15] The fact that the poem is occasioned by the death of a child would seem to confirm and justify the poet's dwelling on the shortness of life; but because the soul of the poem is also the immortal soul/World Soul, the poem also points beyond both mortal man and the sun to an eternity in which man will in fact outlive the earthly sun. Since both man and the sun were regarded in Neoplatonism as emanations of the World Soul, which themselves reflected or embodied that Soul, the comparison is not simply wit on Donne's part but integral with the system of correspondences on which the poem is based.

The contemporary lack of a proportionate relationship between man and the sun that Donne observes ("We're scarse our Fathers shadowes cast at noon," [line 144]—with an obvious pun on "our Fathers") is extended in the last stages of the poem to include the breakdown of sympathetic astrological relationships between man and the heavens:

> What Artist now dares boast that he can bring
> Heaven hither, or constellate any thing,
> So as the influence of those starres may bee
> Imprisoned in an Herbe, or Charme, or Tree,
> And doe by touch, all which those starres could do?
>
> (lines 391–395)

Since the "she" of the poems was the light of the sun, she was also the invisible influence of the stars—an equally common way of presenting the *anima mundi*.

> If this commerce twixt heaven and earth were not
> Embarr'd, and all this trafique quite forgot,
> Shee, for whose losse we have lamented thus,
> Would worke more fully' and pow'rfully on us.
>
> (lines 399–402)

As an invisible influence capable of affecting both man and his world, she is even equated by Donne with magnetism, in a reference to Gilbert's *De Magnete* (lines 219–222); and in fact, Gilbert himself had identified the World Soul with magnetism (though, as Bacon complained, Gilbert tended to identify almost everything with magnetism).

But not only the invisible influences of the heavens have broken down; the regular physical order of the celestial universe, which once confirmed Neoplatonic interpretations of the world as harmonically structured, is no longer observable. Donne's discussion of astronomy in this poem is intended as an illustration of the loss of "proportion" in the world and deals with this breakdown of simple geometrical movements and relationships.

> We thinke the heavens enjoy their Spericall
> Their round proportion embracing all.
> But yet their various and perplexed course,
> Observ'd in divers ages doth enforce
> Men to finde out so many Eccentrique parts,
> Such divers downe-right lines, such overthwarts
> As disproportion that pure forme.
>
> (lines 251–257)

The sun itself is unable to complete a perfect circle, and this lack of geometrical proportion in the spheres has moral implications since "in this / The worlds proportion disfigured is, / That those two legges whereon it doth relie, / Reward and punishment are bend awrie" (lines 301–304). The sun is here, as elsewhere in the poems, a moral symbol of man. The sun is "empayled within a Zodiake" (line 263) in something of the same way in which man's soul is imprisoned within his body. The lines describing the manner by which the sun's movements are controlled by the astrological constellations (lines 263–277) may be pointing forward to the discussion of the weakening of astrological influences on man; but certainly the sun itself is, like man, falling away from order and control, coming nearer to the earth: "And seeming weary with his reeling thus, / He meanes to sleepe, being now falne nearer us" (lines 273–274). The original parallel between man and the sun, based on the longevity of both, is replaced by this point in the poem with a new equation based on the impending death of both.

This transformation of the sun as a symbol is an excellent illustration of the use of symbolism that I am claiming for Donne. The sun symbolizes, on the one hand, the Lord and the World Soul and the redeemed human soul, and on the other, fallen nature and fallen man. It does this not only because of Donne's universally acknowledged skill in logic and in use of the conceit (through which he so skillfully manipulates an image into a *discordia concors*) but also because the multiple and sometimes contradictory meanings of such symbols are inherent in the symbols themselves and a product of their history. For example, the woodcut illustrating Sol in the late medieval and renaissance *Kalendar and compost of Shepherds* shows as Sol's "people" a king, a musician, and a hypocrite. That some of the disparate available meanings for a symbol like the sun might have arisen independently of each other hardly occurred to the mind of a renaissance writer; all the possible meanings actually existed in the symbol itself and must therefore be related in significant rather than accidental ways to each other. The perceived relationship of meanings was, like all products of renaissance analogical thinking, hierarchical, from high to low on the chain of being and from positive to negative in valences of moral value. The kind of critical question, then, that asks, "If symbol x in this work means a, how can it also mean *not a*?" simply does not apply. The decorum of such symbolism has little to do with maintaining a single meaning or even a limited category of meanings. In poems as free from generic restraints as Donne's *Anniversaries,* it also has little to do with the appropriateness of a meaning to any genre. The critical issues here are the questions of, first, the meanings the symbol is actually given in the poem, and then, and much more important, how these meanings are related by the poet to each other and to the subject. In this particular case, the sun is a symbol absolutely appropriate, in all the meanings Donne employs, to the use of a cyclical Christian-Platonic myth of the creation and destruction of a harmonically, geometrically ordered universe—a myth that itself is being used to image the occasion of the poem: a created soul's return to God.

But however important the discredited system of regular geo-

metrical, heliocentric spheres may be as a symbolic structure, Donne
is very careful *not* to say whether it was originally an existential reality—the solution to the questions raised by the discoveries of modern astronomy, which Milton was to suggest in *Paradise Lost*. Given
his statements elsewhere in these poems about the limits of human
knowledge, Donne could not have done otherwise. But the implication
that this ideal order may never actually have existed in this world,
except perhaps momentarily, pushes the poem's nostalgia for original
harmony, which is one of its chief positive thrusts, away from this
world toward that spiritual world where such harmony has always
existed and where it will finally be established for mankind.

> Then, as mankinde, so is the worlds whole frame
> Quite out of joynt, almost created lame:
> For, before God had made up all the rest,
> Corruption entred, and deprav'd the best;
> It seis'd the Angels, and then first of all
> The world did in her Cradle take a fall,
> And turn'd her braines, and tooke a generall maime.
> Wronging each joynt of th'universal frame.
> The noblest part, man, felt it first; and than
> Both beast and plants, curst in the curse of man,
> So did the world from the first houre decay.
>
> (lines 191–201)

"God created man in health," says Donne in a sermon, "but health
continued but a *few hours,* and sicknesse hath had the Dominion 6000
years" (II [1955], 79; cf. IV, 136); even before the Fall, he goes on to
declare, man was subject to mutability—how else could he have
fallen?

The implication that ideal proportion may never have been fully
realized in matter also makes much less exaggerated Donne's claim
that the freed soul of his poem *is* that proportion, that she is harmony
itself. This statement is clearly meant to apply to her redeemed soul,
not to the mortal girl. Harmony and proportion may not exist in this
body or in this world, but they do exist in God and in His reflection,
the virtuous soul—and thus no hyperbole is intended. In the lines

describing the soul of the poem as harmony, Donne makes specific mention of the Neoplatonic philosophical tradition that he is exploiting for his symbolism:

> Shee by whose lines proportion should bee
> Examin'd, measure of all Symmetree,
> Whom had that Ancient seen, who thought soules made
> Of Harmony, he would at next have said
> That Harmony was shee, and thence infer,
> That soules were but Resultances from her,
> And did from her into our bodies go,
> As to our eyes, the formes from objects flow.
>
> (lines 309–316)

There have been several suggestions of which "Ancient" in this long tradition Donne had in mind. Certainly in Donne's period Plato and Pythagoras were most often credited with originating the notion of the soul as harmony,[16] though Donne's contemporaries could be as vague as Donne about the concept's origin; Sir John Davies, for instance, says merely that "*Musitians* thinke our *Soules* are *Harmonies*" as well as that "Some thinke one generall *Soule* fils every braine."[17] Scholars today still debate the origin of the idea of the soul as harmony; but Donne's failure to specify a name here is, I believe, a quite intentional ambiguity, parallel both to his not naming Elizabeth Drury in the poem and to his claim that the world has lost its name. All of these failures to name names are devices to take the mind beyond the equivalencies of definition or even of metaphor to the multiple world of symbols and universal truths. The poem here, as throughout, uses ignorance to produce knowledge; the very plenitude of names that could be substituted for the unnamed "Ancient"— Plato, Pythagoras, Plotinus, Plutarch, "Timaeus the Locrian," etc.— makes Donne's silence and ambiguity amount to a page of footnotes citing proof texts.

The Neoplatonic belief in the soul as proportion is immediately confirmed in the poem in Christian terms, and with equal ambiguity about sources:

> Shee, who if those great Doctors truely said
> That th'Arke to mans proportions was made,

Had beene a type for that, as that might be
A type for her in this, that contrary
Both Elements, and Passions liv'd at peace
In her, who caus'd all Civill warre to cease.

(lines 317–322)

Here as elsewhere the literal truth of the earthly event—whether
or not the ark was built to man's proportions—is left uncertain. What
is certain, however, is the truth of the idea represented in this belief
as that truth exists in the soul. The ark had a formal relationship,
not only to the proportions of man, but to the Christian church, of
which it was a typological foreshadowing ("Every man is a little
world, sayes the *Philosopher*; Every man is a little *Church* too."
Donne's *Sermons* IV, 194).[18] Thus the ark also foreshadowed the virgin, who was herself symbolic of the church. The specific lines quoted
above make no direct allusion to either of these other available meanings, but they initiate a context in which these meanings will also
become available to the reader later in the *Anniversaries* as important
devices for interpreting the symbolic main figure.

The typological significance of the ark is also reinforced by the fact
that this mention of the ark occupies an important place in the chronology of the biblical allusions, which provide something of a temporal, narrative structure to the *First Anniversary,* a loose structure
that none the less allows for a symbolic presentation of the soul as it
reveals itself in parallel events throughout history. Most of the biblical
allusions in the *First Anniversary,* other than the fairly indirect allusions
to the crucifixion of Christ, come from the Pentateuch and in general
occur in the same order in which they are recorded there. Donne
uses the Pentateuch as a repository of symbols as did those Christian
Cabalists and Neoplatonists of his period whose numerological spec-
ulations Donne thought of as an "honest and serviceable curiosity,
and harmless recreation and entertainment."[19] "All arts," said William Ingpen in *The Secret of Numbers* (1624), "all kinde of knowledge
whatsoever, according to the opinion of the Antients, is included in
these Five Books of Moses" (p. 42, sig. G 1,r). The most obvious Old
Testament allusions in the *First Anniversary* are, in order of first occurrence, to the Garden of Eden (lines 81–84, 364) and the fall of

Adam and Eve (lines 100–107, 180, 199–200), to Methusalem (line
128), to the fall of the rebel angels (lines 195–196—not, in this case,
in chronological order, but also, not in the Pentateuch), to the ark
(line 318), to the creation of the rainbow (line 352), to the Egyptian
magicians from Exodus 7 (lines 389–390), and to Moses's song from
Deuteronomy (lines 462–466). Most of these are historically important
typological events in themselves, and all of them are given archetypal
significance by Donne in his poems. The most prominent of them
are related closely to the "she" of the poems, who is for such things
as the paradise within, as for the ark, the ideal spiritual model. In
the beginning of time, says Donne, "every soule / Did a faire King-
dome, and large Realme controule."

> ... the very stature thus erect,
> Did that soule a good way towards Heaven direct.
> Where is this mankind now? who lives to age,
> Fit to be made *Methusalem* his page?
>
> (lines 123–128)

Though this is satire on man's brief mortality, the answer to
Donne's rhetorical question finally lies with the immortal soul of the
poem on its way to heaven, to a life exceeding that of Methusalem.

The fall of the rebel angels is presented as a disease of the brain,
a perversion of the mind, in contrast to the immortal soul who is
pure intelligence. The rainbow is seen as God's revealing through
color the nature of beauty and the balance that was a characteristic
of the creation, while the "she" of the poem was "all colour, all Dia-
phanous" (line 366), having in herself all the elements of ideal beauty.

It is this kind of typology and idealism that can justify, if anything
can, the satiric attack on women in the *First Anniversary*. That woman
first caused the fall of man and continued to do so repeatedly thereafter was perhaps a commonplace so common in the period as to
need no defense, and so unpopular today as to be indefensible. But
the point of Donne's witty attack is the same as that of his other
satire on humanity: it is an illustration of mankind's decay from
original perfection and ideal purpose. Woman was sent by God "For
mans reliefe" and "to good ends" (lines 102–103). She still fulfills these

ends, says Donne, but only as an "accesory" (line 104) to her now predominately evil purposes. This attack is an essential part of the symbolic whole of the poem. If the World Soul is the generative force of the universe, it naturally and inevitably manifests itself in sexual forms. The dissolution of the world will just as naturally turn sexuality back in the direction of chaos. What creative value remains in human sexuality is "Like sonnes of women after fifty" (line 204), a very rare thing and possibly malformed. The poem must include an attack on decadent sexuality (and the attack is, to be just, on male as well as female sexual waste) in order to be true to its symbols. That woman rather than man bears the brunt of the attack is in one sense an historical accident—given the history of man as recorded in the Bible and the history of renaissance attitudes towards women—but in another it is poetically inevitable, since woman stands in the symbolic role of earth in this poem and in her actual role of mother.

> The father, or the mother [heaven or earth] barren is.
> The clouds conceive not raine, or doe not powre
> In the due birth-time, downe the balmy showre.
> The'Ayre doth not motherly sit on the earth,
> To hatch her seasons, and give all things birth.
> Spring-times were common cradles, but are toombes;
> And false-conceptions fill the generall wombs.
>
> (lines 380–386)

Even on the occasional level, the attack on women offers appropriate though indirect praise of Elizabeth Drury's now-eternal virginity. It is, however, praise by contrast—one of the few methods Donne had available for presenting virtue as something more than an abstract concept to a world where virtue no longer existed. But the glorification of Elizabeth Drury's soul in this poem is ultimately a glorification of womankind as well, though one that has its justification in the next world; as Donne said in a sermon, "Woman, as well as man, was made after the Image of God, in the Creation; and in the Resurrection, when she shall rise such as we were here, her sexe shall not diminish her glory" (IX, 192). Even the conventional sexual cynicism of "We kill our selves, to propagate our kinde" (line 110) might not be totally indefensible as a projection of some of the bitter feelings the

death of their child must have produced in the Drurys, though Donne
intends to direct his readers beyond this attitude to a new and very
different kind of marriage and generation in heaven.

This redirecting by the poet, not often gentle in spite of its subtlety,
takes the reader on a journey that moves outward into space and time
and finally beyond space and time; but however high into the clouds
we are permitted to penetrate, we are never allowed to forget that
our feet are still firmly entrenched in the mud, and it is this tension
between the sky and the mud entrapping our feet that provides the
drama of these poems. It would be nonsense to argue that Donne is
either primarily realistic (i.e., cynical and pessimistic) or primarily
idealistic in these poems. He is primarily aware of the complex relationships between these two perspectives. The great cycle of creation,
decay, and regeneration is presented here in all of its parts. As we
look at the corruption of this world, we are asked to direct our eyes
to an earlier world, even though that world might have had only a
brief existence or, indeed, might have been realized only in the mind
of God; and our eyes are also directed simultaneously to the next
world. Donne's question about tall, long-lived, patriarchal man—
"Where is this mankind now?"—by means of its very ambiguity
opens up thought about the eternal fate of the patriarchs, but also
thoughts about the present human condition and man's fate. "Onely
death addes t'our length: nor are we growne / In stature to be men,
till we are none" (lines 145–146). Such lines embody the essence of
the poem: a look at corruption, death, and loss of identity rather than
a turning away from it, but a look that carries the reader beyond the
soulless body to both man's primitive and his final condition. "We
seeme ambitious," says Donne, "Gods whole worke t'undue; / Of
nothing he made us, and we strive too, / To bring our selves to
nothing backe" (lines 155–157), which is an attack on the corrupting
forces at work in man that also, given the situation, anticipates a
consummation, for the flesh at least, devoutly to be wished.

The phrase "for the flesh" saves my last statement from overstate-
ment; but, in fact, it is not only the breakup of the individual mortal
body that interests Donne. Donne seeks and describes a dissolution
of some aspects of individual human identity itself; and it is this

retreat from aspects of individuality that makes the notion of a universal soul, a World Soul encompassing all other souls, imaginatively attractive to him. Such a claim could no doubt inspire amateur psychologists to point Freudian fingers toward Donne's study of suicide, *Biathanatos*; but there is nothing in the *First Anniversary* on this subject for which Donne lacks either important precedents or justification in impersonal terms. None the less, the concept of the self under attack in Donne's poem is that concept of the individual that, some have claimed, was responsible for producing the Renaissance: the sense of one's self as a unique identity existing independent of one's relationships to all other selves.

> Prince, Subject, Father, Sonne, are things forgot,
> For every man alone thinkes he hath got
> To be a Phoenix, and that there can bee
> None of that kinde, of which he is, but hee.
>
> (lines 215–218)

The contemporary belief in the phoenix-like uniqueness of the self is for Donne merely one more example of the dissolution of the harmony of the world. Ultimately, of course, this sense of uniqueness is seen as groundless; the phoenix mentality of his contemporaries is presented by Donne as one of the diseases of the mind and body that parallel the diseased world of the poem. Perhaps the fact that Donne himself was one of the greatest phoenixes of the period enabled him to make this attack on the new concept of selfhood all the more effectively, just as his repeated experience of sickness intensified his skill in creating medical analogies for the world's condition in his poems. The alternative to the phoenix-self is, however, the kind of identity typified by the "she" who is Donne's subject. Elizabeth Drury is never named in the poems because in dying she has symbolically lost her name, just as the world did at the imagined loss of the World Soul; she has lost her unique, seventeenth-century, phoenix-like identity and become what she in fact always really was, a soul whose existence is defined primarily in terms of its relationship to God and to other souls. Donne believed strongly in the doctrine that individual souls would be united with purified bodies at the resurrection, but this is not the kind of survival of the soul Donne is concerned with in the *Anniversaries,* whose poetic moment is one after death but before the resurrection. That Donne actually believed that individual souls were absorbed into the World Soul until the resurrection is unlikely; rather, like Abelard in an earlier century, Donne seems to have regarded these Platonic conceptions of the World Soul as beautiful figures with which to describe the operations of the Holy Spirit. By using Elizabeth Drury's soul as a Platonic symbol, identifying her soul with the World Soul, Donne carries to the opposite possible extreme his period's concern with phoenix-like selfhood.

Seeing her soul as the World Soul allows Donne to present the idea that a human soul is more important in its relationships than in its uniqueness. She *is* the universal pattern, says Donne. Thus it is perfectly appropriate that she is never given a specific name in the poem, and equally appropriate that the unstated name is repeatedly offered as a mystery to be examined, a blank into which any number of possible names may be inserted.

This, then, brings my consideration of the poem back again to its typological structure, a subject that has not in fact been left behind, since it is the sense of the soul as something important through its relationships that justifies a poetic structure dependent on linked parallels, and it is this that allows the poet to associate his heroine with unfallen woman, with the ark, and with Mary. Beginning the poem with allusions to the creation and Eden and concluding it with reference to Moses at the end of his wilderness journey frame the poem as a cyclical structure of creation, loss, and return that parallels its subject's history and allows Donne to see in her "All the old Text" (line 148). In contemplating this death, the poet is given a view of the Promised Land. "This departing," he would later say in a sermon, "is our last *Exodus,* our last passeover, our last transmigration" (V, 210). Indeed, according to one common application of the theory, each man typologically lives out the history of the world in his own lifetime; and in each man, as in history itself, the Word of God, which is the soul of the World, is present and alive, though not always with the same intensity and in the same form.

The typological aspects of the poem, like other areas of the symbolic complex generated by the subject, are multiple. Though the Old Testament (and the New as well) could be seen as foreshadowing events in the life of every man, and thus of Elizabeth Drury, the main typological function of the Old Testament was, of course, to predict the coming of Christ. The biblical allusions of the *First Anniversary* point toward the presence of Christ in that poem and toward the soul as *alter Christus,* a role that must be adopted by every virtuous soul. The phoenix of individual selfhood becomes, in Donne's poem, absorbed by the true Phoenix. Again, this is not hyperbolic praise of Elizabeth Drury; it is a dramatization of a typical soul losing *its self* by finding itself in Christ.

The Christ of the *First Anniversary* is Christ suffering. The death that occasioned the poem is equated from the very beginning with Christ's crucifixion, when "This world, in that great earth-quake languished" (line 11). Other allusions contained in the references to a bath of tears and a wound further establish the image, though Christ's act of intercession is not directly mentioned until lines 167–168: "This man, whom God did wooe, and loth t'attend / Till man came up, did downe to man descent"—lines that are yet another example of the cyclical relationship of emanations and returns that unifies the poems. The suffering body of Christ is reflected in the poem in the sick and suffering body of the world, undergoing agues and fevers and being anatomized, as criminals once had been, while still alive. The world the poem presents is very much the world before the resurrection: "Perchance the world might have recovered, / If she whom we lament had not beene dead" (lines 359–360), which also alludes to Christ's contemporary type, Lazarus. But the poem's final vision is none the less one of the rebirth which follows.

The presentation of the world as a sick body provides an excellent illustration of the ways in which Donne unites the abstract with the concrete in the symbolism of his poem. This image may be related to the poem's specific occasion—to the sickness that led to the death of Elizabeth Drury—though such a relationship is only implied and must be seen as but one of the possible extensions of this particular analogy in the poem. It would not have been inappropriate to speak of the final illness of the deceased in an elegiac poem; but the Eliz-

abeth Drury whom Donne presents is so far removed from the suffering mortal she was when in this world that her former frailty and
mortality are only indirectly recalled. The surface of the poem presents the sickness as that of the macrocosm itself. The detailed description of the progress of the world's disease, as well as the direct
address to this sick world by the poet, personifies this consumptive
figure sufficiently to protect the idea of a sick world from turning
into a cliché or vague abstraction; and yet this ailing world hardly
becomes a realistic character in the poem, nor is it intended to do so.
By his personification of the world and his use of a sickness that is
simultaneously real and metaphorical, Donne presents multiple visions
in one symbolic representation. The image embodies the earth since
the Fall, subject to such vicissitudes as earthquake, flood, and fire; it
includes man subject to disease, deformity, madness, and death. It also
includes Christ suffering on the cross, a criminal suffering from moral
decay, the human race destroying itself with progress (lines 159–160),
a sick prince dying without an heir, and a sick man being treated by
a physician who has no belief in a possible cure and whose patient
does not wish to know that he is ill (lines 441–442). That two of these
meanings are directly opposed to each other—Christ and the degenerate criminal—is indicative of the kind of symbolism being used.

Few of these projected meanings have their importance only or
even mainly in themselves. Even Christ's suffering is not important
as a unique event but as something undertaken for mankind. All of
these meanings of the symbol are important and related to each other
as they typify and give evidence of the results of a disruption of ideal
harmony and balance; they are all both symbolic representations and
specific manifestations of an abstract idea. And since, as Donne
claims, man's salvation and health lie beyond the grave, the idea itself
must have most importance. As Ficino said in his commentary on the
Philebus:

To the extent the soul excels the body, so the soul's health is better than
the body's and its disease worse than bodily disease; and the health of
the soul must never be neglected, even at the cost of everything—of the
body and this life. (p. 212)

The old sciences of alchemy and astrology are present in the poem for the same symbolic reasons as are the new sciences and the imagery drawn from medicine. Alchemy and astrology might be as false as the old astronomy, but it is the true alchemy that matters to Donne— the spiritual one:

> . . . she that could drive
> The poysonous tincture, and the stayne of *Eve,*
> Out of her thoughts, and deeds; and purifie
> All, by a true religious Alchimy;
> Shee, shee is dead.
>
> (lines 179–183)

Such spiritualization and idealization of concrete, faulty human systems leads the reader further into the realms of abstraction without cutting him loose from reality.

Nevertheless, as the poem develops, abstract ideas in pure form become more frequent, as Donne uses his built-up meanings to raise his reader into the realm of the ideal. "Harmony," "colour," "proportion," and "correspondence" become the key terms now, though for each the poet offers examples—the positive ones always being the soul herself, she who literally *is* these abstractions.

> And, Oh, it can no more be questioned,
> That beauties best, proportion is dead,
> Since even griefe it selfe, which now alone
> Is left us, is without proportion.
>
> (lines 305–308)

> She, after whom, what forme soe're we see,
> Is discord, and rude incongruitee,
> Shee, shee is dead, she's dead; when thou knowst this,
> Thou knowst how ugly a monster this world is.
>
> (lines 323–326)

Proportion, Donne goes on to say, has also become a monster, it is so uncommon an occurrence in this world.

The "colours" that matter to the poem are not pigments but spiritual symbols; Petrarchan praise of the fair lady's coloring is transferred by Donne to the realm of divine ideas:

> ... shee, in whom all white, and redde, and blue
> (Beauties ingredients) voluntary grew,
> As in an unvext Paradise; from whom
> Did all things verdure, and their lustre come,
> Whose composition was miraculous,
> Being all color, all Diaphanous.
>
> (lines 361–366)

The breakdown of the harmonic correspondence between heaven and earth gives virtue itself a monstrous appearance and allows it to function within satire:

> So that some Princes have some temperance;
> Some Counsaylors some purpose to advance
> The common profite; and some people have
> Some stay, no more then Kings should give, to crave;
> Some women have some taciturnity;
> Some Nunneries, some graines of chastity.
>
> (lines 419–424)

This type of satire in no way calls into question the abstract virtues themselves, which are not of this world but are embodied and symbolized in the redeemed soul that is Donne's subject.

Sam L. Hynes, in a note published in 1953, recognized the importance of the aesthetic abstractions of harmony, color, and proportion in the later parts of the *First Anniversary*. He attempted to relate these concepts to Aquinas's definition of beauty (in spite of their ubiquitous appearance in most aesthetic theories). Hynes found it impossible, however, to relate these abstractions to the overall structure of the poem, claiming that "in spite of its elaborate organization, the poem is far from successful, and certainly it is, in an intellectual sense, disorganized."[20] But Hynes's failure to see the intellectual organization of the poem stemmed from his misplaced emphasis. The aesthetic principles Donne discusses are no more the subject or organizing principle of the poem than are the discoveries of the new science, the corruption of the world, or any other of the specific instances Donne employs; they are simply more abstract manifestations of the basic structure of relationships between the real and the ideal, body and soul, that holds the poem together. The organization of the poem does not depend upon scholastic aesthetics but upon biblical typology and upon Neoplatonic movements between the concrete and the abstract, the many and the One—movements that themselves incorporate even Christian typology and that are all poetically derived by Donne from the poem's occasion and subject: the departure of the soul of Elizabeth Drury, the Soul of the World.

As *anima mundi*, then, the "she" of the poem is as abstract a personification as a poet could feel called upon to present. Indeed, she is almost as abstract as the concept of God itself, since she is the image of God, whom Origen declared to be *"quasi anima mundi."* Donne saves the concept from becoming lost in a world of bodiless ideas by exploiting its symbolic richness more often than he analyzes any philosophical truth behind the identification. Sir John Davies, John Davies of Hereford, and Henry More all wrote philosophies of the soul in verse; but Donne creates poetry rather than philosophy out of the same material—by developing not an argument but a complex of symbolic relationships. The areas from which he draws his symbolic meanings may be those one would expect from reading Agrippa or one of the other renaissance encyclopedic harmonies; but the compression, suggestiveness, and allusiveness with which he uses his material, together with the tight interweaving by which one meaning points toward others without breaking out into mystical emptiness, result in the fact that the "soul" of these poems is one of the richest symbolic creations in English literature.

That richness is increased by the distinctive presence of the poet himself within his poem—by which I do not mean to suggest that Donne is mimetically reproducing things from his own life or that the style is peculiarly Donnean, though both of these may be the case. The poet appears in this poem in a symbolic manner parallel to that with which he presents his subject. The most important aspect of that projected presence is the poet's role as prophet—a Jeremiah at times perhaps, but, more importantly, a Moses. It is not until the end of the poem that Donne makes specific the connection between the poetic voice and Moses, but the allusions to the Pentateuch and the typo-

logical treatment of his subject have throughout prepared the way for
this identification. This identification unites the speaker himself with
biblical history in the same way in which he has united the soul of
the poem to that universal pattern. The *First Anniversary* is the poet
Donne's own pentateuch, and his own creation (and de-creation)
myth, and a typological prophecy of the return of man to God. As
in the Old Testament, the types have often to be read as inverted
versions of the future truth they anticipate.

It is, in fact, this need to discover truth through negative analogy
in a fallen world that provides the key to the relationship between,
on the one hand, the poetic voice as Moses and, on the other, the
speaker's initially more obvious role as a bitterly satirical "anatomist"
pulling the rotten world to pieces. He is a physician who, in so far as
his patient is sick, has no desire to cure him or postpone his death,
and who, in so far as the world-body is dead, finds little in his pre-
maturely aborted anatomy lesson but that which disgusts him (ll. 439–
440). This bad physician is, in both negative and positive ways, a type
of the Good Physician, just as were Adam and Noah and Moses. The
reader may be aware of the speaker first as anatomist, then as Moses;
both roles are in fact always present. The speaker is simultaneously
satirist, elegiac poet, and inspired prophet, and he can play all of these
roles at once because of the nature of his subject, a subject with which
he is (or seeks to become) totally "involved."

In that he is a bad physician, a cynical satirist, the poet is very
much in and of the body of this rotten world. The only escape possible from this disgusting condition is a separation from this world—
something for which his subject provides a model and a cause for
hope, a personal reason for the elegiac celebration of the death of
someone he never knew. However, what the poet cannot find in the
outer world, except in traces, he can find imaged in his inner world
in the idea of a virtuous, redeemed soul. This is his inspiration, the
subject of his poem, and the factor that makes a biting satirist also a
Moses. Indeed, Moses himself, in the song from Deuteronomy to
which Donne compares his poem, was bitterly satirical about the corruption of his people. When Donne made use of this song again in

a sermon in 1622, he emphasized God's reason for causing Moses to sing it:

God himselfe made *Moses* a Song, and expressed his reason why; The children of *Israel*, sayes *God*, will forget my Law; but this song they will not forget; and whensoever they sing this song, this song shall testifie against them, what I have done for them, how they have forsaken me. (IV, 179–180)

The role of preacher and prophet in this world is necessarily linked to that of satirist and anatomist. This is what Donne calls in another sermon Solomon's method:

Therefore *Solomon* shakes the world in peeces, he dissects it, and cuts it up before thee, that so thou mayest the better see, how poor a thing, that particular is, whatsoever it be, that thou sets they love upon in this world. (III [1957], 48)

The speaker of Donne's poem is himself an image of the world view he is presenting—a fallen, decaying, mortal being, but still representative, through his poetry, of the Idea. The poet's rebirth as Moses at the end of the poem is simply the result of the development of an embryo that has been within the anatomist himself all along. This metamorphosis is a death, something the poet has been desiring throughout the poem, but a death into new life and to an identity like the one he posits for his subject. The poet seeks to know himself as he knows the subject of his poem, in terms of the relationships of the one to the many. As Agrippa said in his *Occult Philosophy*:

Whosoever therefore shall know himself, shall know all things in himself; especially he shall know God, according to whose Image he was made; he shall know the world, the resemblance of which he beareth; he shall know all creatures, with which he Symbolizeth.[21]

Agrippa goes on to relate this doctrine to astrology, magnetism, and alchemy, though without Donne's indifference.

The voice at the end of Donne's poem asks to be heard not as that of the phoenix, but as the impersonal, Divine Voice speaking through men and through poetry:

And you her creatures, whom she workes upon
And have your last, and best concoction
From her example, and her vertue, if you
In reverence to her, do thinke it due,
That no one should her prayses thus reherse,
As matter fit for Chronicle, not verse,
Vouchsafe to call to minde, that God did make
A last, and lastingst peece, a song. He spake
To *Moses,* to deliver unto all,
That song: because he knew they would let fall,
The Law, the Prophets, and the History,
But keepe the song still in their memory.
Such an opinion (in due measure) made
Me this great Office boldly to invade.
Nor could incomprehensibleness deterre
Me, from thus trying to imprison her.
Which when I saw that a strict grave could do,
I saw not why verse might not doe so too.
Verse hath a middle nature; heaven keepes soules,
The grave keeps bodies, verse the fame enroules.

(lines 455–474)

The poet and his verse have the same creative, mediating nature as the World Soul. But, like the earthly creation, this kind of poetic creation only finally succeeds when it fails. The poem takes as one aspect of its theme the Fortunate Fall; it is itself a fortunate failure, and it ends with a celebration of its own defeat. The poet's subject remains to the end "incomprehensible"; it still cannot be named even though the unstated name "refines course lines, and makes prose song" (line 446). The limits of a poem can no more hold a subject like this than a grave can hold a soul, however much they try "to imprison her." And yet the poem may be as glorious a failure as the grave itself; it may point beyond itself to what it cannot contain and by negation and absence imply a presence. "How weak a thing is Poetry? (and yet Poetry is a counterfait Creation, and makes things that are not, as though they were)" (Donne, *Sermons* IV, 87). It may create in the minds of the living ideal images whose only existence is divine.

"A Funerall Elegie"

Though it may have been written before the *First Anniversary*, "A Funerall Elegie" stands, in the completed sequence that Donne published, as a fulcrum between the *First* and *Second Anniversary*, summing up many of the lines of thought developed in the first poem, and opening the way for the new direction to be taken in the second. It begins where the *First Anniversary* ended, with an even stronger statement of the failure of the grave and of poetry to contain and memorialize the immortal soul:

> Tis lost, to trust a Tombe with such a ghest,
> Or to Confine her in a Marble chest
> ... Can we keepe her then
> In workes of hands, or of the wits of men?
> Can these memorials, ragges of paper, give
> Life to that name, by which they must live?
>
> (lines 1–2, 9–12)

Poetry, Donne goes on to say, is a lifeless carcass unless it is inhabited by the soul, the Word, the unspoken name which is his subject. But that soul has left the world, has been transformed by death; "And can shee, who no longer would be shee, / Being such a Tabernacle" (lines 15–16) return to the body of the poet's verse giving it life? Again, the poet declares his ignorance—and also his indifference. "But 'tis no matter; we may well allow / Verse to live so long as the world will now" (lines 19–20). It is the imminent end of the world, and the poet's own anticipated transcendence in the next life of the inevitable failure due to ignorance in this one, that allows him to sing among the corpses and justifies the mirth that continually undercuts the potential solemnity apparently demanded by his poems' occasion and their self-confessed failure.

The "Funerall Elegie" at times approaches the *joyance* of Spenser's vision. Death and Nature enter the poem as abstract personifications engaged in a rather absurd contest, Death failing to find anything to exercise his function upon except the "decrepit" world itself. The soul of the poem, who has now become explicitly a symbolic tabernacle, was, we are told, admired by all men when it was in a body, and this admiration is compared to that of saints for a new church: "As when a Temple's built, Saints emulate / To which of them, it shall be consecrate" (lines 65–66), a humorous vision of competing saints, which is none the less integrated thematically both by continuing the idea of the Unnamed (in this case, an unnamed church), and in anticipating the idea of sainthood at the end of the *Second Anniversary*. The "Funerall Elegie" also presents a witty picture of astronomers (or astrologers), disagreeing about how to classify newly discovered stars, who "Argue, and agree not, till those starres go out" (line 70). Nature is instructed to rejoice (line 55) and the poem ends with a vision of "spirituall mirth" produced in the blessed as they watch "the good play her, on earth" (lines 105–106).

Yet this vision of heavenly mirth is always clearly presented as a condition that can be shared only momentarily and ironically by the earth-bound and ignorant poet. The ideal and the actual retain their dramatic tension. The body, the tomb, the poem, are all empty treasure chests; the jewels they have been built to house can be seen only with the mind's eye. Donne early on in the poem develops an aspect of the microcosm-macrocosm analogy that throughout the *First Anniversary* had been for the most part only implied: that of the body politic as a human body. The comparison begins in an extremely conventional fashion: "The world contains / Princes for armes, and Counsailors for braines, / Lawyers for tongues, Divines for hearts" (lines 21–23); but then this vision of an existing earthly order, so atypical of what Donne has been saying before, is extended and destroyed by a line that shows this "body" to be as corrupt as any other in the poem: "The Rich for stomach, and for backes the Pore" (line 24). Donne then offers two analogies suggesting that the soul will someday return to the body. He pictures death as a clockmaker who takes a clock apart with the intention of reassembling it into a timepiece better that the original (lines 37–40). (Donne in his sermons would frequently make similar arguments from design.) And he compares dying to a river going underground only to surface again somewhere else (lines 41–44). But, as soon as these suggestions are made, their potential comfort is denied by the reappearance of the specter of human ignorance:

> Heaven may say this, and joy in't; but can wee
>   Who live, and lacke her, here this vantage see?
> What is't to us, alas, if there have beene
>   An Angell made a Throne, or Cherubin?
> We lose by't. . . .
>
> (lines 47–51)

One solution to this problem is contained in the possibility that the living, though ignorant and cut off from the heavenly, may still retain the lost ideal in their memories; but the advantages of such a memory are highly qualified indeed:

> . . . And as aged men are glad
>   Being tastlesse growne, to joy in joyes they had,
> So now the sicke starv'd world must feed upone
>   This joy, that we had her, who now is gone.
>
> (lines 51–54)

The alternative to ignorance or futile nostalgia, however, is to be found in the idea of active imitation, "measuring future things, by things before" (line 87). The idea of the pure soul, if we are willing to give up our own corrupt identities to imitate it, allows us to live a life that is in structure her life. Because this form, this pattern, is not that of the life of any single individual alone, we can complete what Elizabeth Drury's early death prevented her from completing in this world:

> . . . if after her
>   Any shall live, which dare true good prefer,
> Every such person is her delegate.
>   T'accomplish that which should have beene her fate.
> They shall make up that booke, and shall have thankes
>   Of fate and her, for filling up their blanks.
>
> (lines 97–102)

As we can conform ourselves to the universal pattern that was her life and the world's true life, we can also imitate her death—though development of that subject is saved for the *Second Anniversary.*

The "Funerall Elegie" is, then, a turning point between the two longer poems. In a more conventional elegiac development, it would have contained a simple turning from grief and bitterness to joy in immortality, a statement that "she" was not really dead. But the *Anniversaries* are not conventional elegies. They are metaphysical poems in a strict sense of that term: poems about the metaphysics of the human soul. Everything in them is conditioned by a belief in the mind as simultaneously ignorant of all but the most basic things, and yet capable of conceiving the ideal. Measuring what is to follow by what came before, we can anticipate that the *Second Anniversary* will not abandon the satire and scepticism of the first poem, but that it will none the less look forward rather than back, that it will seek to imagine the fulfillment of the patterns that have been both poetically and divinely established.

The Second Anniversary: Of the Progres of the Soule

That as our *Genesis* is our *Exodus,* (our proceeding into the world, is a step out of the world) so every *Gospell* may be a *Revelation* unto us. (*Sermons* VIII, 96)

The *Second Anniversary* is parallel to the first and must be read as a continuation of it. It does not have its full meaning on its own. If nothing else, its title and its original publication in 1612 with a second edition of the *First Anniversary* would suggest this dependent relationship; but its content as well constantly refers the reader back to the earlier poem.

In interpreting the symbolic nature and function of the ideal soul in the *Second Anniversary,* the reader must carry over into this poem the meanings given to that figure in the first poem and the "Funerall Elegie." Donne, throughout the *Second Anniversary,* largely assumes an understanding of the significance of his main figure; there is little development of that figure beyond what was presented in the first poem, though different aspects of its meaning are explored. Thus the long panegyrics of the second poem are absurd nonsense if they are taken as referring only to the young girl that was Elizabeth Drury:

> Shee, to whom all this world was but a stage,
> Where all sat harkning how her youthfull age

Should be emploid, because in all, shee did,
Some Figure of the Golden times, was hid.
Who could not lacke, what ere this world could give,
Because shee was the forme, that made it live;
Nor could complaine, that this world was unfit,
To be staid in, then when shee was in it;
Shee that first tried indifferent desires
By vertue, and vertue by religious fires,
Shee to whose person Paradise adhear'd
As Courts to Princes; shee whose eies enspheard
Star-light inough, t'have made the South controll,
(Had shee beene there) the Star-full Northern Pole,
Shee, shee is gone. . . .

(lines 67–81)

Donne makes no attempt here to distinguish between his sign (the young girl) and its Neoplatonic symbolic meanings. A reader might attempt such a distinction, but he would almost certainly run into confusion. The reference in the above lines to the promise shown by her youth could perhaps be taken as primarily biographical, were that promise not immediately explained in symbolic terms hearkening back to the use of Christian and Platonic creation myths in the first poem. The world-stage metaphor directs the reader back to the end of the "Funerall Elegie" where *we* were the players, imitating her. To call her "the forme, that made [the world] live" is to assume the first poem's identification of this individual soul with the World Soul; it is also a recollection of the use of Ramist logic there, which saw her as the formal cause of the world. "Paradise adhear'd" to her person not only because of her innocence but also because she already has been established symbolically as unfallen Eve and the ideal creative principle. As Astraea and Queen Elizabeth, her presence would make any place a court; and reference to the influence of her star-bright eyes is at once Petrarchan praise and Neoplatonic astrology. The metaphysical context of the *Anniversaries* as a whole turns these excessive hyperboles and conventional praises into significant figurative statements of the poems' ideas.

It is true, however, that, though the nominal subject of the *Second Anniversary* is the "progres of the soule" into the next world, this poem contains more direct mentions than the first of the living girl whose death was the poems' occasion, though her name is still withheld. Donne no doubt believed that, having established the symbolic significance of her redeemed soul in his first poem, it was safe to treat her earthly life in a similarly idealized manner, to imagine poetically what sort of body the ideal soul would inhabit (the ideal body being here a symbol of the ideal world). Contemporary and modern misreadings of this poem indicate that he may have been mistaken. Donne was attempting to transform a tradition—that of Petrarchan praise of a beautiful woman—in a way that many readers have not been prepared to accept. Petrarchan poems had, from the first, been subject to allegorical interpretations that gave them religious significance. Donne, however, writes Petrarchan praise in these poems as though he thought the religious significance would be recognized as the primary one. The failure of his contemporaries to understand this confirmed for Donne his skepticism about this world and about the power of poetry in it, which he evidences everywhere in the *Anniversaries*.

But when Donne writes of her "Complexion" (i.e., the balance of the humors in her) that it

> ... was so even made,
> That which of her Ingredients should invade
> The other three, no Feare, no Art could guesse:
> So far were all remov'd from more or lesse,
> (lines 123–126)

he is seeing her as a healthy, beautiful girl who, in these qualities, symbolized the ideal balance of the humors and elements that were present in the Idea, the pattern, of the creation; he is also seeing her soul as the World Soul, through which that ideal balance was in part communicated to matter. The geometrical imagery, which Donne employs concurrently with his references to the four humors and four elements, brings into this poem the ideas of Pythagorean geometric order developed at length in the first poem, and enables the reader to see her life as an example of the abstract idea of order manifesting itself in the flesh:

And as, though all doe know, that quantities
Are made of lines, and lines from Points arise,
None can these lines or quantities unjoynt,
And say this is a line, or this a point,
So though the Elements and Humours were
In her, one could not say, this governes there.

(lines 131–136)

To whose proportions if we would compare
Cubes, th'are unstable; Circles, Angulare.

(lines 141–142)

She was, Donne adds, the Golden Chain of Homer. And yet, lest we take this symbolic picture of her spiritual and physical health as an indication that what the first poem showed to be impossible—the survival of good in the world—is yet possible within individuals, all of this ideal picture is destroyed by the sickness, the disturbance of the humors, that destroyed Elizabeth Drury: "Shee, shee embrac'd a sicknesse, gave it meat, / The purest Blood, and Breath, that ere it eat" (lines 147–148). The ideal, the Christian ideal inherent in the "purest Blood," is finally realizable only in death, which must therefore, like Elizabeth Drury's sickness, be embraced: "Death must usher, and unlocke the doore" (line 156).

As her soul is both actually and symbolically a redeemed soul, so her body before its sickness is offered as an image of the ideal human body as it was at the creation and as it will be after the resurrection:

Shee, of whose soule, if we may say, t'was Gold,
Her body was th'Electrum, and did hold
Many degrees of that; we understood
Her by her sight, her pure and eloquent blood
Spoke in her cheekes, and so distinckly wrought,
That one might almost say, her bodie thought.

(lines 241–246)

One might almost say this because her body represents—as far as anything mortal can—the Idea, the Divine Thought, realized in matter. Whether Elizabeth Drury actually was beautiful does not matter. Donne never saw her, and his ignorance of her functions in the same way as all ignorance functions in these poems: as a means of directing the mind toward ideal images and away from earthly corruption.

The mortal body of Elizabeth Drury serves in this poem the same function as that served by the notion of a harmonious, geometrical physical universe in the first poem. The same brevity and early corruption characterize both, the same pointing beyond themselves to an unchanging order. On the one hand this is a return from the realm of abstractions to the world of particulars, though only a temporary one; the *Second Anniversary* parallels the first in a general logical development from specifics to abstractions, "essential joy" being the final concept toward which this poem is moving. The most important relationship between the two poems, however, is typological rather than logical.[22] The girl as an individual receives somewhat more emphasis in the *Second Anniversary*, not because Donne is retreating from the concept of the soul's absorption in God, which justified the symbolism of the first poem, but because the *Second Anniversary* is a typological application of the universal history behind the *First Anniversary* to the "self." I place "self" in quotation marks because the self that matters to this poem is not so much that of Elizabeth Drury as it is that of everyman, including the reader and the poet.

This pattern of meditation, which involves contemplating the broad historical pattern and the significant events of Christian history, and then applying these to the individual as everyman, was a common one employing an extension of biblical typology to individual applications. This kind of typology was as old as Tertullian.[23] It may have functioned as part of larger patterns of Catholic and Protestant meditation, but it also occurs independently. Donne and many other preachers followed the pattern in funeral sermons. The best known poetic example is George Herbert's "Easter-wings":[24]

Easter-wings
Lord, who createdst man in wealth and store,
Though foolishly he lost the same,
Decaying more and more,
Till he became
Most poore:
With thee

O let me rise
As larks, harmoniously,
And sing this day thy victories:
Then shall the fall further the flight in me.

My tender age in sorrow did beginne:
And still with sicknesses and shame
Thou didst so punish sinne,
That I became
Most thinne.
With thee
Let me combine
And feel this day thy victorie:
For, if I imp my wing on thine,
Affliction shall advance the flight in me.

The first stanza of this poem parallels Donne's *First Anniversary* in its presentation of Christian history as a pattern of descent and return; the second stanza parallels the *Second Anniversary* in seeing this pattern reflected in the life of the individual.

Thus the true "heroes" of the *Second Anniversary* are potentially the reader, together with the poet and Elizabeth Drury, and each becomes the hero the poem celebrates through loss of his phoenix individuality and absorption into the universal pattern. This heroic self-sacrifice can be approached by imitation of the good, the ideal; but, more importantly, it can finally be achieved only through death. Donne in his sermons often speaks of death as a "transmigration" of the soul, converting the Pythagorean doctrine into Christian terms. We are not reborn on earth but in heaven where our souls will be different—purer, and filled with knowledge instead of ignorance—and our new bodies, after the last judgment, will be ideal, purified versions of the corrupt clay vessels we now inhabit. Because of the corruption of man and the world, imitation of the ideal while here on earth can be only a partial and temporary, though necessary, measure. The metempsychosis offered by death and resurrection is the only important change for the good. The "Progres of the Soule" is not therefore about its earthly progress. References to Elizabeth Drury's ideal body are imaginings of the lost world and anticipations of the one to come.

The main subject of the *Second Anniversary* is, of course, death; and Donne's purpose is to reconcile himself and his reader to it. This is achieved by a brilliant transformation of that subject during the course of the poem, a transformation achieved through image and symbol. The first image of death the poet offers is as graphic and violent a memento mori as any baroque artist ever presented, and not an image the reader associates at first glance with the death of an innocent girl:

> Or as sometimes in a beheaded man,
> Though at those two Red seas, which freely ran,
> One from the Trunke, another from the Head,
> His soule be saild, to her eternall bed,
> His eies will twinckle, and his tongue will roll,
> As though he beckned, and cal'd backe his Soul,
> He graspes his hands, and he puls up his feet,
> And seemes to reach, and to step forth to meet
> His soule; when all these motions which we saw,
> Are but as Ice, which crackles at a thaw:
> Or as a Lute, which in moist weather, rings
> Her knell alone, by cracking at her strings,
> So strugles this dead world, now shee is gone;
> For there is motion in corruption.
>
> (lines 9–22)

This is the kind of death the corrupt world of the *First Anniversary* deserves; it is also the kind of death every guilty man—i.e., everyman—fears, and one that he would not willingly embrace. It is the most mimetic description of a human action to be found in the *Anniversaries,* and it consequently seems almost subhuman or inhuman in context. It is kept, however, from being purely a horrific or grotesque picture of violent death by its symbolic meanings. It means, of course, what Donne says it means: that "there is motion in corruption," that the world in these latter days survives on mechanical reflexes, which mock true life; but it means a good deal more than that. The severing of the body from the head is the severing of the senses from the mind, of the passions from the controlling influence of the soul, of the lower souls from the rational one, of the corporeal from the spiritual in both man and his world. Agrippa, in his *Occult Philosophy,* says:

There is a certain Nerve found by the Anatomists about the nod of the neck, which being touched doth so move all the members of the body, that every one of them move according to its proper motion; by which like touch Aristotle thinks the members of the world are moved by God. (p. 276, sig. T2, v)

Donne, the anatomist of the world, has touched this nerve in a most violent manner. The motions of his beheaded world-man are those expressing a desire for proper unity of body and soul, but this severing has denied him the power of speech, the power of the Word.[25]

However, as one would expect with this type of symbolism, there are aspects of the image that simultaneously point in another direction. The reference to "two Red seas" links this image with the typological use of the Pentateuch in the *First Anniversary* and offers even this death as a type of the entrance into the promised land of heaven. This, and the statement that the soul has gone "to her eternall bed," imply that the death described might well be that of a martyr rather than of a vicious criminal. Ice cracking at a thaw may be another example of motions in an inanimate object, but it is also a common herald of spring, of release. The random sounding of the single lute string is, however lifeless a sound, a musical note; and music is to be a major source of symbolism in this poem. The "moist weather" links with the thawing ice and the two Red Seas to create a pattern of water imagery that is extended into the lines that follow, tying Donne's apparently disparate images together into a symbolic image of redemption. Our forgetting of the ideal soul is "a new Deluge, and of Lethe flood" (line 27), in which the poet discovers himself struggling for life, a life he will find through praise of the "Immortal Mayd" of the poems. In the midst of all this water imagery, the poet desires more of the same, a deluge and a Red Sea that he will enter only at his own death:

> Thirst for that time, O my insatiate soule,
> And serve thy thirst, with Gods safe-sealing Bowle.
> Bee thirsty still, and drinke still till thou goe;
> 'Tis th'onely Health, to be Hydropique so.
>
> (lines 45–48)

The imagery of water and blood comes to mean what all such imagery in the Bible was taken to symbolize—the blood of the Eucharist. The beheading of the world-man is joined poetically by Donne to the Crucifixion. Yet the desire for such a draught can only appear to be a gross sickness in this sick world, a world where death, which is a release and a reward, looks like a punishment.

But in this poem shadowy types give way to truth. The loss of Eden, the wandering in the wilderness, the corruption of the world, the death of an innocent young girl, are all justified in the only way Donne knew how to justify them—as part of a redemptive pattern, as part of a circular process, which will eventually take us to heaven. Louis Martz has complained that "the omission of Grace may be said to indicate the fundamental flaw of the *First Anniversary*: it lacks the firm religious center of the *Progresse*."[26] But this is to criticize what is an essential part of the design of the poems, and a design ultimately not of Donne's creating but of God's.

The *First Anniversary* contains only foreshadowings of Grace because its world is the Old Testament world, the world of history and the individual before the coming of Christ. There is a firm religious center to the *First Anniversary,* but it is masked by the world's corruption, just as it was in the biblical world before the Incarnation. With the entrance of Grace, the past takes on new meaning, typological meaning, for both the world and the individual. Paradoxically, however, when Christ comes, the past might just as well be forgotten. This too applies to the individual: "And unto thee, / Let thine owne times as an old story be, / Be not concern'd" (lines 49–51). Grace not only makes the old new, it transforms everything, including meanings. Through his own use of symbols, Donne transforms the most grotesque examples of man's mortality into indications of his salvation. The imaginative movement from the image of the beheaded man to the poet's thirst for the time of "Gods great Venite" (line 44) is unbroken, swift, and sure; he *can* embrace such a death, just as Christ did—because Christ did.

But the progress, in reality and in the poem, is not over yet. The end of the pattern is anticipated, but the reality of the moment is still corruption. The surface imagery dealing with death is still replete with the kind of *contemptus mundi* appropriate to the early stages of a meditation on this subject. "The World is but a Carkas; thou art fed / By it, but as a worme, that carcas bred" (lines 55–56). Yet here again, man, whom Donne speaks of in his sermons as a "rational worm," is offered the opportunity to transform this image by an act of the mind—two acts in fact, one negative: "Forget this world, and scarse thinke of it so, / As of old cloaths, cast of a yeare agoe" (lines 61–62); the other positive: "Looke upward; that's towards her, whose happy state / We now lament not, but congratulate" (lines 65–66). This is sound advice, impossible to be followed consistently even by the poet in his poem. The bitter reality of death and corruption is simply too clearly present in the world and in Donne's poem to be dismissed with a simple forgetting. The world is "not worth a thought" (line 83), but it is given a good many thoughts in the *Anniversaries*. Again Donne fails magnificently. The *Second Anniversary* consists of repeated attempts by the poet (parallel to that contained in the image of the beheaded man) to transform the horrid actuality of death into a symbolic image of man's salvation. That each attempt is a partial success gives the poet grounds for belief in the truth of the ideal he envisions behind these gross realities. That he is unable to sustain any of his visions is proof of his limited, ignorant condition in this world.

The "Contemplation of our state in our death-bed" (marginal gloss), which extends from line 85 to line 156, is one such attempt at converting apparent realities to ideal truths, though its direction is the reverse of the meditation on the beheaded man. It begins with images of death as a guide to heaven and as a release of the soul: "death is but a Groome. . . . thinke that but unbinding of a packe, / To take one precious thing, thy soule, from thence" (lines 85, 94–95). But the discrepancy between the idea and the actuality begins to undermine the consolation. The reader is asked to imagine his laboring breath on the deathbed as "broken and soft Notes" (line 91), which are simultaneously "Division, and thy happiest Harmonee" (line 92). He is invited to see his fatal sickness as his cure, his death knell as a call to the church triumphant; he should imagine himself returning his sins as a legacy to the devils from which they came. All of these things are, of course, capable of being believed; but the paradoxical truths the mind is being asked to accept become too many, and the poet moves without transition from the believable to the unbelievable.

> Thinke thy friends weeping round, and thinke that thay
> Weepe but because they goe not yet thy way.
> Thinke that they close thine eyes, and thinke in this,
> That they confesse much in the world, amisse,
> Who dare not trust a dead mans eye with that,
> Which they from God, and Angels cover not.
>
> (lines 107–112)

This is witty, but it is too clearly *not* why people behave as they do at a deathbed; and this failure to sustain a serious paradoxical acceptance of death throws the poet back into the macabre where he began:

> Thinke that thy body rots, and (if so lowe,
> Thy soule exalted so, thy thoughts can goe,)
> Thinke the a Prince, who of themselves create
> Wormes which insensibly devoure their state.
>
> (lines 115–118)

The direction of thought here is, as the verse itself announces, downward, and the only alternative to this failure is the one the poet takes: a turning away from thoughts of one's self and of one's own death to a contemplation of she who is already redeemed.

> . . . and if thou bee
> Drowsie or slacke, remember then that shee,
> . . . hath taught us that though a good man hath
> Title to Heaven, and plead it by his Faith,
> And though he may pretend a conquest, since
> Heaven was content to suffer violence,
> Yea though he plead a long possession too,
> (For they'are in Heaven on Earth, who Heavens workes do,)
> Though he had right, and power, and Place before,
> Yet Death must usher, and unlocke the doore.
>
> (lines 121–122; 149–156)

The remainder of the poem consists of swings of the pendulum between beatific visions of the redeemed soul and cynical realizations about the corrupt self and the world. The poet calls attention to his failure to maintain a visionary experience by his desperate attempts to sustain it, and the willful demands he makes upon his own soul, demands that are incapable of fulfillment:

> Returne not, my soule, from this extasee,
> And meditation of what thou shalt bee,
> To earthly thoughts, till it to thee appeare,
> With whom thy conversation must be there.
>
> (lines 321–324)

But his poetic soul responds with an immediate plunge into satire:

> Shalt thou not finde a spungy slack Divine
> Drinke and sucke in th'Instructions of Great men,
> And for the word of God, vent them agen?
> Are there not some Courts [etc.] ...
> Up, up my drowsie soule.
>
> (lines 328–331; 339)

During the discussion of the soul's joys in heaven, Donne announces a pause to consider the "essential" joy of that place (lines 383–384), but the reader must first find his way through fifty lines of satire on the empty joys of this world before Donne instructs his soul "to thy first pitch worke up againe" (line 435) and finally defines "essential joy" as "The sight of God" (line 441). The poet cannot succeed except temporarily in forgetting this rotten world. "Onely in Heaven joyes strength is never spent" (line 487). As in the *First Anniversary*, failure proves his point. But in spite of the repeated failures to maintain a beatific vision, there is a progress that takes place in the *Second Anniversary*. By his series of rises and falls, the poet does move from his image of the beheaded man to a vision, however temporary, of the resurrection, of a heaven where

> Joy of a soules arrivall neere decayes;
> For that soule ever joyes, and ever stayes
> Joy that their last great Consummation
> Approaches in the resurrection;
> When earthly bodies more celestiall

> Shalbe, then Angels were, for they could fall;
> This kind of joy doth every day admit
> Degrees of grouth, but none of loosing it.
>
> (lines 489–496)

The twitching body of the felon is finally superseded by the celestial bodies of the redeemed.

Human ignorance is not altered by such visions. Man will, as always, forget the good he has seen. The attitude toward human knowledge established in the *First Anniversary* continues throughout the *Second*. The proposals of the New Science have made the truth or error of scientific notions "an even lay" (line 268).

> Be not concern'd: study not why, nor whan;
> Do not so much, as not beleeve a man.
> For though to erre, be worst, to try truths forth,
> Is far more busines, then this world is worth.
>
> (lines 51–54)

> Poore soule in this thy flesh what do'st thou know.
> Thou know'st thy selfe so little, as thou know'st not,
> How thou did'st die, nor how thou wast begot.
> Thou neither knowst, how thou at first camest in,
> Nor how thou took'st the poyson of mans sin.
> Nor dost thou, (though thou knowst, that thou art so)
> By what way thou art made immortall, know.
>
> (lines 254–260)

Only in heaven can we expect a true transformation of the understanding, the will, and the memory. "In Heaven thou straight know'st all, concerning it, / And what concerns it not, shall straight forget" (lines 299–300). Donne finds himself in a particularly unfortunate position in attempting to exercise memory in a poem occasioned by the death of someone he never knew, and at any rate one cannot will visionary experiences. And yet, as the poem demonstrates, one may have visionary experiences none the less. This is possible because of nothing in the mind of man, but because of the survival in the world of images of God's Word; and that Word the poet finds imprinted in the soul, in the Bible, and in prophetic poetry of the type he is writing. It is therefore not simply a seventeenth-century literary convention that

causes Donne to present the redeemed soul of Elizabeth Drury as a
symbolic book. The poet, through his theology and aesthetics of the
Word and through his use of biblical typology, has been establishing
the basis of this metaphor from the very beginning.

> Shee whose example they must all implore,
> Who would or doe, or thinke well, and confesse
> That aie the vertuous Actions they expresse,
> Are but a new, and worse edition,
> Of her some one thought, or one action.
> . . . shee tooke,
> (Taking herselfe) our best, and worthiest booke.
>
> (lines 306–310; 319–320)

The Word has left the world; the World Soul has abandoned creation; and yet something has been left behind to sustain us until the
end: the Holy Spirit, the *spiritus mundi*, the book in which the Word
is recorded. The soul of Donne's poems symbolizes the Bible, in both
the Old and New Testaments. "Shee rather was two soules, / Or like
to full, on both sides written Rols" (lines 503–504). And Donne's two
poems are themselves such a double roll, depending for what successes
they have upon the Bible and the redeemed soul as sourcebooks to be
imitated. It is this that justifies Donne's presentation of himself in a
prophetic stance, in spite of his admitted human ignorance. In the
First Anniversary the prophetic voice was that of Moses; in the *Second,*
John Donne seeks to allow the speaking voice to become the voice of
St. John the Divine, and the poem is Donne's Book of Revelation,
including even, as in the biblical original, the attacks on earthly corruption.

The success such books can have in this world is limited. At best,
says Donne, they serve to embalm the corpse, to stave off a little of
the putrefaction. Building structures of words is a folly that also has
a biblical type—the Tower of Babel, another pattern of rise and fall:

> They who did labour Babels tower t'erect,
> Might have considered, that for that effect,
> All this whole solid Earth could not allow
> Nor furnish forth Materials enow;
> And that this Center, to raise such a place

> Was far to little, to have beene the Base;
> No more affoords this world, foundatione
> To erect true joye, were all the meanes in one.
>
> (lines 417–424)

The best one can hope for is the "watch-towre" of line 294. But though the world may not provide material or foundation enough for the grand structures man would erect, the success of the sort of structure Donne is attempting to build with words does not finally rest in this world, where he is certain to fail. At the end of the poem Donne presents himself as the Trumpet of the Lord, an image that in itself combines Old and New Testament allusions (Ezekiel and Revelation), and that is a final dissolving of individual selfhood into divinely ordained vocation:

> And that the world should notice have of this,
> The purpose, and th'Authority is his;
> Thou art the Proclamation; and I ame
> The Trumpet, at whose voice the people came.
>
> (lines 525–528)

God [promises] that his Prophet, his Minister shall be . . . a Trumpet, to awaken with terror. But then, he shall become *Carmen musicum,* a musical and harmonious charmer, to settle and compose the soul again in a reposed confidence, and in a delight in God: he shall be *musicum carmen,* musick, harmony to the soul. (*Sermons* II, 166–167)

This last is as direct a statement as one could wish of the purpose and the aesthetics of the *Second Anniversary.*

When the poet abandons the efforts of his individual memory, understanding, and will in his meditation on death and the redeemed soul, then the divine Word becomes the poetic words. This experience is described in the poem as an ecstasy—a getting outside of the self, a symbolic death. It is, in one of its aspects, a musical ecstasy, which restores on the ideal plane the broken harmony described in the *First Anniversary.* The involuntary sounding of the lute-knell in lines 19–20 of the *Second Anniversary* has given way by the end of the poem to the divinely willed trumpet. The *Anniversaries* themselves are "Hymns" (lines 37 & 43) that will be superseded when "Gods great Venite" (line

44) changes the song. The bells rung at a death are calls to the church triumphant (lines 100–101), where one "Shall in the Angels songs no discord heare" (line 340), no discord of the sort one certainly does hear in these poems.

The purpose of Donne's music is both Christian and Platonic-Pythagorean. Iamblicus said of Pythagoras that

he established that to be the first erudition which subsists through music, and also through certain melodies and rhythms, from which the remedies of human manners and passions are obtained, together with those harmonies of the powers of the soul which it possessed from the first. (*Life*, pp. 31–32)

The same didactic and restorative purposes underlie Donne's "Hymns." The prophetic voice in the ecstatic visions is also an Orphic one. Leo Spitzer reminds us that "Archytas, Plato's Pythagorean friend, sought (after 400 B.C.) to find the essence of the individual soul, as of the world soul, in the tones of music," and Kepler revived this doctrine for seventeenth-century England.[27] The harmonious joining together of various Platonic-Pythagorean concepts that Donne achieves in the *Anniversaries* has its precedent in Plato's *Timaeus* where, to cite Spitzer again, "the world soul (a religious concept), the regulation of the cosmos (a concept of physics), world harmony (a musical concept), and the soul of man (a psychological concept) are fused" (p. 11). Donne, like Ficino, has little difficulty in combining these concepts with Christian theology, particularly since, unlike Ficino and Kepler, he is primarily interested in the metaphorical and analogical possibilities of these Platonic concepts and not in their literal truth.

Because of the presence of this musical Pythagoreanism, the sounding lyre at the first of the poem ceases to be heard as an accidental phenomenon, but can be reinterpreted as a sign that there is still some principle producing imitation of the divine music, however feeble, on earth. The universe of the Pythagoreans was, according to Quintilian, constructed as a lyre, and sound itself was a product of celestial motion.[28] Donne's ecstasies in the *Second Anniversary* are intended as Platonic-Pythagorean *catharsis* as well as Christian prophetic visions. *Catharsis,* as the return of the soul to harmony, was a word used by

the Pythagoreans for the effects not only of music, but also of philosophy: indeed, for them philosophy *was* catharsis. For Ficino and other
Neoplatonists, the music of the spheres was identical to the muses who
inspired the arts:

And so we name the nine sounds of the heavens, from their musical
harmony, the Muses. Our soul was from the beginning endowed with the
principle of this music, for the heavenly harmony is rightly said to be
innate in anything whose origin is heavenly. This harmony is then imitated
by various instruments and songs. This gift like the rest was given us
through the love of the divine providence. (*Commentary on the Symposium*,
p. 181)

As Donne put it:

God made this whole world in such an uniformity, such a correspondency,
such a concinnity of parts, as that it was an Instrument, perfectly in tune:
we may say, the trebles, the highest strings were disordered first; the best
understandings, Angels and Men, put this instrument out of tune. God
rectified all again, by putting in a new string, *semen mulieris,* the seed of
the woman, the *Messias*: And onely by sounding that string in your ears,
become we *musicum carmen,* true musick, true harmony. (*Sermons* II, 170)

The analogy is ubiquitous in Donne's works.

In the *Second Anniversary,* however, there is a marked difference
between the ecstasy and catharsis that the poet achieves and the heavenly condition of the ideal soul. The catharsis of death is a process
different in kind from that produced by meditation or song. Thus,
though the description of the soul's journey to heaven included in this
poem might seem, on first reading, to be an account of the progress
of the soul of Elizabeth Drury, it is nothing of the sort. It is the
progress of the soul of John Donne and, with him, of the reader. The
redeemed soul who is in heaven at the "moment" of the poem got
there by means of no such Cook's Tour through the spheres as Donne
takes his reader upon. When a soul leaves its body, Donne says in this
poem, it "Dispatches in a minute all the way, / Twixt Heaven, and
Earth" (lines 188–189). "But ere shee can consider how shee went, /
At once is at, and through the Firmament" (lines 205–206). The
poem's contemplative journey through the spheres, which she never

saw, serves to emphasize once again man's ignorance of cosmology, but its major function is to establish for the reader and poet the upward directional pattern of the thought and imagery through which Donne achieves his visions of heaven. The "she" of the poem is never described as on her way to heaven; both in heaven and on earth she is and was the symbolic embodiment of perfection. On the theme of journeys to heaven, S. K. Heninger, Jr. says, "The physical journey through the heavenly spheres, a favorite motif in literature from Cicero to Donne, is only a metaphor for the inward search for absolutes."[29] That Donne presents his journey in negative terms (what she did *not* see) emphasizes the purely metaphorical and symbolic nature of the device.

Donne, in his imagined journey through the spheres, has in mind precedents such as the ascent of Philology in Martianus Capella's *Marriage of Philology and Mercury,* but the idealized soul of the poem has more in common with Martianus's figure of Harmony than with Philology. "Having long since taken her departure from earth, Harmony has rejected mortals and their desolated academies."[30] "Long shee'ath beene away, long, long" (*First Anniversary,* line 41). The title of Donne's poem then, "The Progres of the Soule," does not refer to the soul of Elizabeth Drury except in so far as that soul is reflected in the poem and reader and in their parallel but essentially different progress into visionary experience.

Donne had, of course, written about ecstasy before, albeit rather ambiguously in a love poem. But there is no question about the divine cause producing the movements out of the self in this poem. "A Rapture," says Agrippa,

is an abstraction, and alienation, and an illustration of the soul proceeding from God, by which God doth again retract the soul being fallen from above to hell, from hell to heaven. The cause of this is in us a continuall contemplation of sublime things. (*Occult Philosophy,* p. 508; sig. K 6,v)

This passage which can profitably be set beside the following, from one of Donne's early sermons:

The contemplation of God, and heaven, is a kinde of buriall, and Se-pulchre, and rest of the soule; and in this death of rapture, and extasie, in this death of the Contemplation of my interest in my Saviour, I shall finde my self . . . enterred and entombed in his wounds. (*Sermons* II, 210–211)

Donne would have found similar statements in Agrippa's intellectual heirs (e.g., in *Batman uppon Bartholome*).

But though the ecstasy of the *Second Anniversary* is religious rather than erotic, it has its sexual implications. It has already been noted how strong the emphasis on sexual corruption is in the *First Anniversary,* extended there to the very concept of earthly generation itself. This is continued in the *Second Anniversary* and applied to the self: "Think further on thy selfe, my soule, and thinke; / How thou at first wast made but in a sinke" (lines 157–158).

> Thinke but how poore thou wast, how obnoxious,
> Whom a small lump of flesh could poison thus.
> This curded milke, this poore unlittered whelpe
> My body, could, beyond escape, or helpe,
> Infect thee with originall sinne, and thou
> Couldst neither then refuse, nor leave it now.
>   (lines 163–168)

The foulness of human conception parallels the foulness of the beheaded man; but like that image, this one is also transformed by a recognition of the idea behind and distorted by it, and by a poetic restructuring of the act itself in a vision of its spiritual original. This act of contamination becomes a type of purification. The second womb is the tomb; the first blotted the soul with original sin, the second frees it: "Thinke thy sheell broke, thinke thy Soule hatch'd but now" (line 184). The Platonic world-egg opens up again for the individual at his death, and destruction becomes creation. This third birth of the soul ("Creation gave her one, a second grace," [line 215]) opens the way for a kind of generation and creativity impossible in this world, yet imaged in the examples of Mary and the virgin saints[31] as well as in the patriarchs, prophets, martyrs, and apostles who have left their memories—and their writings—behind. The redeemed soul, who at the first of the poem was asked to be a "father" to Donne's muse, is at the end envisioned as the Bride of Christ; she "by a faithfull confidence, was here / Betrothed to God, and now is married there" (lines

461–462). Even possessing the ideal human body and soul, she was not before death capable of the kind of creativity this union makes possible. She is now symbolically the True Church, Wisdom, the Faithful Virgin, and the muse who inspires Donne and makes the creation of these poems possible, starting a line of generation through imitation of the ideal that Donne prays will continue: "These Hymes may worke on future wits, and so / May great Grand-children of thy praises grow" (lines 37–38).

This presentation of the ideal soul's creative potential in terms of sexual reproduction is part of a long tradition of Christian Platonism, best epitomized in the words of Ficino:

According to Plato, the soul is as pregnant as the body, and they are both aroused to procreation by the stimuli of love. But some men . . . are better equiped for offspring of the soul than for those of the body. Others, and certainly the majority of them, are the opposite. The former pursue heavenly love, the latter earthly. (*Commentary on the Symposium,* p. 207)

Donne's soul seeks its fulfillment in a creative union with the redeemed soul of his poem, his Venus Urania. Birth and death are therefore transformed. "This death," says Donne in a sermon, "this dissolution, this change, is a new creation; this Divorce is a new Marriage; this very Parting of the soul, is an Infusion of a soul, and a Transmigration thereof out of my bosome, into the bosom of Abraham" (I, 231).

Toward the end of the *Second Anniversary* Donne disclaims his metaphors and displays his poetic license just as at the end of the first poem he had disclaimed the apparent inclusiveness of his poetry.

> Here in a place, where mis-devotion frames
> A thousand praiers to saints, whose very names
> The ancient Church knew not, Heaven knowes not yet,
> And where, what lawes of poetry admit,
> Lawes of religion, have at least the same,
> Immortall Maid, I might invoque thy name.
> Could any Saint provoke that appetite,
> Thou here shouldst make mee a french convertite.
> But thou wouldst not.
>
> (lines 511–519)

She, who is in one sense "invoked" in these very lines, is not a saint to be worshipped. The laws of poetry, which have freed Donne to create the poetic symbol that is Elizabeth Drury, are not to be mistaken for his religion. There is no misdevotion in Donne's *Anniversaries*; there is the brilliance of a great poet drawing on the imaginative wealth of the syncretic Christian-Platonic world view to create what he hopes is an image of the truth in a world that must confine itself to images, "Since his will is, that to posteritee, / Thou shouldest for life, and death, a patterne bee" (lines 523–524). Man in general, and a poet in particular, is a clouded mirror, who can none the less creatively shape himself and his objects through *virtus* and *ars*.

The *Anniversaries* as Consolations

Surely the parents of the lamented Mistress Elizabeth Drury would have been better pleased with a simple and recognizable eulogy of their daughter.[32]

How could such elaborate symbolic structures as the *Anniversaries* have succeeded in fulfilling the immediate purpose for which they were written—the consolation of the Drurys for the loss of their child? By that very symbolic metamorphosis that is Donne's method throughout. One of the several things that go through a metamorphosis during the course of these poems—death, birth, the self, the poet, the soul— is the idea of grief itself. Modern readers may regret the absence of the elaboration of any *personal* immortality for the young daughter of the Drurys; but to do so is to miss the point. Though Donne's metaphor of the World Soul may be poetic license, the idea behind it is an orthodox one: the redeemed soul returns to God and to its original form as the image of that abstract essence. Whether personal identity as we know it continues, whether we will recognize one another in heaven, is a subject on which Donne is here content to be silent. Thus, to follow the symbolic transformations of these poems is to lose that sense of death as something personal and particular that makes grief so apparently unbearable;[33] it is to transform personal grief through recognition of the event which caused it as part of a universal, providential pattern. The mourner who follows the poet into rapture is taken out of himself in several ways. The unnamed "she" is always the soul of Elizabeth Drury, whatever else she may become symbolically; her living, physical being receives more rather than less emphasis as the sequence progresses. But this kind of development is possible because of the symbolic transformations that are simultaneously taking place. Donne is able to drop his metaphors at the end of the second poem and declare that she is not really a saint to be invoked because the reality of what she has become has been established by those very metaphors. The emphasis of the last lines is on subservience to God and selfless acceptance of His will, and that is the cure for grief Donne offers. Dwelling on the realities of the life and death of Elizabeth Drury could never have made this the positive experience it is shown to be.

This is the technique Donne also uses in his sermons, many of which have specific occasions, including deaths, as their subjects, and all of which treat their subjects first in universal terms, descending to particulars only after the pattern has been established, and then only to such particulars as would be relevant to a large number of listeners. It was the method not only of Donne but of his time. One need only read seventeenth-century biographies such as those by Walton to see how human life was regarded as important and definable mainly in its conformity to general, pre-established patterns. The kind of particularized "real" life that Shakespeare is sometimes said to have given his characters was seldom if ever given to real people in renaissance biographical accounts of them, however skilled the writer.

Donne also had, if he needed it, classical precedent for his treatment of the dead in his poems of consolation. Though Christian Neoplatonism provided a basis for his symbolism and, with Petrarchism, for his praise, the methods of consolation he employs are largely those of Christian Stoicism. Enough has been written in recent years about the influence of the Christian reading of Seneca's philosophy in the Renaissance to justify the claim that Donne's readers would easily have recognized the mode. As a specific model for his Senecan poetic consolation, Donne would have had available Seneca's own "Consolation to Marcia," a poem that was also drawn upon by Ben Jonson. Seneca's poem, like Donne's, is about the death of a child and is

118 THE QUIET HERO

written for her parents. It too presents a sordid picture of the world and argues persuasively that the child is better out of it. It too looks forward to the end of the world. The following passage from Ralph Freeman's translation of 1635 may perhaps have the translator's memory of Donne somewhere behind it, but it demonstrates effectively the way in which Seneca anticipates Donne in turning a child's short life into something to be celebrated rather than mourned:

> But beside this, that future things are still
> Doubtfull, and never certaine but to ill.
> The passage is more easie, when the soule
> Is speedily dismissed from her foule
> Abode, for she doth then contract less slime,
> And to her station may more lightly clime.
> Great spirits cannot willingly reside
> Long in the body, nor those straights abide,
> But to breake through, and mount aloft, desire,
> And to their first originall aspire.[34]

Like the *Anniversaries,* Seneca's poem also sees death as a move from ignorance to knowledge:

> Thy father there (O *Marcia,* though that place
> Makes all of kinne) his Grandchild doth embrace,
> And there instructs the new enlightened youth
> Not by conjecture, but assured truth.
>
> (p. 43)

The prefatory poems that Joseph Hall wrote for the original publications of Donne's *Anniversaries* reveal that he, at least, recognized the major aspects of Donne's symbolism and their relationship to the themes of consolation. However poor Hall's own poetry here, the response he records is the type Donne would have expected on the basis of the techniques he was employing. Hall, for one thing, recognizes the dependent relationship between the failed earthly sign and that sign's eternal symbolic meaning. Of Elizabeth Drury in the *First Anniversary* he writes:

> . . . wee
> Give more unto thy Ghost, then unto thee.

Yet what we give to thee, thou gav'st to us,
And maist but thanke thy selfe, for being thus:
Yet what thou gav'st and were, O happy maid,
Thy grace profest all due, where 'tis repayd.
So these high songs that to thee suited bine,
Serve but to sound thy makers praise, in thine.

("To the Praise of the Dead, and
the Anatomy," lines 29–36)

"Well may we walk in blacks, but not complaine" says Hall (line 6), in an image which, however much it is praise of the poem, also characterizes the proper response to that poem—a response that retains the memory of the loss and the knowledge of man's darkness, but without regrets.

Sing on, thou Virgin soule, whose lossefull gaine
Thy love-sicke Parents have bewayl'd in vaine;
Never may thy name be in our songs forgot
Till we shall sing thy ditty, and thy note.

(lines 45–48)

In the "Harbinger" before the *Second Anniversary*, Hall shares Donne's desire "to see / The worlds last day, thy glories full degree" (lines 5–6), as well as the realization of man's ignorance of this condition: "I envie thee (Riche soule) I envy thee, / Although I cannot yet thy glory see" (lines 17–18). Hall also recognized that the progress of this poem involved the poet's own growth, and that he as reader was expected to "move" in the same direction. In accepting the meanings of Donne's symbol, Hall shared Donne's perception of death and this world; but more important for him, as for Donne, is the vision of and desire for the next world, which he says the poem has given him.

Hall's response would no doubt have been shared, in even stronger form, by the Drurys, who were so much more intimately involved in the poems' occasion. But one need not even share Donne's beliefs to recognize the transformation of grief that takes place in these poems. The vacillations between bitterness and acceptance (which none the less move steadily from the former to the latter), the manner in which Donne substitutes for the memory of a growing, changing child, whose future the parents would constantly be imagining, an image unchanging and complete—these are the human mind's own methods of coping with such a loss. The memory of a dead child is not the child; it does not grow and change, but it instead becomes part of the selfhood of the parents; what growth, what progress it has is our own. Donne offers his picture of the next world as an ignorant man's vision of what that world might be like, for which his only confirmation lies in the hope that he is inspired. But his understanding of grief is as capable now as then of confirmation.

The Third Anniversary

In the *Anniversaries* Donne says that he will continue to write such poems annually, but there are no others after the *Second*. It is fashionable today to claim that the great unfinished works of literature (like Spenser's *Fairie Queene*) actually are complete: that they somehow completed themselves in spite of their author's original intentions—a fact realized only afterward by the author himself, who then abandoned his project without apology. We might call this notion the "finale fallacy." But certainly my argument about the *Anniversaries* is capable of that kind of extension. Given the typological parallelism between the two poems, where could Donne have gone from here?

In fact, he could have gone in any number of directions. As neat as binary structures are, they are not the only possible ones even in typology. The Pentateuch and Revelation do not exhaust the Bible as a field for harvesting structures and images. Applications of these to the self are not the only use that can be made of biblical types. (The Puritans after Donne's lifetime would apply them even to the history of their own actions in the Civil Wars.) Beauty and "essential joy" do not exhaust the abstract ideas realized in heaven. In some ways, however, future *Anniversaries,* had they kept to the principles established by the poet in the first two, would often have found themselves merely filling in the blanks and restating in different ways what had been said before. Indeed, the *Second Anniversary* itself is not free of this kind of repetition.

In the "Harbinger" to the *Second Anniversary,* Hall calls on Donne to fulfill his promise to continue. At the same time, however, he asks Donne to go beyond these first two poems and to make a significant change in his methods:

> Yet still thou vow'st her more; and every yeare
> Mak'st a new progresse, while thou wandrest here;
> Still upwards mount; and let thy makers praise
> Honor thy Laura, and adorne thy laies.

(lines 33–36)

This is not backhanded criticism, suggesting that Donne may have been wrong to make the use he has of Elizabeth Drury. It is a perceptive recognition on Hall's part of what should be the next stage of the development that has taken place during the first two *Anniversaries*. The movement of the soul from this world into the next is a movement into the presence of God. The movement from individual selfhood to the image of God in the self has as its next stage a direct contemplation of the Divine Being rather than another consideration of God in His image. The poet's own progress in these poems is to a point where he can now praise his Maker directly, a change that will not involve abandoning the idea imaged in the *Anniversaries* ("thy Laura"). It will, however, constitute a reversal of one aspect of Donne's technique: writing and singing about God will now honor the image rather than the reverse.

That Donne himself realized this as the next stage of his progress is confirmed by the remaining productions of his life. Quotations from the sermons in my discussion should by now have demonstrated that many of the aspects of Donne's later works were already developed by the time he wrote the *Anniversaries*. The direct service of God as preacher and as author of poems such as his later hymns fulfills the promise made by Donne as nothing else could.

[4]
"Temperance Invincible":
Paradise Regained and the Second Adam

... *"Hast thou seen my servant Job?"*
Famous he was in heaven, on earth less known,
Where glory is false glory, attributed
To things not glorious, men not worthy of fame.
They err who count it glorious to subdue
By conquest far and wide, to overrun
Large countries, and in field great battles win.
(*Paradise Regained* III, 67–73)[1]

The Christ of Milton's *Paradise Regained* is a direct imitation of the archetypal idea of Heroic Temperance as it exists in Christian tradition. The major precedent for such a hero in an epic poem was the hero of Book II of Spenser's *Faerie Queene*; but where Spenser synthesized Christian and classical models, both the form and content of *Paradise Regained* invoke Greece and Rome and renaissance classicism only in order to transcend them. Milton attempts to outgo both Spenser and Homer by the directness of his approach to the Idea.

Satan, and a number of modern critics, are unable to accept and employ the different standards that this type of heroic characterization requires.[2] Milton's Christ has, as a result, been described as an unsympathetic, static, negative figure. Yet not only Christ's words and actions (as well as his inaction), but also the various epithets used in the repeated formulae that introduce Christ's replies to Satan, identify him as the temperate (II, 378), patient (II, 432), calm (III, 43), sage (IV, 285), though sometimes fervent (III, 121) type of hero whose symbolic importance this book has been examining.

On the other hand, most modern criticism of *Paradise Regained* that has not adopted this negative view of Milton's hero could be described as an attempt to rescue the poem from the relative disfavor into which it had fallen by reading it as a neo-Shakespearean drama with a psychological conflict between two realistic characters, Satan and Christ, in which the first is defeated and the second gains knowledge through the experience and is confirmed in his vocation.[3] Some objections have recently been made to this view, but the alternative readings proposed (for instance, *Paradise Regained* as pure ritual, or as Platonic dialogue),[4] while containing a measure of truth, do not seem to explain satisfactorily much of what happens in this rather unusual poem. I should like, then, to approach the problems of Milton's brief epic through a consideration of Milton's Christ in terms of his roles as the second Adam and as a quiet hero—a reading that offers an alternative to some current conceptions of what happens in the poem.

That the Christ of *Paradise Regained* is to be viewed as the second Adam is the main thrust of Milton's induction:

> I who erewhile the happy garden sung,
> By one man's disobedience lost, now sing
> Recovered Paradise to all mankind,
> By one man's firm obedience fully tried
> Through all temptation, and the Tempter foiled
> In all his wiles, defeated and repulsed,
> And Eden raised in the waste wilderness.
>
>   (I, 1–7)

During the poem Milton extends his typology to include many other figures who were types of Job (as has been admirably demonstrated by Barbara Lewalski).[5] But the primary comparison, even though not always stressed directly, remains throughout that between Adam and Christ. Milton, after pointing out the parallel at the beginning of the poem, could have assumed that his readers would make the necessary connections elsewhere, not only because the Adam-Christ figure was the most commonly used typology in seventeenth-century literature and theology, but also because he had titled his poem *Paradise Regained,* which invites a direct comparison between the main characters of the two Miltonic epics.

But more than that, Milton's title invites a contrast, for it is a reversal of the name of the earlier epic. Appreciating the real importance of the Adam-Christ link in *Paradise Regained* requires a recognition that theologically this typology was far more important as an antithesis than as a parallel. As Martin Luther phrased it: "Therefore Adam is an image of Christ, as Paul says in Rom. 5:14, where he enlarges on both. However, the latter is far better and different, indeed, it effects the direct opposite of what its antitype, Adam, effected."[6] It is oppositions that Milton stresses in his title and induction: oppositions between the old and the new Eden, between the first and the second Adam. Even the rhetoric of the induction uses antithetical structures along with parallels to emphasize this point. The origin of the typological contrasts between Adam and Christ is in the origin of the typology itself. In I Corinthians 15, for instance, Adam is described as "natural" man and Christ as "spiritual," Adam as "of the earth," Christ as "the Lord from heaven." In Romans 5.14, Paul says that Adam brought death into the world, but Christ came to remove it. In all of these biblical ways the Christ of *Paradise Regained* is set against the first Adam, and he is in other ways as well dramatically opposed to the Adam of *Paradise Lost*.

Several contrasts might be made, such as that between Adam's culpability in his passion for his wife in *Paradise Lost* and even Satan's recognition that Christ could not be tempted by such means in *Paradise Regained*; but one major contrast, highly important in the interpretation of *Paradise Regained* and functioning both theologically and dramatically in the poem, is that between Adam's fallibility and the infallibility of Christ. The point needs to be stressed, because much recent criticism seems to have adopted, though sometimes in modified or implied ways, Barbara Lewalski's argument that "for the encounter between Christ and Satan to constitute a genuine dramatic action and a real conflict, Christ's character must be conceived in such a way that the test or temptation is real: he must be able to fall, must be capable of growth, and must be genuinely (not just apparently) uncertain of himself" (p. 135). Lewalski goes on to argue that Milton's Christ does indeed meet these criteria for dramatic action.

Two of the eighteenth-century editors of *Paradise Regained* made the same reading of Christ's character and suspected Milton of being a Socinian or, to quote Warton, "at least an Arian."[7] However, theologically and dramatically the Christ of Milton's poem is incapable of falling, nor does he ever suspect it possible that he might. Milton's

Christ cannot fail because his success has been divinely predestined. This is quite different from the temptations of Adam and Eve, whose fall was only foreknown, not predestined, by God. Milton's Christ had, of course, free will, since all creatures in Milton's theology (and Christ was for him a creature) had such freedom; but freedom of the will is not important to *Paradise Regained* as it was to *Paradise Lost*. Indeed, freedom of the will is never directly mentioned in the second epic; it is God's will that gets the emphasis.

Milton himself, in his role of narrator, tells the reader early on in the first book of *Paradise Regained* that Christ's success is predestined. In describing Satan's journey to the Jordan to subvert "this man of men, attested Son of God" (I, 122), Milton comments, "But contrary unweeting he fulfilled / The purposed counsel *preordained and fixed* / Of the Most High" (I, 126–128, italics added). God Himself then informs the angels of the certain outcome of the event. He describes it, not as a test, but as an "exercise" in which Christ "shall first lay down the rudiments / Of his great warfare, ere I send him forth / To conquer Sin and Death" (I, 156–159). The frame of reference is military; but it is a war game, not a real battle, that is anticipated, a preparation for the real thing, which will come later. The angels listening have no doubt of the outcome: "The Father knows the Son; therefore secure / Ventures his filial virtue, though untried, / Against whate'er may tempt" (I, 176–178). It was even before the Fall in *Paradise Lost* that God willed the eventual salvation of man ("and," as He says elsewhere, "what I will is fate" [*PL* VII, 173]). Nor is it a contradiction in Milton's theology that he presents Christ's victory as predestined; both in Book III of *Paradise Lost* and in *Christian Doctrine* Milton had stressed the ability of God to destine events so that they will produce good, and to select some individuals "of peculiar grace / Elect above the rest" (*PL* III, 183–184).

All of this, given to the reader prior to the temptations, makes a dramatic interest in whether or not Christ will succeed rather difficult to maintain. It would be hard to argue that, at line 182 of Book I, the reader is expected to suspend suddenly his knowledge of the preordained outcome and observe Christ simply as a man facing a trial. We know throughout that he is more than just a man, and he knows it as well. He has had a heavenly announcement that he was God's "belovèd Son" (I, 32), or, as he remembers it later, "his belovèd Son, in whom alone / He was well pleased" (I, 285–286); and his reading of Scripture has told him something of this even before. He does not put off his divinity to behave solely as a man. Though there was, as Elizabeth Pope has pointed out, a tradition for regarding Christ in this episode of his life as acting only as a man, there were as well traditions opposed to such a view (also acknowledged by Pope).[8] That Milton believed Christ acted solely *quasi homo* during the temptations is a modern critical assumption that cannot be demonstrated from the poem or from Milton's other works. The epic repeatedly emphasizes both Christ's human origins ("a man / Of female seed" [I, 150–151]) and the fact that his Father is "the Eternal King" (i, 236). Milton answers for himself in *Christian Doctrine*:

Once his two natures have coalesced hypostatically into a single person, whatever Christ says of himself he must say it (unless he makes a distinction himself) not as if he possessed one nature or the other, but as a whole person speaking about a whole person. Those who take it upon themselves to tear apart this hypostatical union, as it is called, rob Christ's speeches and replies of all sincerity. They substitute for Christ an unknown quantity, now one person, now another, and everything it says is ambiguous and uncertain, true and false at the same time. When dealing with such opponents, one may aptly ask Horace's question: With what knot shall I hold this face-changing Proteus?[9]

There is nothing the Christ of *Paradise Regained* does as a man that he could not also have done as a member of the Godhead. Some things he says and does indicate that he is at least no ordinary man. That he goes without food for forty days and does not hunger shows him as neither God nor man, since divine intervention applies. As John Calvin said, "God worked a great miracle when he released His Son from the necessity of eating."[10] That he finally does hunger makes it no more certain that he is behaving as a man, for, as Milton went to great lengths to explain in *Paradise Lost,* eating and hunger are characteristic of heavenly creatures as well as earthly. "And food alike those pure / Intelligential substances require / As doth your rational," says Raphael (V, 407–409), and then falls to "with keen dispatch / Of real hunger" (436–438). Christ's words to Satan during the banquet temptation ("I can at will, doubt not, as soon as thou, / Command a table in this wilderness, / And call swift flights of angels ministrant, / Arrayed in glory, on my cup to attend" [II, 383–386]) demonstrate conclusively that the Christ of *Paradise Regained* sees himself and presents himself to Satan as something more than a higher form of Adamic man. It is the power of Christ's *will* to perform miracles that is being asserted at this point. He does not distinguish between his two natures even in his words from the top of the pinnacle (an argument that I shall take up again later).

Another important way in which the Christ of *Paradise Regained* is a reversal of at least the fallen Adam of *Paradise Lost* is in the type of knowledge that is available to him. One of the main purposes of Michael's narration to Adam, in the last books of *Paradise Lost,* is to supply historical knowledge as a substitute for the great intuitive knowledge Adam possessed, according to Milton and rabbinic tradition, before the Fall. *Paradise Regained* reverses the learning process of *Paradise Lost.* The growth of Christ's knowledge began with the study of the old law and especially of those parallels with Christ that Adam in *Paradise Lost* saw as future events but that Christ studied as history. However, the Christ we meet in *Paradise Regained* has already augmented that historical knowledge obtained through the use of reason with divine intuition. There is little he has left to learn when he goes into the wilderness.

The soliloquy in the desert (I, 196–294) deals with Christ's growth of knowledge; it is all in the past tense. Christ tells the reader that some time ago (it is mentioned just after the visit to the temple "ere yet my age / Had measured twice six years" [209–210]) he had thought about "victorious deeds" (215):

> To rescue Israel from the Roman yoke,
> Then to subdue and quell o'er all the earth
> Brute violence and proud tyrannic pow'r,
> Till truth were freed, and equity restored;
> Yet held it more humane, more heavenly, first

By winning words to conquer willing hearts,
And make persuasion do the work of fear.

(217–223)

Having made this decision already, he cannot be said to make it subsequently when tempted by Satan with military power. Christ knows that he is the fulfillment of all the prophecies concerning the Messiah that he has read (I, 262). He knows that he alone is the chosen Son of God (284–287) and that it is now time for his ministry to begin. What, then, can Satan really offer, or Christ learn, except minor things? All Christ is unsure about is why he is drawn into the wilderness, but the answer to this he trusts to revealed knowledge: "For what concerns my knowledge God reveals" (293). All of this is at the beginning of the forty days in the wilderness, and Satan does not appear until after those days are over. His thoughts during these forty days, we are told, are all along the same lines as those in the soliloquy (299–302).

Toward the end of Book I, Christ informs Satan that "God hath now sent his living Oracle / Into the world, to teach his *final will*" (460–461, italics added), which would also indicate that he has knowledge of his mission already. After the first temptation Christ again:

Into himself descended, and at once
All his great work to come before him set:
How to begin, how to accomplish best
His end of being on earth, and mission high.

(II, 111–114)

This is not in question form, and it is presented as an instantaneous event rather than as part of a reasoning process. Christ is by this point fully aware of his vocation and knows that it will be a spiritual, not a material, victory he will seek. Critics seem sometimes to forget that the narrative portions of *Paradise Regained* present *two* events in the life of Christ, the baptism as well as the temptation. It was traditionally the baptism, not the temptation, that was regarded as the beginning of Christ's public mission, though the temptation could be seen as a secondary confirmation of it. Satan himself interprets the baptism as a public revelation of Christ's role:

> And he himself among them was baptized,
> Not thence to be more pure, but to receive
> The testimony of Heaven, that who he is
> Thenceforth the nations may not doubt.
>
> (I, 76–79)

As Thomas Becon wrote in the sixteenth century: "Christ, although sent down for that purpose, took not on him the office of preaching till he was openly called of his heavenly Father, having his vocation confirmed by a visible sign of the Holy Ghost, which came down from heaven upon him in the likeness of a dove."[11]

That Milton accepted this view of the baptism is confirmed by a major change he makes in the Bible story. Where all the scriptural accounts have Christ going directly from the baptism to the wilderness, Milton has his Christ remain "some days" (I, 183) in Bethabara where he spends the time, not only in meditation, but also in talking and lodging with Andrew and Simon (II, 6–7), who were by this convinced that Christ was the Messiah, that God had "sent his Anointed, and to us revealed him, / By his great Prophet, pointed at and shown, / In public, and with him we have conversed" (II, 50–52).[12] They do not yet know the spiritual emphasis of Christ's mission; but Milton's Christ does and has already publicly begun it. Milton links the baptism with the temptation for the same reasons that they were often linked in commentary: because both were regarded as fulfillments of the law and as examples to be followed by every man.

Christ's knowledge, I suggested earlier, is largely revealed knowledge, though this revealed knowledge is complemented with an unerring reasoning ability. Revelation was usually described in this period as having two main forms, and Milton emphasizes both of them: the revealed word of the Scriptures and direct spiritual inspiration—the "inner light." Milton's emphasis on and consideration of these two kinds of knowledge in combination with various types of "reason" (natural, Socratic, etc.) place *Paradise Regained* within an identifiable late seventeenth-century context, that of the contemporary debate about the nature and value of "enthusiasm."

Christopher Hill, in *Milton and the English Revolution,* attempts to associate Milton and his ideas with various seventeenth-century sects of radical "enthusiasts"; and the view of reason that is presented in *Paradise Regained* Hill specifically links to the Muggletonians who, like other contemporary radical sects, rejected both reason and Scripture in favor of the inner light. Muggleton himself, as Hill points out, saw reason as the devil and referred to the Temptation of Christ in the Wilderness as "the reason of man" tempting Christ with this world.[13] Such sectarians, though willing to use Scripture in this way as a rhetorical support, rejected the Bible as an absolute authority in spiritual matters. When these radical enthusiasts were subjected to questioning by church authorities, the standard pattern of such interviews was a repeated citing of relevant scriptural texts by the orthodox churchmen (attempting to convince the radical of his errors) and a repeated rejection of the validity of such arguments by the devotee of the inner light.

Though the radical sects of the seventeenth century often met with intolerance and abuse, as Hill's books have demonstrated, their claims to divine inspiration were also given some serious examinations. Meric Casaubon's *Treatise concerning Enthusiasme* (1655) is such a study and set the pattern for all later serious considerations of the subject in seventeenth-century England, and after. Casaubon's full title was *A Treatise concerning Enthusiasme, as it is an effect of Nature; but is mistaken by many for either Divine Inspiration or Diabolical Possession.*[14] Like all later writers who were not merely satirizing the enthusiasts, Casaubon is concerned to distinguish true and false versions of inspiration.[15] Enthusiasm in either form can occur, according to Casaubon, in divination, in philosophy, in rhetoric and poetry, in prayer, as well as in other activities of the mind and passions. The only possible test that can be applied to distinguish the true from the false is that of the Scriptures.

Casaubon's book might well have served Milton as a model for his general presentation of the theme of knowledge in *Paradise Regained,* and particularly for Christ's rejection of classical wisdom. Though Casaubon was one of the great scholars of his age, when he set pagan claims to inspired knowledge beside true Christian inspiration, he had no hesitation in rejecting the former. The ancient orators, he says, lacked true inspiration and substituted art; oratory may indeed have its peculiar fire, but "if good language may ravish, how much more excellent matter, delivered in ravishing language?" (p. 267). Plato's philosophy was useful to early Christianity, "yet of Christians it hath [made] many Hereticks; and is to this day the common refuge of contemplative men, whether Christians, or others, that have run themselves besides their wits" (pp. 69–70). Some men do have visions, either in their minds only or, in some cases, actually visible to the eyes; but the common people in particular are susceptible to delusions, and such sects as the Quakers mistake the nature and source of their supposed inspiration. True inspiration, for Casaubon, is most readily identifiable when it is manifested as the elevating effect produced on the Christian's spirit by prayer.

Henry More took up the theme in *Enthusiasmus Triumphatus* (1662) in which More, himself a Platonist, attacked those who rejected reason for the inner light. More, like Causabon, believed in the reality of inspiration, and for him, too, a conflict between inspiration and reason could not exist within true Christianity. The fancies of the Anabaptists, Quakers, and other sects were simply "the *Dreams* of men *awake*."[16] His prescribed cure for enthusiasm was "*Temperance, Humility,* and Reason" (p. 36)—those qualities that are the major characteristics of Milton's Christ in *Paradise Regained*.

The same attitudes toward enthusiasm are ubiquitous among later seventeenth-century thinkers. John Locke in his *Essay Concerning Human Understanding* said that enthusiasm "takes away both reason and revelation, and substitutes in the room of them the ungrounded fancies of a man's own brain."[17] George Hickes, in 1680, preached a sermon called "The Spirit of Enthusiasm Exorcised" on the text, "Now there are diversities of Gifts, but the same Spirit" (I Cor. 12:4); in it he attacked those who claimed "that this spirit of immediate Revelation or Spiritual light, is not, like the *Spirits* in Primitive times, to be tryed by the Scriptures, and reason, but that both of them are to be tryed by it."[18] This false doctrine "makes every private Christian a Pope" and "utterly overthrows the Authority of the Scriptures, and makes them an useless rule of Faith" (ibid.).

This triumvirate of reason, Scripture, and inspiration, fully in agreement with each other, was rejected by the radical sects in favor of the monarchy of the inner light; but it was adopted by Milton in *Paradise Regained.*

Milton's Christ makes claims to direct revelations, as a consequence of which Satan tries to tempt him to abuse his mission as a prophet. To take Satan's advice would be to substitute demonic inspiration for true revelation. But the kind of inspiration with which *Paradise Regained* is concerned is something which takes place "in pious hearts, an inward oracle" (I, 463)—an experience the poet seeks for himself in the opening invocation.

Satan, throughout the brief epic, tries to rouse up in Christ an enthusiastic response, to inspire him through the attractions of such things as spiritual power, fame, glory, and knowledge. Christ responds with temperance, occasionally with righteous indignation, but never with the enthusiasm Satan is seeking. Satan presents Christ with visions: "By what strange parallax or optic skill / Of vision multiplied through air, or glass / Of telescope, were curious to inquire" (IV, 40–42). Satan even offers Christ his own diabolic version of prophetic signs in competition with the divine announcements of the Bible: "So many terrors, voices, prodigies, / May warn thee, as a sure foregoing sign" (IV, 482–483); but Christ rejects these as "false portents."

The end of the contest is almost a metaphysical conceit, as Satan literally "in-spires" Christ by taking him up to the golden spire of the temple. But Christ's elevation is Satan's downfall, and the bearing of Christ "through the blithe air" by the angels is an unambiguous revelation of divine supernatural realities.

Because Christ's inner light (his inspiration) cooperates with reason and Scripture, it remains uncontaminated by Satan's enthusiasm. *Paradise Regained* has as one of its models the Socratic dialogue, and—at least until the middle of Book IV—the alteration of argument and counter-argument between Christ and Satan is an important dramatic technique. Satan, however, is justly criticized for his "weak arguing, and fallacious drift" (III, 4), a criticism that would be rather inappropriate if Satan were meant to be a figure representing reason. In arguing the worse to be the better reason, as in his attempt to inspire Christ to worldly actions, Satan serves as a foil to Christ's

Right Reason, which is rational, inspired, and in harmony with Scripture.

The Christ of the Bible answers Satan with scriptural quotation. In *Paradise Regained,* Milton, like some of the earlier commentators, presents scriptural knowledge as an adequate defense against the devil and superior to all other forms of knowledge, short of direct revelation. Even Satan seems to agree and attempts to argue by scriptural precedent, but always to an obviously false conclusion (see II, 306–318 and IV, 556–559). Thomas Becon, in the sixteenth century, wrote a dialogue between a Christian knight and Satan, in which the devil employed these same techniques of perverting Scripture and citing the old law rather than gospel truths in order to elevate works above faith. Becon's Satan is accused by the knight of

calumniating and depraving the scripture, and of not reciting the same purely and wholly. For where my God hath spoken and taught those things that do agree and ought to be joined together, these dost thou partly allege, and partly leave out.[19]

The development of this dialogue follows the dramatic pattern Milton would adopt for *Paradise Regained*: as "Satan moveth into desperation, the knight comforteth himself with the sweet promises of the Holy Scripture" (p. 626). Both Becon and Milton have thus produced dramas of ideas in which the hero's static firmness counters his opponent's desperate activity. Though it has been suggested by critics that *Paradise Regained* is concerned with heroic knowledge more than with heroic rejection, it must be recognized that this "knowledge" is not the kind found either in the world of secular learning or in experience; and from a worldly point of view it looks very much like rejection.

The importance of the shield provided by Scripture is part of the reason for the emphasis Milton places on Christ's early studies. It is also why the highest dramatic moment of the poem is reached in a scriptural quotation. Those readers who suggest that Christ reveals himself as a member of the Godhead in his answer from the pinnacle often leave out the first four words of Christ's speech: "*Also it is written,* / 'Tempt not the Lord thy God'" (IV, 560–561). Christ is asserting nothing about himself;[20] he is quoting. There is thus little ambiguity in the reply; or at least Satan does not seem to have much time to work out any ambiguities before his fall. Though Milton chose to follow the order of the temptations in Luke, he makes this speech a modified version of that in Matthew: "It is written again, Thou shalt not tempt the Lord thy God" (4:6). The version in Luke was much more direct: "It is said [etc.]" (4:12). Milton's "also" delays the dramatic effect and calls attention to the fact that this is a quotation and related to the other quotations.[21] Satan's fall, then, is not the result of any direct announcement by Christ that he is the second member of the Trinity; it is rather the symbolic and type-fulfilling antithesis of Christ's miraculous stand.

As Adam's fall had raised Satan and his crew from hell to reside in middle air, so Christ's triumph dislodges him from that position. It is a foreshadowing of Satan's final fall, which will come after Christ's last victory; and it is also the lessening, the binding of Satan's powers that Christ's appearance in the world brought about. Satan's fall is as inevitable as Christ's triumph over the temptations. Both were predestined, and predestined so that they might serve as examples of what was to come and of how man should behave until the Second Coming.

The temptation has traditionally been regarded as an exemplum for every man. That is why biblical commentary stressed so heavily the nature of Christ as the second Adam in this episode, for as all men were involved in the sin of the first Adam, so all men are involved in the triumph of the last. It is not really Christ who is being attacked by Satan in the temptation; it is, as Calvin said, "our salvation that he attacked in the Person of Christ."

I have no doubt that God displayed in the Person of His Son, as on a brilliant screen, how hostile and persistent an adversary Satan is against the salvation of man.... So often as Satan attacks us, let us remember that we can in no other way sustain and repulse his assaults than by the protection of that shield.[22]

This aspect of the temptation meant little, however, until after the Crucifixion. It was only then that, by Christ's imputed righteousness, man could be saved. Thus, for the time being, the deed remained "in secret done" (I, 15), an example only to the angels of what would later be an example to all men (I, 163–167). The way this event would become known to all men was, of course, through the Scriptures.

One other major contrast between the first Adam and the second is the contrast between man under the law and man under grace. The Christ of *Paradise Regained* is involved in both, for, as Milton emphasized in *Paradise Lost,* mercy does not eliminate justice. Adam fell under the law, but had the promise of grace; Christ brought grace, but also fulfilled the law—and fulfilling the law was an impossible task for anyone except Christ.

The superimposition of law and grace is pointed up by the numerical structure of the epic. The four-book structure was chosen for the brief biblical epic, as Barbara Lewalski has noted, because of the parallel with the four gospels. Four is the number representing the New Law, the covenant of grace. Within this four-book structure Milton has set ten linked temptations arranged in the following order:

Book I:	Stones-to-bread temptation
Book II:	Banquet temptation
	Riches temptation
Book III:	Glory temptation
	Throne-of-Israel temptation
	Parthia temptation
Book IV:	Rome temptation
	Learning-of-Greece temptation
	Storm temptation
	Pinnacle-of-temple temptation[23]

The number of temptations in each book appears to be equal to the number of that book, thus providing one kind of dramatic build-up in the accelerating imposition of temptations. All of these are temptations under the law, and ten is of course the number of the Decalogue, the "ten words" of Moses, here set against the Divine Word.

Milton emphasizes the numbers four and ten also, for instance, in the forty days' wandering in the wilderness, which Christ rather awkwardly refers to as "four times ten days" (II, 245), and in the discussion of the ten tribes of Israel. In addition, in the rhetoric of Book IV, Satan tends to catalogue things in rather cumbersome groups of ten:

> Since neither *wealth*, nor *honor, arms* nor *arts*,
> *Kingdom* nor *empire* pleases thee, nor aught
> By me proposed in *life contemplative*,
> Or *Active*, tended on by *glory*, or *fame*,
> What dost thou in this world?
> . . . .
> *Sorrows*, and *labors, opposition, hate*,
> Attends thee, *scorns, reproaches, injuries*,
> *Violence* and *stripes*, and lastly cruel *death*.
> (IV, 368–373, 386–388; italics added)

And Christ lays down the law to Satan in his last speech from the pinnacle in ten words. Thus, in the events, structure, and rhetoric of *Paradise Regained,* the life of Christ encompasses grace and the law.

There is one precedent among many for this numerological interpretation of the temptation, in Ludolphus de Saxonia's *Vita Jesu Christi*:

Quadraginta autem diebus et quadraginta noctibus dominus jejunavit; quia quadragenarius numerus ex quatuor constat et decem: quater enim decem vel decies quatuor, faciunt quadraginta. Per quatuor autem Novum Testamentum, quod in quatuor Evangelistis consistit, significatur; per decem vero Vetus, quia in decem manditis Legis continetur. Quadraginta ergo diebus jejunare, est utrisque Testamenti præcepta servare.[24]

[So the Lord was fasting for forty days and forty nights; because the number forty is made up of four and ten; for four times ten, or ten times four, makes forty. Now by four is signified the New Testament, which is based upon the four Evangelists; and by ten is signified the Old Testament, because within it is contained the ten commandments of the Law. Therefore, to fast for forty days is to obey the precepts of each Testament.]

A new edition of Ludolphus had been published in Lyons in 1642.

Though many modern readers find such numerological thinking so strange that they deny its existence in literature, it was part of a long and accepted tradition. St. Augustine himself said:

Ignorance of numbers, too, prevents us from understanding things that are set down in Scripture in a figurative and mystical way. A candid mind, if I may so speak, cannot but be anxious, for example, to ascertain what is meant by the fact that Moses and Elijah, and our Lord Himself, all fasted for forty days. And except by knowledge of and reflection upon the number, the difficulty of explaining the figure involved in this action cannot be got over. For the number contains ten four times, indicating the knowledge of all things, and that knowledge interwoven with time. . . . Now while we live in time, we must abstain and fast from all joy in time, for the sake of that eternity in which we wish to live; although by the passage of time we are taught this very lesson of despising time and seeking eternity.[25]

The numerological interpretation of Christ's Temptation was first popularized in English literature in the *Stanzaic Life of Christ*:

> The new lawe also ys sette
> in four ewangilistes lore,
> so bi four withouten lette
> gone alle the thinges sayde bifore.
>
> Also by ten comoñdement3
> the olde lawe well ordeynet was,
> and to bothe lawes with grete offense
> oft tyme we doon trespasse.
>
> Ther-fore to bothe amende most be.
> 3if we to blisse woln be worthy,
> bi ten sithe four, as 3e schun se,
> and four sithe ten, as telle wol I.
>
> Takes hede now, I ow pray,
> to vnderstond this thing oright,
> by noumbre of ten, as I 3ow say,
> the olde lawe to vs was dy3t,
>
> The new lawe god 7 verray
> by faur ewangeliste3 lore,
> so by faure 7 ten our fay
> ys schewet frely vs byfore.
>
> faur sith ten that is faurty,
> 7 ten sith faur faurty also,

so noumbre of ten to multiplie
faur is set to, may not be fro.

And so by noumbre of ten i-wis
the olde law ʒiuen to vs was,
7 now confermet wel hit is
By noumbre of faur in tyme of *grace*.
(II. 4509–4536)[26]

The theme seems to have been a common one for explication on Quadragesima.

In the late sixteenth century, the numerological interpretation of the Temptation was summarized in *Batman uppon Bartholome*:

Lent, is the time of chivalrye of christen men in the which time wee fight sharplye against vices and sinnes. . . . And well in these number of dayes wee fast. For this number ten doubled foure times, presenteth and beto-keneth the ten commaundements, and the foure Gospells, by the which Gospells armes and weapon nowe of our adversary is putte off, and lande of life is there got by lawe of heritage, as the lande of behest was graunted to the children of Israel after that battaile and fighting of fortie yeere, in desert and wildernesse.[27]

The biblical meanings and parallels of ten, four, and their product are incorporated in Milton's poem not in some magical game but as an integral part of the inherited doctrine and archetypal/symbolic significance of the event. That rhetorical and poetic structures should reflect these ought to surprise no one who believes that poetry contains more than meanings susceptible of paraphrase.

As Adam is visited by angels before his fall, so Christ is visited by the angels following his triumph. Their songs again point up the Adam-Christ antithesis:

. . . Now thou hast avenged
Supplanted Adam, and by vanquishing
Temptation hast regained lost Paradise,
And frustrated the conquest fraudulent.
He never more henceforth will dare set foot
In Paradise to tempt; his snares are broke.
For though that seat of earthly bliss be failed,
A fairer Paradise is founded now

For Adam and his chosen sons, whom thou
A Saviour art come down to reinstall;
Where they shall dwell secure, when time shall be
Of tempter and temptation without fear.

(IV, 606–617)

The angels go on to interpret this event as a foreshadowing of the future victories of Christ over Satan. The "fairer Paradise ... founded now" will not be fully realized until "time shall be / Of tempter and temptation without fear." It is not the paradise within that has been established here so much as the paradise beyond, which will come to fulfillment in its proper time. This has been the first step in that establishment, not an interval after the baptism. The foundations have been laid, not for Christ, but for man: "Now enter, and begin to save mankind" (IV, 635).

Milton's seventeenth-century readers would have needed no more than the initial emphasis on the Adam-Christ typology in order for them to identify with Christ. They knew that as all men were involved in Adam, so all were involved in Christ. Christ went through the temptations in the wilderness to give an example to every man of how temptations should be met; but more important than that, he went through them so that men would not have to meet the Devil's tempting power in such direct confrontations. Because Christ bore for us the brunt of Satan's assault, Satan was forever thereafter restrained in his dealings with men. It is this surrogate action by Christ that linked the Temptation to the Crucifixion for Milton and his contemporaries. As Jeremy Taylor said of the Temptation:

As soon as it was permitted to the devil to tempt our Lord, he, like fire, had no power to suspend his act, but was entirely determined by the fulness of his malice as a natural agent by the appetites of nature; that we may know to whom we owe the happiness of all those hours and days of peace in which we sit under the trees of paradise, and see no serpent encircling the branches and presenting us with fair fruits to ruin us. It is the mercy of God we have the quietness of a minute; for if the devil's chain were taken off, he would make our very beds a torment, our tables to be a snare, our sleeps fantastic, lustful, and illusive, and every sense should have an object of delight and danger, a hyena to kiss, and to perish in its embraces. But the holy Jesus having been assaulted by the devil and felt his malice by the experiments of humanity, is become so merciful a High priest, and so sensible of our sufferings and danger by the apprehensions of compassion, that He hath put a hook in the nostrils of Leviathan.[28]

It is this aspect of Christ's life that makes possible George Herbert's response to his temptations:

> Yet when the houre of thy designe
> To answer these fine things shall come;
> Speak not at large; say, I am thine;
> And then they have their answer home.[29]

I doubt that Milton even questioned whether his readers could identify imaginatively with Christ, though modern critics have found this one of the main problems of the epic. Lawrence W. Hyman has perceived the widest gulf between Christ and the reader, arguing that Christ must in fact give up part of his humanity rather than his divinity, that he must "separate himself from us, and that, degenerate and inwardly enslaved as we are by the world around us, we cannot be like Christ."[30] Such identification, however, was one of the "givens" of the tradition in which Milton was working. Of course, no man is as good as Christ, but the imitation of Christ was always understood to have limits, for Christ is always more than just an example. Christ in *Paradise Regained* is teaching us to use Scripture against temptation; but even more importantly, he is using it for us. The point lies in the concept of imputed righteousness. We watch a defeat of the devil in what is ultimately, to cite Calvin again, an attack on our salvation. Because Christ is victorious in this second of his three battles with Satan, we know he will win the last as well, for that is the way typology works. Because Christ takes on our sins and meets the devil for us, we can be saved. Christ is not regaining paradise for himself in this poem; he is regaining salvation for the reader and doing so both under the law and through grace. Thus, we identify with Christ as we do with any dramatic hero who embodies the ideal virtues of a people and who uses those virtues in their defense.

Even though the work is an epic poem, it deserves to be treated as drama. Indeed, aside from a few descriptive and narrative passages, the epic is nearly all in dialogue. But it must be recognized what sort of drama this is. It is not a realistic drama of psychologically complex characters engaged in an intellectual struggle for an uncertain victory. It is a biblical drama,[31] a ritual drama, which is also (it should be added) something more than simply a ritual. Because we as readers are expected to be totally familiar with the main events and characters and even some of the speeches, their appearance in *Paradise Regained* is ritual. But because Milton has changed the story, has added some things and has been very specific about others, we are constantly being dramatically surprised. In fact, not only are the changes and additions thrown into relief by their appearance within a ritual performance, but they emphasize the author's interpretation of the story and force us to meet it in terms of these glosses and not with the soothing effects of ritual.

I think most readers of the seventeenth century would have been pleased with what they saw (even though they might have liked *Paradise Lost* better). Compared with other treatments of the story, *Paradise Regained* is dramatically forceful while remaining doctrinally moderate. Where John Bale, in his play about the temptation, went to great lengths to show that Christ's long fast was not one of the things in the story to be imitated—a very Protestant view of the matter—Milton has one short speech:

> ... That fast
> To virtue I impute not, or count part
> Of what I suffer here; if nature need not,
> Or God support nature without repast
> Though needing, what praise is it to endure?
>   (II, 247–251)

Where the pseudo-Bonaventura's *Life of Christ* stressed heavily the Savior's return home to his mother after the temptation, even to the point of claiming that the food the angels brought Jesus came from Mary, Milton has only those moving last two lines of the poem: "He unobserved / Home to his mother's house private returned," lines that call attention to the as-yet-private nature of his active and contemplative life—a quiet ending for a poem about a quiet hero.

Because of the private nature of the action, as well as because of the high value placed on passive endurance, Milton's Christ is the quiet hero par excellence. Milton chose to present the archetypal source of this kind of heroism in one of the least dramatic, and hence most symbolic, of the events of Christ's life. His chief literary model was clearly Book II of *The Faerie Queene,* and there are many points of comparison.[32] In penetrating to the heart of quiet heroism in this manner, however, Milton has made an important and telling change of emphasis. Spenser's is a secular epic, and the image of radical temperance he presents in Book II has a large public purpose; it offers a model for relations between men in this world and a call for the externalizing of a virtue whose outward appearance does not always seem honorable. Milton's epic offers no hope of the public, secular realization of temperance. When Christ encounters a Bower of Bliss where "nature taught art" (II, 295), he leaves it intact; the people of Christ's world are "rabble.... Of whom to be dispraised were no small praise" (III, 50; 56). Both the action and the emphasis of this epic are private, meant "to dwell / In pious hearts, an inward oracle" (II, 462–463).

Milton's opposition to violence is therefore much greater than Spenser's and extends to a total rejection of the possibility of heroism in war, something that would have been impossible to Spenser. Quiet heroism in *Paradise Regained* is a major extension of the use of the concept in a narrative, perhaps to its limits, perhaps—at least according to some readers—beyond. Though the epic does contain characters and some action, these are, until the last half of Book IV, so lacking in physical detail and real conflict, and the embodied (symbolized) ideas are so prominent, that *Paradise Regained* almost seems to stand closer to Donne's *Anniversaries* than to *The Faerie Queene* in its methods of presenting its exemplary hero. But in any case, the proper way to read Milton's epic is as a symbolic poem, not as a mimetic narrative; to realize the fullness, complexity, and interest of *Paradise Regained,* the reader must attempt to follow the development of the idea embodied by the main character, not his imagined psychological development.

Milton's poem is about "deeds / Above heroic, though in secret done" (I, 14–15), that is, about the quiet heroism of temperance. The antithesis to this is the noisy public heroism valued by Milton's Satan. Satan, it has been said, sees himself in *Paradise Lost* as the hero of a classical epic; in *Paradise Regained* he first believes Christ to be that kind of hero and then attempts to argue him into accepting such a self-image. But because Christ is characterized by "temperance invincible" (II, 408—where it is ironically attributed to him by Satan), he is untempted by the image; and no reader could possibly regard the attractions of this kind of heroism as a serious threat to Christ's inner stability. What does hold our interest during Satan's speeches are the poetry in which Satan presents the glories of public heroism (wealth, fame, power and—most subtly—knowledge) and the arguments he uses in their defense, arguments that become, as Christ remains invincible, self-destructive. Though we know Christ cannot be tempted, we are tempted ourselves. Against this we are given a Christ who has nothing in his favor except the fact that he is absolutely right.

Christ is undergoing an act of symbolic humiliation here, not fighting a real battle; and it is Satan's ignorance of this that constantly frustrates his attempts on the hero and causes him to accomplish unaware the divine purpose. Christ's victory is the result, as the Most High predicted, of "humiliation and strong sufferance: / His weakness shall o'ercome Satanic strength / And all the world" (I, 160–162). Not that Christ's counterarguments do not matter, but they none the less remain a secondary part of what Christ represents in this epic. Christ conquers Satan with something more than arguments; he wins simply by being himself, Christ, perfect God and perfect man, the great exemplar who is himself aware of his Old Testament foreshadowings in this archetypal event (I, 350–355). The epic answers the question that troubles Satan throughout: what does it mean to be the son of God? And "sons of God both angels are and men" (IV, 197), not just Christ. The answer lies in imitation of the Archetype.

Christ walks through the wilderness of *Paradise Regained* like Guyon through the house of Mammon or Joyce's Bloom through the streets of Dublin, persecuted but inviolate, quietly enduring (except in moments of righteous indignation), and observing. He is misunderstood not only by Satan but by his own disciples who, thinking that "now, for sure, deliverance is at hand, / The Kingdom shall to Israel be restored" (II, 35–36), suddenly find themselves deprived of the cause of their hopes—an archetypal loss such as Milton himself personally experienced in the Revolution. The true heroism of Christ, and of his followers ancient and modern, consists in waiting. "And think'st thou to regain / Thy right by sitting still or thus retiring?" asks Satan (III, 163–164). The answer is yes, for God's kingdom will come in its own due time. The repeated loss of Christ to the world calls forth a response from the poet parallel to that of Mary: "Afflicted I may be, it seems, and blest; / I will not argue that, nor will repine. / But where delays he now?" (II, 93–95).

Christ enters the epic amid the noise of "the great Proclaimer, with a voice / More awful than the sound of trumpet" (I, 18–19), and leaves it in a quiet, "unobserved" return "to his mother's house" (IV, 638–639); for Christ the development of the epic has been one into quietness. In spite of attempts readers have made to save the situation, Milton means what he says in the rejection of classical learning he places in the mouth of Christ. All Socratic dialogue—which has steadily become less Socratic and more a straightforward rejection of Satan by the hero—ends after the dismissal of learning in the middle of Book IV. In the last half of this Book Christ is almost silent; and his final words, as was noted, are a brief biblical quotation. He wins neither by combat nor by argument but by literally and figuratively standing still (see IV, 420–421, and 561). Satan, on the other hand, moves from his initial quiet deception to open violence; his actions in the storm, and perhaps even the pinnacle scene, are not real temptations even in his own terms: "By this his last affront resolved, / Desperate of better course, to vent his rage / And mad despite to be so oft repelled" (IV, 444–446). Argument is dropped by Christ not because he has been wrong in using that method but because, in the hierarchy of values and in the nature of things, quiet endurance is a superior response to hostile attacks when such endurance is supported by the wisdom of Scripture and of revelation. The movement was also Milton's own, in his life and in his epic, where he now seeks to surrender his own voice completely to God who will then "inspire, / As thou art wont, my prompted song, else mute" (I, 11–12). The same spirit he invokes here is that which led Christ into the wilderness (I, 189). "Light from above, from the Fountain of Light, / No other doctrine needs" (IV, 289–290).

Unconquered Bloom:
The Prudent Member

*He found in the world without as actual what was in his
world within as possible.*

(*Ulysses*)[1]

May his forehead be darkened with mud who would sunder!
(*Finnegans Wake*)[2]

*Whereas a voyage was considered by the Romanticists a means
of enlarging space and populating time, a means of releasing
physical energy and increasing exterior stimuli, the voyage that
will now be evolved will seek, on the contrary, to limit and
concentrate time and space to the minimum, divest it as much
as possible of physical movement, free the explorer little by
little from exterior stimuli and horizons, and surround the
traveller with such landscapes as will reveal a changed relationship in regard to nature. This voyage was to represent the
poet's orientation toward his inner absolute image of exterior
entities.*

(Anna Balakian on the dominant symbol of
French poetry from 1885 to the early 1920s)[3]

James Joyce was "coulinclouted" long before he coined that word
on Spenser's pastoral pseudonym for *Finnegans Wake*. The methods of
symbolic narration and characterization that Joyce employs in *Ulysses*
are essentially Spenserian methods, with no work of fiction in English
providing a closer precedent for the symbolic techniques of *Ulysses*
than does *The Faerie Queene*.[4]

When Spenser chose to write his epic as an interwoven narrative,
using Ariosto as his model, but using such interweaving for a very
un-Ariostan purpose—the symbolic creation of a "conceit" of the
ideal renaissance man—he produced a most unusual epic. Though
Spenser borrowed from the entire tradition of epic and romance, the
focusing of all of his materials upon an image of Man in his Mag-

nificence makes *The Faerie Queene* unique; it makes it something of the kind of poem Spenser and renaissance allegorizers mistakenly believed Homer and Virgil had created, and for which Tasso did provide a partial precedent; but no one, in fact, had ever written such an epic before.

Certainly its nationalistic and humanistic aims are typical enough of the genre. *The Faerie Queene* is a historical epic, closely tied to the events of Spenser's lifetime and the concerns of his world (and also to events and concerns personal to Spenser himself); it is an epic celebrating the highest values of European culture, while at the same time ridiculing contemporary abuses. Yet Spenser chose not to follow the realistic methods of those of his European counterparts who had also attempted to enshrine the values of the Renaissance in epic forms. Rather, he chose to write allegory, with a surface that highlighted the marvelous rather than the natural. But instead of imposing a trivial allegory on top of historical reality, Spenser saw and presented phenomenal reality itself as the "mask" of the symbolic forms that he brings to the surface in the imagery and allusions of his narrative.

In Spenser, surface realities and symbolic meanings are inseparably related, for truth cannot appear without its veil in this world. However, in that process of abstraction called writing, where one is forced to describe parts in order to suggest the whole, Spenser, unlike Joyce, could assume knowledge in his reader of the realities he was penetrating and could anticipate that, where the source of an image was not obvious (Who would not have recognized Duessa's relationship to Mary Stuart?), his readers would have had the necessary intellectual equipment to discover the symbolized meaning for themselves. Or rather, the symbolized meanings; for, as this book has demonstrated, the economic advantage of symbolic presentation lies in its plurality of application, when such application is directed by the work itself and not left indefinitely vague.

Joyce, too, expected his reader to discover the connections and realities presented in his symbols, but he could not assume the universal understanding of the world as a system of analogies that lies behind Spenser's confidence in his sixteenth-century reader. (Or at least in *Ulysses* Joyce did not assume it—*Finnegans Wake* is another matter.)

In writing a twentieth-century Spenserian epic, Joyce not only developed a coherent system of inherited and original symbols into a pattern imaging his modern Ulyssean man, he also sought to present the phenomenal world itself through a plethora of specific details. For a greater part of the novel, the symbolic patterns of *Ulysses* exist within those realistic details themselves; but as the novel—and Joyce's method—develop, obvious symbols soon demand recognition in their own right as part of the system of analogies that is ubiquitous in the novel and has connections going far beyond the world of Dublin on 16 June 1904.

As Edmund Wilson noted early on in the history of *Ulysses* criticism, Joyce "exploited together, as no writer had thought to do before, the resources both of Symbolism and Naturalism"[5] though Wilson mistook the symbolism of *Ulysses* for the indefinite Symbolism of the French movement in poetry, which attempted "to approximate the indefiniteness of music" (p. 18). Joyce was influenced by the Symbolists; but, though the symbolism of *Ulysses* is at times complex, it is seldom indefinite. It is capable of schematic analysis and was given just such an analysis by the author himself.

Readers of Spenser in need of help in interpretation could go to Spenser's sources and to published commentaries on them, or they could at least consult the popular encyclopedic "harmonies" and dictionaries of mythology. Readers of Joyce can do—and have done—the same sort of thing. But since Joyce had so often to create as well as to discover the analogies of *Ulysses,* he himself provided and promoted the kind of commentary he felt his book needed. The reader of *Ulysses* today has the advantage not only of Joyce's schemata outlining the symbolic analogies of *Ulysses,* but also of two works by critics who knew Joyce well and who consulted him about his intentions in *Ulysses*: Stuart Gilbert's *James Joyce's Ulysses: A Study* (1930),[6] on which work Joyce was in fact himself a collaborator, and Frank Budgen's *James Joyce and the Making of "Ulysses"* (1934).[7] Joyce could not have chosen two more complementary commentators: Gilbert with his emphasis on symbols and allusions, Budgen with his celebration of the human body and of physical realities; and together they outlined the soul and the body of *Ulysses.* Modern critics have, of course, resented this immensely. For them the artist should have been the absent God of Joyce's youthful aestheticism, quietly paring his fingernails. When the Creator himself starts explaining what he meant, the priestly cast finds itself rather devalued; and Joyce should perhaps have signed his schema "E. K."

If, however, one refuses to accept that tired article of faith that says that a work of literature has its meanings independent of its writer's intentions, there still remains the difficult critical task of relating intentions, as they are recorded both in the work itself and in authorial commentary, to the total work, a task that admittedly begins with testing the reliability of the author's or narrator's own comments. Had only the Linati schema of *Ulysses* survived, for instance, we would be in something of the same position as we are in with the "Letter to Raleigh" appended to the first edition of Books I–III of *The Faerie Queene*, a letter that contains information based on a version of the poem different from the one published, but that is still valuable as a description by Spenser of his methods.[8]

But Joyce's public-relations campaign on behalf of *Ulysses* has provided us with a very full demonstration that the novel is simultaneously held together by the classical unities of Aristotelian mimesis and by a system of analogies identical in structure, and in some cases in content, to the kind of symbolic complexes that my previous chapters have described in renaissance literature.

Whether or not Joyce, like Spenser, actually believed in the existence of the world as such an analogical symbolic construction is perhaps an unanswerable question. Certainly his biography reveals him as a superstitious man, and most of his superstitions depended on a belief in occult connections between apparently unrelated phenomena. Both in his life and in his novel the "real" could also be the "symbolic" (which makes nonsense of the kind of criticism that tries to show that an item in the novel cannot be symbolic because it really existed in Dublin).

Joyce seems at first to have been willing that the analogies of *Ulysses* should make their way to the reading public without authorial directions; he removed the Homeric chapter headings and for some time denied all but a few critics access to his schema. He may have thought that his art alone, or else the nature of reality itself, would make his symbolic structure clear; but when readers failed to perceive the connections, he eventually had few qualms about pointing them out. He may possibly have regarded his system as he did his use of the interior monologue: whether it was a reflection of reality or not, it enabled him to write *Ulysses*. Nor would there have been anything particularly unusual in such an attitude. As we have seen in previous chapters, Donne was able to use the Neoplatonic doctrine of the human soul as part of the World Soul for symbolic and structural purposes without implying any measure of belief in the concept, and Spenser could exploit the Pythagorean-Ovidian idea of metempsychosis/metamorphosis without in any way suggesting a departure from Christianity.

Joyce's schema and the analogies and techniques pointed out by Gilbert and Budgen represent the *methods* of *Ulysses,* but not necessarily the content.[9] Recognition of this early on might have cleared away a good deal of the rancor that has existed between Joycean symbolists and their realist opponents. It is true that many of the items of the schema might never have been recognized in the novel without its aid (though given the history of twentieth-century symbol hunting, I think this point has been overemphasized); indeed, some items in Joyce's lists still seem to be without significant relationships to the text. But, though a Michelangelo may choose to leave some of the original rock showing, it is not common for artists to exhibit their tools as part of the finished sculpture. Nor, when one looks at the David, is it always necessary to keep hammers and chisels in mind. Awareness of how an artist worked, however, can heighten appreciation of the finished masterpiece. To change the metaphor slightly, the schema is the foundation of *Ulysses*; some of it is hidden below ground, but the building could not have been erected without it.

Symbolic patterns do not need to be perceived readily when employed to structure a work; they appear only when they form part of the content intended for conscious communication. Joyce uses symbols in both overt and covert ways, as did Spenser. It was almost four centuries after the poem was written when A. Kent Hieatt discovered that Spenser's *Epithalamion* was structured as both a twenty-four hour clock and a calendar. The discovery was made within the poem itself rather than through the uncovering of any external evidence; but generations of readers had loved the poem and praised it as a work that successfully gave eternal life to the most important day in Spenser's life, without ever recognizing this structure. The discovery added depth to the poem's significance, but was much more important as an indication of the nature of Spenser's art and, indeed, of renaissance art generally. The comparison with Joyce is an almost exact one, for his book is also an epithalamion enshrining the single most important day of his life in a symbolic structure.

In *The Faerie Queene* Spenser, despairing at the dullness of his contemporaries, chose to write fiction rather than ethical philosophy because he knew that men "delight to read" fiction for its own sake ("Letter to Raleigh"); he believed that if he could keep the reader interested in his story, his ideas might still be communicated to men of "common sense" through fictional examples instead of through sermons. Joyce's purpose was almost the reverse of this. For him the work of art was the main object, but art for him as for Spenser had to realize itself in the middle course between the rocks of Aristotelian realism and the whirlpool of Platonic ideas; or, rather, it had to use the forces of both the rocks and the whirlpool. Consequently, in spite of their very different objectives, the methods of Spenser and Joyce were similar.

Joyce had few lessons to teach in *Ulysses,*[10] but he employed a good many ideas. They exist in the novel as realities to be perceived rather than as doctrines to be communicated, and they are as essential to making the novel what it is as are the details of the Dublin streets. These ideas and the images in which Joyce chose to embody them are those he saw as characterizing his own time (in economics, politics, theosophy, medicine, and the sciences generally) and those he saw as linking all time together (theology, astrology, magic, sexuality, commerce in cattle, etc.). Joyce's ethical positions with respect to these things hardly matter within the novel; the ideas are there or are responsible for what is there. As in *The Faerie Queene,* the symbolic structures built upon these ideas are what give the work significant form, as Joyce demonstrated when he chose to explain them to detractors who could see only the meaningless chaos of modern life in the novel. Joyce would no doubt have been happy had the initial reaction to *Ulysses* been a celebration of its realistic art rather than a condemnation of its supposed world view. His propaganda on behalf of his system was, as Gilbert himself acknowledged, corrective. Joyce was pointing out the aspect of reality—symbols—that such criticism missed.

The Spenserian nature of *Ulysses* is not necessarily the result of direct borrowings by Joyce, and my point is not that he imitated *The Faerie Queene*. Because of the similarities in technique, comparing the two works is a way of understanding both better and of setting Joyce's novel in its proper historical genre, a Spenserian epic. Joyce had, of course, read Spenser, although he seldom alludes to him directly; but he also drew on many of the same sources that shaped Spenser's poem, upon Spenser's heirs, and upon twentieth-century revivals of some of the occult symbolic thinking of the Renaissance. It is, however, what Joyce chose from his reading and from his experience, and the ways he chose to employ that in fiction, that make his work distinctly Spenserian. Joyce too combined elements of classical "realistic" epic with the symbolic traditions of romance (where watches stop exactly on the moment when the hero is being betrayed), all in service to a composite picture of universal man. When T. S. Eliot spoke of Joyce's parallel use of the *Odyssey* and a story of contemporary life as having the importance of a scientific discovery, he forgot that the discovery had already been made in the sixteenth century by Spenser. If Joyce's object was, as Richard Ellmann has said, "to blend the two ends of the Western tradition like a multitemporal, multiterritorial pun,"[11] he had clearly been anticipated by Spenser, whose images and events constantly conflate historical occasions and geographical locations within an intricate web of allusions.

The purpose of the present chapter is to describe Joyce's "Spenserian" characterization of Leopold Bloom rather than to make a full comparison of *Ulysses* and *The Faerie Queene*. However, it can at least be pointed out in passing that not only are their methods of symbolic characterization similar, both works are fragmented "interwoven" narratives in which the various characters and plot lines constantly meet and diverge. In addition, both works present their heroes journeying through landscapes where they are repeatedly subject to unpredictable encounters (cf. the Dublin streets and the Wandring Wood) and where their journeys are repeatedly punctuated by stops at "houses" of thematic significance, both exploit the comic possibilities of mock epic in what is a "straight" comic epic, and both draw on the devices of the morality play. Furthermore, Joyce's decision to use a different stylistic technique for each chapter of *Ulysses* is paralleled by similar shifts in technique between the books of *The Faerie Queene*. Both works employ a "reflexive" technique, through which "an understanding of any one part involves a grasp of the whole,"[12] and because of which one is expected to remember early details and make connections later. Both works employ multiple symmetry of their structural units: in *Ulysses* the first three chapters have important parallels with the last three, the first nine chapters are symmetrical with the last nine, and Richard Ellmann finds that each group of three chapters treats time and space in similar ways, while Clive Hart has found links between chapters one and four, two and five, and three and six. Even more intricate patterning has been proposed for *The Faerie Queene*, though everyone agrees that Books I and II are symmetrical, III and IV are linked, and V is concerned with some of the same themes as I. Both are encyclopedic works; as Hugh Kenner has said, "*Ulysses* is an epic in the Renaissance sense, a manifestation of every province of rhetoric and compilation of every form of learning."[13] Finally, both works are significantly Irish in both inspiration and content.

The Spenserian nature of Joyce's characterization has its foundation in the idea, shared by both writers, of a character as a composite creation which can itself combine by positive and negative analogy with other figures to generate a larger symbolic human image. In a letter about *Ulysses* written to Carlo Linati, Joyce said:

My intention is not only to render the myth *sub specie temporis nostri* but also to allow each adventure (that is, every hour, every organ, every art being interconnected and interrelated in the structural scheme of the whole) to condition and even to create its own technique. Each adventure is so to speak one person although it is composed of persons—as Aquinas relates of the heavenly hosts.[14]

—and as Spenser said of *The Faerie Queene*.

For Spenser, too, the idea of the composite character no doubt has its inspiration in the theological doctrine of the Trinity; but for Spenser, even more than for Joyce, the idea is secularized. In *The Faerie Queene* IV, Priamond, Diamond, and Triamond, whose three souls become lodged together in the body of Triamond, form Spenser's most direct use of trinitarian characterization; but these three are the children of Agape, are created rather than the Creator, and their main symbolic function is to represent the idea of brotherly love. The union of the Father and the Son in Bloom and Stephen is also a secular use of the theology, but the mirror of symbolism does not block out nearly as much direct reflection of the Original in Joyce as in Spenser, for whom such direct secularization might have appeared blasphemous.

Composite characterization in Spenser means that his super hero, Arthur, is all of the virtuous knights of the epic compacted into one image of "magnificence," a virtue that "is the perfection of all the rest, and conteineth in it them all" ("Letter to Raleigh"). As a result, Arthur seldom appears in the poem. He is meant to be seen as present in the other heroes, but only in so far as they are reflections of him. In such a composition the parts must be both similar to, yet in some major ways different from, the whole. The knights are thus also independent beings, who may at times depart from the Arthurian norm. But above even Arthur stands the figure of the Faerie Queene herself, Gloriana, who, though she is often invoked, never appears in the action of the narrative at all except in dream or memory or in her lesser manifestation as "a most vertuous and beautiful Lady" rather than as a queen, and who then has the name Belphoebe (i.e., she appears as a different character). Not only are Spenser's heroic characters symbolic aspects of larger characters and ultimately of glory and magnificence itself; they are also capable of being reduplicated in negative forms. Florimell in Book III has her name and place in the narrative usurped by the False Florimell. Duessa, disguised as Fidessa, attempts to take the place of Una. Guyon as Temperance meets his anti-self in the brotherhood of Pyrochles and Cymochles, figures of irascibility and concupiscence.

In *Ulysses* the title also refers to a figure who, like the Faerie Queen,

nowhere enters the action *in propria persona* but who is the generative
principal behind it all. Ulysses is Gloriana and Arthur combined; he
is the glory and magnificence of Man. To be sure, Joyce interpreted
these virtues in a way rather different from Spenser; but the contrast
is by no means a major one. Though Joyce would not have given his
Ulysses positive manifestations of Holiness or Chastity, he does give
him the other virtues of the knights of *The Faerie Queene*: Friendship,
Justice, Courtesy, and, above all, Temperance. Leopold Bloom stands
in the same type of relationship to Ulysses as Belphoebe does to Gloriana: he represents the complete Ulysses in one chief aspect—as corporeal man. In the course of his day he meets many other aspects of
Ulysses, positive and negative, with some of whom he has direct
analogies; others represent aspects of the Ulyssean self that Bloom
does not fully possess.

Maeterlinck says: *If Socrates leave his house today he will find the sage seated
on his doorstep. If Judas go forth tonight it is to Judas his steps will tend.*
Every life is many days, day after day. We walk through ourselves, meeting robbers, ghosts, giants, old men, young men, wives, widows, brothers-
in-love. But always meeting ourselves. (*Ulysses*, p. 213)

Blazes Boylan mates with the (possibly) chaste Penelope-Molly in
the fabled bed, because he too is Ulysses and fulfills, with Bloom's
ultimate consent, an aspect of the role in which Bloom is deficient.
Boylan is the "conquering hero" but Bloom is the "unconquered
hero" (p. 263), and the two are grammatically confused by Molly in
her soliloquy.

Stephen Dedalus is the largest supplementary self Bloom meets;
and, as the novel makes clear and the schema supports, Stephen supplies the spiritual dimension to the image of Ulysses that Joyce is
creating, and is himself in need of the earthly and earthy stability of
Bloom.[15] In *The Faerie Queene* we anticipate throughout an eventual
union in marriage of Gloriana and Arthur, but it never comes about.
This is perhaps because the epic is unfinished, but it is more likely
because reality itself prevented it: Elizabeth never married. The unity
of the complementary natures of Stephen and Bloom also remains a

largely unrealized potential at the end of Joyce's novel, though the idea—the symbol—has been firmly established.

Joyce's methods of linking Stephen and Bloom are a complex system of their own. Richard Ellmann has pointed out that the two figures are linked in *Circe* "chiefly in terms of one trait which the two men share, their essentially inactive roles";[16] throughout the novel, in fact, the important connections between the two are established by means other than those of dramatic action and interaction. When they discuss what they have in common, at the opening of *Ithaca*, they find very little; yet the novel constantly violates the autonomy of the two characters in ways that link them together into a symbolic unity. This is reflected even in the styles in which the novel is written. The different styles, which are seldom impersonal, often reflect the consciousness of one of the characters even when not employing his voice. But whose consciousness should one say the style of *Circe* reflects? Most of the *content* of *Circe* is drawn from the private recesses of Bloom's mind, but the style (which we would recognize even without the schema) is that of a drunken or drug-induced hallucination. But who is hallucinating? Certainly not sober Bloom, who in his later remembering of the experience in the brothel has no recollection of such a striking mental aberration. The style, in fact, reflects the consciousness of *Stephen* who, Bloom later suggests, may have been drugged by his "friends." A similar technique is used in *Ithaca,* where the main subject is Bloomian science, but the form is that of a religious catechism.[17] Even their names, the one device of characterization that preserves individuality in spite of all other changes, are temporarily blended by the novel to become Blephen and Stoom (p. 603).

In its methods of characterization, the world of *Ulysses* is a world of funhouse mirrors (and, literally, of cracked, tiny, and shadowed mirrors) where Ulysses always sees himself, but in all manner of forms. When in *Circe* Stephen and Bloom gaze together into a mirror, they see the same face—that of William Shakespeare (p. 508). William James wrote about such perceptions, mistaking one image for another, in his *Principles of Psychology,* where he identifies it with that process through which the mind abstracts from an object placed before it what it needs in order to identify that object with something already known; the mind seeks to name what it perceives at all costs, even that of reason. James quotes an essay by one of his students who mistook a portrait of Shakespeare for one of Hawthorne on the basis of facial features shared by both writers, an identification that the student saw as psychologically satisfying, in that it put a name to the object, but as a product of fancy rather than reason, because it served no purpose other than self-satisfaction.[18] In the reality of the events of *Circe,* if indeed there is such a thing, Bloom and Stephen may be fancying the likeness of each other to Shakespeare. In the symbolic reasoning of the novel, however, it is more than a fancy or hallucination; it indicates not only their shared interest in writing, but their overall unity with each other and with the self-reflective Shakespeare of Stephen's aesthetic theory.

The other selves of *Ulysses* would, by Stephen's theory, include everyone Bloom meets, though Stephen's theories are never to be swallowed whole. In one sense, the theory is too narrow, for it is not only the characters who join together to make *Ulysses* the shadow of a man; it is all the scenes, hours, organs, arts, colors, symbols, and techniques. In walking through himself, Bloom is walking through a book. In another sense, however, Stephen's theory is too general; it does not deal with the different kinds of relationships that exist between aspects of the Ulyssean self. Bloom is given not only parallel and supplementary selves, but false selves like Reuben J., the stage Jew of the anti-semitic mind whose image repeatedly comes between Bloom and other characters distorting their view of him. There is an apparent double, who pops up momentarily as Bloom the dentist, but who turns out to be unrelated to the hero (unless the relationship is a symbolic one.—Query: Why does the schema not include teeth?) *Eumaeus* offers a long list of disreputable characters whom Bloom has the potential to become through "reverses of fortune" (p. 646).

Bloom meets his most obviously anti-Ulyssean self in the returned sailor, W. B. Murphy, of *Eumaeus*; but the narrative, which is a reflection of Bloom's consciousness in this episode, exposes the fraud. Not only is Murphy the False Ulysses-Bloom, it is also comically revealed that he knows the False Simon Dedalus, a sharpshooter. And as Stephen and Bloom together form the most complete image of the

Ulyssean character, so Murphy has an anti-Ulysses-Stephen counterpart in Buck Mulligan, another potential usurper of the honors due
to the true hero.

But in positive and negative, close and distant, spiritual and physical forms, the spirit of Ulysses walks through *Ulysses*; not, to be sure,
as Homer created him, but as Joyce inherited him and recreated him
after centuries of interpretation and reinterpretation, praise and blame,
and allegorization, a prudent Wandering Man. He is the Holy Ghost
to Bloom's and Stephen's Father and Son; the mystery of the relationship of the three is the mystery of the Trinity, which demands
recognition both of the unity of the Persons and of their diversity.
Bloom's individual identity, as many readers have noted, becomes less
and less important as the novel develops. Bloom himself does not
"develop" as a main character in a nineteenth-century novel normally
does; rather, he has a tendency toward the cinematic "dissolve." Analogical links gather force, especially in the last chapters, allowing us
to see Bloom as symbolically joined to such diverse figures as Hamlet
Senior, Shakespeare, the Wandering Jew, Moses, Elijah, Simon Dedalus, Dante, etc., and finally as an archetypal image of the universal
memory of which every individual memory forms a part (i.e., the
anima mundi).[19] "Why, look at the man's private life! Leading a quad-
ruple existence!" (p. 444)—a major understatement.

Yet in spite of this, Bloom never really loses his individual identity;
Joyce was not a Unitarian. The symbolic union of Stephen and Bloom
over identical cups of cocoa has no greater significance to the characters than it does because multiplicity, diversity, and separation are
as important to the novel as is the organic system that holds it all
together. As Stuart Gilbert has said:

These two complementary personages, at last united in intimate conversation, talk at cross purposes: As Mr Bloom would say, it is a case of East
is East and West is West. But that, perhaps, is the secret of true "atonement." (p. 356)

This is the same kind of preserving of the integrity of the individual
character while stressing analogical connections with other figures
that is an essential feature of most of Spenser's symbolic characterization.

In Joyce, however, many of the links the book makes take on the nature of a joke (though, as Ted Cohen has pointed out, all meta-phorical combinations of apparently unrelated objects have the nature of a joke).[20] The kind of multiplicity that Spenser was capable of imaging produces a spirit of *joyance* in the reader, a smile at the surprising plenitude of the world, and there is something of the same spirit in Joyce; but there is also another kind of smile accompanied with ironic laughter at the bathos of many Joycean combinations. Spenser's *joyance* was coupled with direct attacks on the evils of his world; Joyce's basic amorality and aestheticism caused him to make almost every positive at the same time a negative, a technique that theoretically cancels out any emotional response of attraction or rejec-tion in his art (the sort of static response that Stephen, in his advocacy of the classical temper, would have wanted) but that in fact produces a mixed reaction, adding a further level of complexity to the charac-terizations in the novel. Christ will sit at the right hand of the Father; Bloom in *Eumaeus* takes Stephen's right arm with his left hand. The secular atonement of Stephen and Bloom is also a mock atonement. Joyce gives and Joyce takes away.

When symbolic associations and acts are given opposite and yet equal meanings in a literary work, those meanings become far less important than the form of the symbol. Joyce's symbols are forms that give his novel and its world their form; they may not ultimately *mean* anything, but they are no less real on that account, since reality itself may not ultimately "mean" anything. For Spenser, on the other hand, the plenitude of his symbols and the complexity of their combinations image a world overflowing with important meanings, not simply with analogous forms.

Even some of those critics of *Ulysses* who are not willing to toss out the non-mimetic aspects of the novel tend today to devalue the importance of these multiple analogies, but they are essential to any reading of the work. Of course, Joyce, like Spenser, can be enjoyed for his narrative and linguistic surface alone, although I personally would find such an exclusive reading the most difficult of all; when one strikes a chapter like *Circe* or figures in Spenser like the serpent named Error or the giant called Grantorto, there seems to be no real alternative to a reading based on symbolic connections. The most dogged of Joyce's realistic critics have met the problem by a process of allegorizing in which the symbolic surface is seen as a dispensable mask hiding the mimetic reality beneath—a method of reading as mistaken in its way as the older conception of renaissance allegory as a negligible surface hiding ideas and historical allusions.

There are also critics of *Ulysses*, just as there are of Spenser, who advise the reader to make occasional rather than sustained use of analogies. David Hayman, for instance, says:

Though there is no reason to maintain in so rich a context a constant awareness of subidentities which are only periodically underlined, we take pleasure in the sudden discovery of a subtly stated parallel and the consequent enlargement of the being of one of the protagonists.... If we bear in mind their existence and are not disturbed by their subtle glow, the analogies have many practical functions. Through them, the characters can complete not one but many actions, live many lives, resume history, achieve heroic or divine stature. They can be united metaphorically or be made to conform to the structures of various logical system. Since these are no more than analogies, no such identifications need in fact occur and the realistic "curve" is maintained.[21]

Some of this is on the right track, but it does not go nearly far enough. In a world, real or imagined, where the primary structural principle is analogy, the phrase "no more than analogies" is nonsense. The symbolic analogies are an essential element of the "realistic curve," and thus a constant awareness of them can only add to our understanding of the world of the novel.[22]

Granted that the "hero" of *Ulysses* is a composite symbolic figure, an abstract "Ulysses" whose fullest materialization in a character is in Leopold Bloom: what, in fact, is being embodied by this symbol? What are the characteristics of Ulyssean man?

Above all else, he is the quiet hero. Indeed, just as Spenser includes an episode (discussed in Chapter 2 above) where Guyon lies unconscious while the action proceeds around him, so Joyce's Bloom is allowed to sleep out the long last chapter of the novel. Joyce, like

Spenser, casts some doubts upon the passive nature of his representative figure; but he never seeks to reverse it, because the key ethical position that Joyce could not abandon even for aesthetic reasons was his abhorrence of physical violence. As Richard Ellmann has said, "Joyce's version of the epic story is a pacifist verion. . . . The victories of Bloom are mental, in spite of the pervasive physicality of Joyce's book."[23] The same thing applies to Bloom's quiet counterpart, Stephen. Joyce regarded the idea of physical heroism as a lie. "The task was to exhibit heroism of a new kind, undistinguished by any acts, distinguished maybe by the absence of act."[24] But, as I have been arguing in this book, there is nothing new about this kind of heroism in English literature.

Bloom, more Christian than the Christians of his novel, repeatedly turns the other cheek to his opponents. His heroism is that of the Good Samaritan. He is the friendly dog who will walk a piece of the road with any man. Constantly humiliated, like Milton's Christ, Bloom is "stained by the mire of an indelible dishonour" (*Ulysses*, p. 414); but, as the context of this last characterization makes clear, his stain of dishonor is in fact a badge of honor to be respected equally with "the dust of travel and combat" (ibid.). The True Christian Knight, like Sir Gawain in *Gawain and the Green Knight*, wears his dishonor publicly, the green girdle, sign of Gawain's deception and repentance, which was emulated by the whole court of Arthur.

Like Spenser's Guyon, Bloom repeatedly appears dishonorable from the distorted perspectives of the other characters; but his true heroism is known to the reader through the symbols, the psychological insights, and occasionally the direct comments of the narrative voice. Bloom's unheroic appearance results from the fact that he, like Guyon, is the Knight of Temperance, the "prudent member" (pp. 296 and 302), who normally offers only verbal rejoinders in "moderate and measured tone" (p. 417). "Punctual Bloom" is soberly present in Stephen's hour of need, and, "disgustingly sober" (p. 534), later preaches Stephen a sermon on the "dangers of nighttown."

Bloom's own moral development has taken place before the novel begins. Like Guyon and Milton's Christ, Bloom does not learn temperance but evinces it and sees it subjected to tests. As a child, we are told, Bloom had experienced "immature impatience" over Jewish beliefs and practices.

How did these beliefs and practices now appear to him?
    Not more rational than they had then appeared, not less rational than other beliefs and practices now appeared. (p. 645)

He, like all figures of temperance, experiences temptations, but generally manages to meet them with his characteristic virtue. As with Guyon and Milton's Christ, moments of righteous anger are not incompatible with his dominant characteristic.

Bloom's chief angry outburst is in the *Cyclops* episode, where two of his features, his temperance and his Jewishness, are subjected to a complex analysis. The chapter is fraught with apparent ambiguities as challenging as those in Spenser's Cave of Mammon episode or in the angry and apparently ill-tempered responses of Milton's Christ to Satan. Part of the cause of the ambiguity is in the narrative voice, the voice—according to the schema—of Noman, the anti-self of the everyman Ulysses. It is hardly a reliable voice, or that of a mimetically realized character; yet with its formulas, catalogues, inflations, and often-repeated anecdotes, it identifies itself as the voice of a bard, of the kind of storyteller who communicated the Homeric epic in its earlier oral tradition. At times the primitive epic voice breaks through the contemporary jargon; at other times the clichés of journalism, law, and other professions replace the devices of the old oral tradition. The present metempsychosis finds the soul of the bard in the body of a garrulous retailer of gossip in an Irish pub, who, in a sense rather different from his original, "was just passing the time of day with old Troy" (p. 290). Like Yeats's antithetical selves, however, Noman is capable of revealing important truths about the self from the distance of its opposed position. Though he can see little more than the mask of the primary self ("old sheepsface"—p. 343), he has the same power of ironic revelation of all unreliable narrators. As an antithetical self, however, the narrator is not simply opposed to the true Ulysses, but is himself also contained within Bloom. Ulysses *was* Noman in Homer. The narrator regards Bloom's own loquacity with envious hostility, for Bloom too has the repressed soul of a writer and is himself the kind of storehouse of "phenomena" that the ancient bards attempted to become through their use of the repeated formulae of their *memoria technica*. Like other artists, the narrator of *Cyclops* is meeting himself.

This notion of the combined self/anti-self is important in shaping the relationships all of the characters of the episode have to Bloom. Bloom faces hostility nominally because he will not treat the others to a drink; but the Citizen, who also fails in this custom, is forgiven. The Citizen is as much an antithetical self for Bloom as is the narrative voice. David Hayman has suggested that "it is perhaps the supreme irony that Bloom is finally driven to play the citizen's game, naming famous ancestors";[25] but the irony here is by no means a simple one. Bloom, like his Homeric analogue, escapes from the Cyclops by deceit. He is invulnerable to the Citizen's attack because, since the Citizen does not see behind the sheep-faced mask at all, he misses the real Bloom completely. Bloom's parting taunts, which drive the Citizen to throw the biscuit tin after him, are not impassioned defenses of the true self but exploitations of the mask, intended to teach his enemies a lesson. "Christ was a jew like me" (p. 340), for all of its ironic truth, does not belong to the self-image of the thrice-baptized Bloom whose mind we have spent the day traversing; its raison d'être is strategic.

The truth of Bloom's Jewishness makes him the Patriotic Irish Citizen's antagonist, but also his counterpart. By raising the question of Bloom's nationality here, Joyce may be wittily invoking a tradition through which Bloom would qualify as almost more Irish than the Irish. Herbert Howarth has pointed out Joyce's familiarity with Douglas Hyde's *Literary History of Ireland,* which traced the Irish race back through Hebrew origins as far as Adam. Leon Hühner pointed out, in a paper read before the Jewish Historical Society of England in 1905 (published, 1908), that the Irish are one of the few races that have made such serious claims to Jewish origins: "Many are the books written at different times by Irish authors, seeking to trace the descent of the Irish people from Japheth, the son of Noah" and identifying the Irish with the lost tribe of the Jews.[26] (The Citizen, by extension,

laments the "lost tribes" of the Irish—p. 324). Like Ireland, Bloom-
as-Jew is the victim of continued persecution. Haines claims that German Jews are the "national problem" of England (p. 27), but the book
shows another race that merits the description as well.

When asked directly what his nation is, Bloom, of course, replies
"Ireland" (p. 330). By birth as well as perhaps by heritage he has the
right to call himself an Irishman. But then, he has the right to call
himself a good many things, as the context of the novel demands.
"He is Greeker than the Greeks" (p. 201) and, ever the wily Ulysses,
can even claim to be British when the need arises. Nationalism is
made to appear such a one-eyed distortion in the *Cyclops* episode
because true Ulyssean man belongs to all of the nations he has trav-
elled through in space and in time. Bloom's Jewishness and his Irish-
ness, whether or not they are the same thing, are by no means
dismissed as unimportant in his characterization; they are given heavy
emphasis. But Bloom's "nationalism" is valuable, while that of the
Citizen is ridiculous, because Bloom's plurality of national associations
balances, tempers, his character and places him beyond narrow-
minded patriotism. "Jewgreek is greekjew. Extremes meet" (p. 471);
and like Stephen Dedalus (Irish-Roman-Greek-Christian late of
France) meeting Leopold Bloom (Irish-Hungarian-Roman-Greek-
Protestant-Jew with a Spanish, etc., wife), the extremes do not cancel
each other out.

Spenser's Guyon is by race an elf, one of the few heroes from that
pre-Christian tribe in *The Faerie Queene.* Yet he is the heir of the
Greek Ulysses's *sophrosyne* (as the Renaissance saw it) and consequently of Christian temperance. He is a knight of the English court
who wanders through a landscape that has specific characteristics associating it with England, Ireland, the Greek Islands, Italy, and ultimately with the world of romance as it exists everywhere. The world
of Spenser's epic is not the generalized, shadowy world of dreams; it
is a brightly lit, international world, which includes the dream world
as one of its nations. Bloom's characterization parallels Guyon's multiple heritage; and Dublin itself, so specific in the details with which
it is described, repeatedly reminds the reader, through those very
details, of how many different nations have contributed to the history

and nature of that city and its inhabitants, and of how many other cities and nations (including the City of the Dead and the Island of Circe) stand in primary and antithetical relationships to it.

Both Guyon and Bloom are important as culture heroes of a "typical" rather than an "exceptional" heroic variety, but the culture each hero represents exceeds that of any one nation. When Guyon and Arthur visit the chamber of Eumnestes in the Castle of Alma, Arthur reads *Briton moniments,* a book drawn chiefly from the best-known British chronicles; Guyon, however, reads a comparable book with no known source: *The Antiquitie of Faerie lond.* Arthur's chronicle is full of the treachery and internecine warfare that was English history; Guyon's book is an almost unbroken record of the success of a people who ruled "all Nations" (II, x, 72).[27] Guyon's volume, however, parallels Arthur's in its allegorical references to English history, and both volumes lead up to the reign of Gloriana-Elizabeth. But the historical process that leads up to now and England in Guyon's book is not simply an idealized rewrite of English history; it is a view of recent English history within the context of universal human history.

That the history of a particular nation and the history of mankind are parallel structures, which unite and culminate in the present moment, is Joyce's point as well as Spenser's. It is the broader perspective of universal human, international history that balances without devaluing the sufferings of any one nation, for man's home is only temporarily his country. Spenser's Arthur is capable of remembering this even at the height of his emotional patriotic response to *Briton moniments*: "Deare countrey, O how dearely deare / Ought thy remembraunce, and perpetuall band / Be to thy *foster* Childe" (69; italics added). Mortal men are fostered by their countries; but Spenser's "Elfin Kind" is equivalent to Joyce's Ulyssean man, and Guyon's chronicle is a history of mankind's "wandring through the world with wearie feet" (71) but at the same time making a heroic progress. Though Joyce might not have found man's true home to lie where Spenser sought it, Bloom is still heroic Wandering Man, Universal Man yet Ireland's foster son—and one of her best.

In the coolness of reflection several hours after the events of *Cyclops,* Bloom asks himself: "Mistake to hit back. Or? No. Ought to go home and laugh at themselves" (p. 378). That they probably will not laugh at themselves does not affect Bloom's teacherly, priestly motivation ("ben Bloom Elijah") nor the fact that he simultaneously "got my own back there"—symbolically as well as actually, for, as we have seen, the swillers were Bloom's own. "Perhaps not to hurt he meant." The novel asks us to give the temperate man's display of anger the same charitable interpretation he gives to the violence of the Citizen, and makes it almost as difficult to do so. Almost, because the Citizen, like many of the minor characters of both Spenser and Joyce, represents far too narrow a range symbolically and mimetically for him to exist as much more than a caricature. His lack of even a human name in the novel suggests that he is an immediate heir to simpler traditions of allegory rather than to those full Spenserian methods that govern the symbolic characterization of Leopold Bloom.

Bloom is given several other symbolic analogies which are part of the image of him as a quiet hero. He is, for example, both the Jewish scapegoat and the sacrificial lamb of Christianity. He is the Squire of Dames (p. 435—A character who goes by this name appears in *The Faerie Queene* III, engaged in a search for chaste women). One particularly renaissance and particularly Spenserian characterization of Bloom is that of him as the womanly man, a hermaphrodite. The hermaphrodite for Spenser and Joyce is a symbol of the Neoplatonic unity of opposites that makes up love, humanity, and indeed all that exists. Presenting Bloom as a hermaphrodite in *Oxen of the Sun* (pp. 464–465) is another stage in breaking the limits of mimetic characterization and in insuring that Everyman is also seen as Everywoman, containing in one image the full creative process.

When in the hallucinations of *Circe,* however, Bloom is forced to play the role of a subservient woman, the meaning is somewhat different. The source of this episode is in the Hercules myth where Hercules, as an act of penance, is required to act as a female slave to Omphale, queen of Lydia. The Joycean interpretation of this myth, however, is Spenserian. Spenser offers his version of the story in Book V of *The Faerie Queene,* where his theme is the old medieval one of mastery—the question of who should have the upper hand in male-female relationships. Artegall, fighting the amazonian Radigund, takes a rash oath to serve as her thrall if he should lose. Radigund then reveals her beauty, and Artegall is self-defeated; he is forced to dress and work as a woman slave. Spenser, however, fails to draw the expected medieval moral in his evaluation of Artegall:

> Some men, I wrote, will deeme in *Artegall*
>> Great weaknesse, and report of him much ill,
>> For yeelding so himselfe a wretched thrall,
>> To th'insolent command of womens will;
>> That all his former praise doth fowly spill.
>> But he the man, that say or doe so dare,
>> Be well adviz'd, that he stand stedfast still:
>> For never yet was wight so well aware,
> But he at first or last was trapt in womens snare.
>
> Yet in the streightnesse of that captive state,
>> This gentle knight himselfe so well behaved,
>> That notwithstanding all the subtill bait,
>> With which those Amazons his love still craved,
>> To his owne love his loyaltie he saved:
>> Whose character in th'Adamantine mould
>> Of his true hart so firmely was engraved,
>> That no new loves impression ever could
> Bereave it thence: such blot his honor blemish should.
>
> (vi, 1–2)

Not only does the image of Britomart in his heart preserve Artegall from any real dishonor—and here again honor does not bear an honorable exterior—Britomart herself rescues him in a scene that is a Ulyssean homecoming, with Ulysses dressed as a woman: "Not so great wonder and astonishment, / Did the most chast *Penelope* possesse, / To see her Lord ... But Stood long staring on him, mongst uncertaine feares" (vii, 39).

Joyce also rewrote the Hercules myth as a study of sexual dominance, and he too presents his hero as faithful to himself and his beloved during an attack on his integrity and on his male identity. Joyce's Bloom saves himself by remembering his Penelope: "To drive me mad! Moll! I forgot! Forgive! Moll! ... We ... Still ..." (p. 494); and with this charm he returns to male form. He wins all of his victories in *Circe* by responding to the "etherial" hallucinations of guilt with a tenacious clinging to what he is and what he has known, however humiliating such solid realities may seem. *Ulysses* may be in part a psychological novel, but it presents the psychology of guilt as little more than a ghost. Spenser, on the other hand, believes in the solid reality of guilt, but he too refuses to generalize it. In both authors, the honorable man must pay the humiliating price for his failings, but he does not thereby become dishonorable.

When Spenser used the *Odyssey* for a model in Book II of *The Faerie Queene,* he made one striking change of plot. The intended end of Guyon's voyage past the Gulfe of Greedinesse and the Rocke of vile Reproch, the Wandring Islands, the Whirlepoole of decay, etc., is not Ithaca and Penelope but the Circean Bower of Bliss, where Acrasia's sexual attractions turn men to swine. Guyon is seeking temperate revenge against the False Venus rather than union with the True. Joyce, however, always doubling, presents Venus in both of her aspects in his Penelope. Bloom's home may be Ithaca, but it is also the Bower of Bliss; and if it does not possess "all the ornaments of *Floraes* pride" (*F. Q.* II, xii, 50), it has its symbolic "Plumtree's" making it, for those who pluck the "fruit" in Molly's bed, "an abode of bliss." Over the Bloom bed hangs "The Bath of the Nymph"; in the Bower, Guyon is tempted by two bathing nymphs. And as Guyon and the reader were prepared for his encounter with Acrasia by the pre-temptations of Phaedria (whose gondola seems to have been inherited by Rabaiotti at the opening of *Circe*), so Bloom's encounter with Bella seems to have brought him to terms with the Circean elements of Molly; the conclusion of the theme of mastery in *Ulysses* is that Bloom does not feel dominated by Molly, nor is he likely to dominate her. The opposed symmetry of their sleeping arrangements is the visual image of this, and of the entire theme of temperance as it exists in the novel.

Bloom is, as I have said, a single and somewhat limited manifestation of Ulyssean man. The full characterization of Ulysses is the book itself. As the emphasis on Bloom's physical nature makes him symbolically the Body, so the book as a whole, after the Telemachia of spiritual Stephen, is structured like the human body, with each chapter highlighting a particular organ. This has been the least appreciated of Joyce's symbolic techniques, but it is the most obviously Spenserian.

To defend the technique on grounds other than those of literary precedent is much easier today than it was when Joyce employed it. To many of the first readers who were made aware of it, the device looked like the most absurd extension of mechanical allegory possible. What real importance could this system of human organs have to the interpretation of the novel or to anything else? But, as a result of recent work in anthropology and sociology, we now know that structural systems based on the organs of the human body are perhaps the most common systems in existence: the body may, in fact, be the meta-system to which all other forms of human organization relate. Mary Douglas has argued in *Purity and Danger* (1966) that the organic system is universally analogous to social systems; and in *Natural Symbols* she points out that "the human body is the most readily available image of a system" and that "the body is capable of furnishing a natural system of symbols."[28] Joyce understood all of this over a half-century ago. "Organizing" his book according to the organs of the human body may turn out to be one of the most universalizing of the structural techniques he employed, rather than the most absurd.

But however "natural" the system, Joyce was not a sociologist, and he wrote a novel rather than a study of human systematizing. His most important justification must therefore be a literary one. The image of the human body as a symbolic analogy, parallel to such things as the organization of the macrocosm and the political structure of the state, occurs in the art of all ages, but structural symbolic use of particular organs in a narrative is, in English literature, a Spenserian technique. Joyce was attracted to this technique not, it seems, by the work of Spenser himself, who makes important but only occasional use of it, but by one of Spenser's seventeenth-century imitators, Phineas Fletcher. Fletcher's twelve-book Spenserian allegory, called *The Purple Island,* contains, in Books II–IV, a physical allegory equating features of the landscape of the Island to the various organs of a man. It has all of the specificity of a medical treatise, and may simply be intended as entertaining instruction in anatomy. All of the allegorical meanings are explained in the text or in marginal glosses, and there seems to be no "dark conceit" at all. Nevertheless, the structural principle appealed to Joyce.

Frank Budgen, who read Fletcher's epic at Joyce's prompting, records a conversation between himself and Joyce in the Astoria Cafe, a location that perhaps determined Joyce's example:

"Among other things," he said, "my book is the epic of the human body. The only man I know who has attempted the same thing is Phineas Fletcher. But then his *Purple Island* is purely descriptive, a kind of coloured anatomical chart of the human body. In my book the body lives in and moves through space and is the home of a full human personality. The words I write are adapted to express first one of its functions then another. In *Lestrygonians* the stomach dominates and the rhythm of the episode is that of peristaltic movement."

"But the minds, the thoughts of the characters," I began.

"If they had no body they would have no mind," said Joyce. "It is all one."[29]

Whether he was aware of it or not, Joyce, like Fletcher, was employing a Spenserian technique; but Joyce's use of that technique produced something much closer to the original than did Fletcher's. Though Spenser made some relatively simple uses of the method, as in Book III, where the mount of Venus in the Garden of Adonis is anatomically the *mons veneris,* his major development of it was, as every reader knows, in the description of the Castle of Alma in Book II. Spenser's allegorical castle of the human body shares with Joyce's *Ulysses* an acceptance of all things natural; Spenser treats both the profundities of the tripartite human mind and the function of the anus where waste "was close convaid, and to the back-gate brought, / That cleped was *Port Esquiline,* whereby / It was avoided quite, and throwne out privily" (ix, 32), a pun Joyce would have enjoyed. (Also like Joyce, Spenser has been condemned by critics for discussing defecation.)

The Castle of Alma is not a static image, like Fletcher's Island, but closely related to the action and symbolism of the book as a whole. Symbolically, the Castle relates to Guyon and Arthur in the same way in which the organs of *Ulysses* are related to Bloom: the larger structure mirrors aspects of the particular heroes. The Castle is the Temperate Man's body, besieged by external forces; Arthur and Guyon are temperate men. In the "memory" chamber they come upon history books personally relevant to themselves. Within the Castle, Guyon meets Shamefastnesse and is informed that "She is the fountaine of your modestee; / You shamefast are, but *Shamefastnesse* it selfe is shee" (ix, 43). Similarly, Arthur meets a major aspect of his own personality in Prays-desire. Like Bloom walking through the "organically" structured world of *Ulysses,* Guyon and Arthur touring the Castle of Alma are walking through themselves and meeting themselves.

The identifications suggested by Joyce's schema by no means exhaust the symbolic realities of Ulysses, though those not included there cannot, of course, be identified with the same kind of certainty. I would suggest, for instance, that the tarot pack could be used to form yet another column in the schema by assigning the Tower to *Telemachus,* the Hanged Man to *Cyclops,* the Queen of Batons to *Circe,* the Star to *Nausicaa,* Death to *Hades*—beyond which relationships become less obvious.

I also believe that there is also another schema behind the existing one, lodged in the etymology of some of the symbols listed, because *Ulysses* has as one of its linguistic bases the renaissance principle that the etymology of a word contains part of its true meaning. Joyce's autobiographical *Stephen Hero* tells us that Stephen/Joyce "read Skeat's Etymological Dictionary by the hour" and that he started to hear the words of ordinary conversation in terms of their tradition rather than of their denotation.[30]

In *Ulysses,* the symbol of *Proteus,* tide, provides the basis for the strong development of the theme of time (A. S. *tid*). "Nymph" according to Skeat first meant "bride," and *Calypso,* for which "nymph" is the symbol in the schema, certainly features Bloom's bride more prominently than it does the pictured nymph over the bed, though later we see the two blending together in Bloom's mind (another symbolic analogy that is realized *within* the novel). That Skeat thought the verb "sail" derived from a word that might have meant "drive" is what places the sailor of *Eumaeus* in the cabdriver's shelter, and it is what causes the chapter to end with a mysterious, silent "driver" watching Stephen and Bloom. The same sort of information has been gleaned by identifying the original meanings of some of the Greek names in the schema. Such etymological research does not yield a new column with an entry for every chapter, but then some of Joyce's own columns have blanks. The schema and its details and extensions are valuable only in so far as they work; and they work not by layering symbols from the outside onto the novel in order to exhaust a preconceived system, but rather by relating what, in a world of analogous systems, is related anyway.

"Horse," for example, is the symbol of *Nestor.* Literally, horses appear in the pictures on Deasy's wall with their "Elfin riders" (p. 38). They are mentioned briefly in the conversation and in Deasy's letter. They relate to the scene "The School" through implied allusion to Blake's horses of instruction. They relate mythologically to Deasy in his role as Nestor, the old horse thief of the *Iliad,* XI. Etymologically, however, the word "horse," according to Skeat, may come from a word meaning "a runner," and this symbolic relationship is carried over to the running children of the episode, Deasy's hockey-playing human horses. ("Run on, Stephen said. Mr. Deasy is calling you" [p. 35]; "the joust of life" [p. 38]; and again to Deasy himself who comes running after Stephen at the end of the episode [p. 42].)

There are a number of other symbols in the same chapter that are not mentioned in the schema—coins and shells, for instance, which are directly identified by Stephen as symbols (p. 36). There are also the symbols of mathematics:

Across the page the symbols move in grave morrice, in the mummery of their letters, wearing quaint caps of squares and cubes. . . . In long shady strokes Sargent copied the data. Waiting always for a word of help his hand moved faithfully the unsteady symbols. . . . Like him was I. (p. 34)

And these symbols, like those associated with horses, have a recurring presence throughout the novel. The schema does not describe the limits of Joycean symbolism but simply elaborates the pattern of some of the more fully developed parts of the analogical system.

Joyce's Ulysses is a character whose essence is all of these realities as they exist in the novel. This may seem a vaster claim than the older proposal that he is Everyman, but it is not. Any novel, even one as full as *Ulysses,* is a closed system, far more limited than the world of reality itself. A novel may *imply* a good deal of reality, but what it actually includes in its pages must always be a very limited selection. What is included in *Ulysses* is included purposefully, and the process of selection was—judging by both internal and external evidence—a rational, coherent one. The schema is an anatomy of *Ulysses* and of Ulysses.

Thus Leopold Bloom, as the most Ulyssean figure in the novel, stands at a nearer or greater distance to all the items of Joyce's system and—potentially at least—includes them all. Understanding his characterization does not consist of attempting to find more limits to his identity than the novel gives him. Bloom, while never ceasing to be a unique individual, becomes much more important for the universals he embodies and with which he associates himself than for his unique personality. He is a quiet, symbolic, epic hero, like Guyon and Milton's Christ, undergoing an apotheosis like that of Donne's Elizabeth Drury—who also remains a unique individual while being symbolically absorbed into the World Soul.

The same thing applies to the other main characters—it must apply to them, given the unity of the multiplex Ulysses. Stephen is always something more and something less than the human soul, while still symbolizing that soul. Molly is identified (once again, *in* the novel) with "Gea-Tellus, fulfilled, recumbent, big with seed" (p. 658). On the one hand, this is only a simile describing her appearance; it has a realistic, descriptive function. On the other hand, however, it reverberates as a symbol through all that has gone before in the novel, setting up sympathetic vibrations in the many images of fertility that the book includes and conditioning the meaning of other symbolic associations.[31] It implies a possible identification of Bloom (and also of Stephen) with Uranus, the heavens, Gea's husband and son, that ambiguous god whom "it does not appear that the Greeks at any time or place worshipped."[32] Yet Bloom's Uranian nature generates the discussion of astronomy and astrology with Stephen, which occupies the same chapter as the association of Molly with Gea.[33]

"It is a paradox of *Ulysses,*" writes a contemporary "realist" critic of the novel, "that although no character has ever been subjected to such intense scrutiny as Mr. Bloom, neither has any character ever so triumphantly escaped final definition."[34] It may be so, though no major literary character that I know of has been caught by a critic in anything approaching a "final definition." It might be more correct to say that few characters have ever been given so many different definitions *by their author.* And because these definitions are all systematically connected by a system whose elements extend beyond the character to the world of analogies and to an analogy-rich world, there is a plenitude to Bloom that is the result of the plenitude of concrete meanings rather than the vagueness of a masked personal psychology or history such as realists attempt to penetrate.

The mind behind the characterizations in *Ulysses* is a renaissance, a Spenserian mind. It considers names to be significant indexes to character. It presents individual temperaments that are related to the four elements and humors (cf. Blazes Boylan and Spenser's Pyrochles). It conceives of human actions in terms of biblical and classical archetypes (cf. the Temptation of Christ and Mulligan's temptation of Stephen in *Telemachus*). It sees symbols contained in reality ("Signatures of all things I am here to read" [p. 42]). It is attracted by the possibilities of metamorphosis and metempsychosis. It can make use of a pagan ethos without, like the "new pagan" Mulligan, actually being part of it. It can impose the ancient microcosm / macrocosm analogy upon "the incertitude of the void" (p. 618), just as Spenser did upon his well-loved enemy Mutability—the ineluctable modality of the visible.

Both writers feature numerological and geometrical forms in their epics; both treat history as a cyclical process, in which the repetitions are not identical to the original ("history repeating itself with a difference" [p. 575]). Like Spenser, Joyce enters his own work as a character, but in a form distanced from his actual selfhood, an ironically "lower" character; maturity and irony separate Joyce from Stephen, while Spenser's Colin Clout is the poet-courtier himself as a simple shepherd. Both writers chose to create distinctive styles by making a combination of available contemporary and historical styles, something no one else has ever successfully accomplished. The language of *The Faerie Queene* calls attention to itself as an artificial language combining medieval and renaissance English, because Spenser is celebrating in his epic not only English history but the English language and its literature, particularly that of Chaucer; the multiple styles of *Ulysses* and the multiplex language of *Finnegans Wake* have a similarly expansive function.[35] Like Spenser and many of Spenser's contemporaries, Joyce chose to violate genre while in other ways following Aristotelian norms, incorporating elements of tragedy in what is structurally a comedy. That Joyce's renaissance mind was also the most representative modernist mind in English literature offers a striking support to the historical theory behind *Ulysses*: literary history too repeats itself with a difference.

After Joyce, quiet heroes became almost the norm in modernist literature, though no one ever created such a hero with the fullness and complexity of a Leopold Bloom. Indeed, possibly the chief difference between Joyce's Ulysses and his fictional heirs is that between a form replete with content and the same form relatively empty. Joyce as an artist was largely indifferent to the materials he included within his structures; if something fit well, it was likely to be included. He could accept the most abstruse and most absurd notions and precedents on purely aesthetic grounds. Later writers have been more committed or more hostile to the ideas they have embodied (or disembodied) in art, and thus more limited.

The most typical examples are the characters of Samuel Beckett— a disembodier. Beckett's main characters are, as everyone knows, quiet heroes who do little more than wait for something to happen. Their general lack of mimetic action and of individual characterization qualify them to be symbolic figures, and certainly the ordinary reader or theatre patron responds to them with the question I described as proper for quiet heroes in the Renaissance: What do they symbolize? But whereas the plurality of answers to this question produces for renaissance and Joycean characters a vast system of related specific meanings, for Beckett the possible answers are unconvincing, contradicted, and finally unimportant. Beckett's characters are symbolic structures whose meaning centers in their lack of meaning. Put another way, Beckett's symbolic structures are important in themselves rather than for any meaning they might seem to contain; and one of Beckett's chief techniques is the presentation of obviously symbolic

figures as if they were nothing more than phenomenal realities—
which is the natural result of emptying such structures of meaning.
The difference (and the similarity) between the methods of characterization of Joyce and Beckett is thus something like that between
the positive and negative paths of mystical experience.

Beckett's first, English fiction has, as one would expect, the most
obvious relationships to Joyce. The description of "Murphy's mind" in
Murphy (1938) is based on renaissance conceptions and visualizations
of the human mind, but it is a parody of them:

> Murphy's mind pictured itself as a large hollow sphere, hermetically closed
> to the universe without. This was not an impoverishment, for it excluded
> nothing that it did not itself contain. Nothing ever had been, was or would
> be in the universe outside it but was already present at virtual, or actual,
> or virtual rising into actual, or actual falling into virtual, in the universe
> inside it.
>
> This did not involve Murphy in the idealist tar. There was the mental
> fact and there was the physical fact, equally real if not equally pleasant.[36]

Like the mind imaged in Spenser's Castle of Alma, this mind has
three zones, "each with its speciality" (p. 76). (Beckett would create a
similar symbolic visualization of the inside of a mind in *Endgame,*
where again the point is "what is felt and pictured itself to be"; what
the set of that play "means" is not a question to be answered.) "Murphy," we are told, "was one of the elect, who require everything to
remind them of something else" (p. 47); but the allusions to mythological characters, works of literature, and historically established symbols that pepper this novel have an almost purely bathetic effect, not
the outward expanding quality of Joyce's symbols and allusions. "The
nature of outer reality remained obscure" (p. 122).

Beckett's passive heroes become heroic not so much through what
they represent but simply by the fact of their enduring, though they
are never given personal credit for that. In *Watt,* the hero, struck with
a stone thrown at him by Lady McCann,

> faithful to his rule, took no more notice of this aggression than if it had
> been an accident. This he found was the wisest attitude, to staunch, if
> necessary, inconspicuously, with the little red sudarium that he always

carried in his pocket, the flow of blood, to pick up what had fallen, and to continue, as soon as possible, on his way, or in his station, like a victim of mere mischance. But he deserved no credit for this. For it was an attitude become, with frequent repetition, so part of his being, that there was no more room in his mind for resentment at a spit in the eye, to take a simple example, than if his braces had burst, or a bomb had fallen on his bum.[37]

The world of *Watt* is a world of forms, the generality and repetition of which seem to make them symbolic forms, but with no significant content:

What distressed Watt in this incident of the Galls father and son, and in subsequent incidents, was not so much that he did not know what happened, for he did not care what had happened, as that nothing had happened, that a thing that was nothing happened, with the utmost formal distinctness, and that it continued to happen, in his mind, he supposed though he did not know exactly what that meant, and though it seemed to be outside him, before him, about him, and so on, inexorably to unroll its phases. . . . If he had been able to accept it, then perhaps it would not have revisited him, and this would have been a great saving of vexation, to put it mildly. But he could not accept it, could not bear it. One wonders sometimes where Watt thought he was. In a culture-park? (p. 73)

All of Beckett's later works are concerned, of course, with the same theme; nothing happens, and it happens to characters who endure because they seem to have no choice but to do so. Like the heroine of *Happy Days,* they fill the forms with whatever content they might have available in their bags, and they wait.

Other writers have tended to use symbolic characterization intermittently in their works. When, for instance, the hero of Saul Bellow's *Humbolt's Gift* is taken by his gangster nemesis to the top of a building under construction and, on this precarious perch, is offered the kingdoms of the Chicago world, the association between the passive hero and Christ is mainly comic and is not extended through the novel. On the other hand, richly symbolic writers like John Barth create heroes who are the embodiments of multiple mythical and literary sources but who are seldom "quiet" in the manner of Joyce's temperate Bloom, though they do often share his insignificant place in the world.

But whatever the differences in later writers, the major break from the conventions of realistic characterization as established by the nineteenth-century novel was made by Joyce's *Ulysses*; and it was made by developing the resources for multi-dimensional characterization provided in symbolic imagery and the use of prominent mythological and literary associations, by a return to the methods of the Renaissance.

Appendix: *Paradise Regained* and Jean Michel's *Le Mystère de la Passion*

Milton drew on many extra-biblical traditions connected with Christ's temptation when he wrote *Paradise Regained*. Attention is most often called to biblical commentaries dealing with the temptation,[1] to the tradition of the brief epic based on the book of Job (although only one brief epic dealing with the temptation has been found),[2] and to the one previous epic treatment of the theme in English, Giles Fletcher's *Christ's Victory and Triumph*. But the content and method of *Paradise Regained* have their closest affinities—outside the Bible—with the biblical dramas of the Middle Ages and the early Renaissance. These analogues for Milton's epic have been unjustly dismissed or neglected by recent criticism.

Allan H. Gilbert, in a 1920 article, argued that Milton's epics were influenced by the English mystery plays.[3] His view has largely been ignored, perhaps because he was "source hunting" in a somewhat vague way and because most of the parallels he found concern things that would have been more readily accessible to Milton in Bible commentaries; it does seem unlikely that Milton would have read the rare manuscripts of these plays. But without attempting to posit any one mystery play as a direct source for Milton's epic, it could still be argued that the early continental and English biblical dramas dealing with the temptation are in form and content closer than anything else now known to Milton's poem. I am convinced that Milton was aware of the tradition.

Milton had, we know, some familiarity with the decayed form of medieval biblical drama that still survived in his lifetime as "the motions"—puppet shows. If he did not have access to the manuscripts of the English mystery plays, he could have come in contact with the form when he was on the Continent; for it survived in isolated pockets there for quite a long time. In fact, the Oberammergau Passion Play did not begin its performances until well into the seventeenth century.

In English, John Bale's play "The Temptation of Our Lord" was in print and, as the early nineteenth-century editor Todd suggested, may have influenced Milton. Finally, Milton could certainly have read at least one of the continental mystery plays dealing with the temptation, Jean Michel's *Le Mystère de la Passion,* which had been printed a large number of times during the late fifteenth and early sixteenth centuries.[4]

Though Michel's play is the most interesting of the early plays dealing with the temptation, I have never before seen it mentioned in connection with *Paradise Regained.*[5] This play, however, draws together more of the same traditions about the temptation that Milton employed than any of the other literary analogues suggested by scholars; and, in addition to such specific parallels, Michel in his play has created a Satan whose subtlety and whose penchant for scholastic disputation is surpassed only by Milton's own Satan. As is conventional in the treatment of this episode in literature, Michel follows the order of the temptations in Matthew rather than in Luke. But there are, besides the parallel events that come from the story as given in the Bible, many specific points of contact, not all of major significance to be sure, but great enough in number to indicate that both Milton and Michel were working within the same tradition and toward similar ends.

To cite some of the most obvious parallels: Both Michel and Milton add to the Bible story by including lamentations of Mary worrying about her missing son. Both Marys look forward to changes and sorrows to come:

> O mon filz, pence qui je suis,
> te souvienge des grands ennuys
> que pour toy porte! . . .
> Je sçay que ta vie sera brefve
> et que tu n'auras paix ne tresve
> ob tes hayneux.
> Mon filz, mon vray Dieu glorïeux,
> te es tu ja tiré vers les lieux
> ou suffrir doye?
>
> (Oh my son, think who I am
> remember the great sorrows
> I bear for you. . . .

I know that your life will be short
and that you will know neither peace nor truce
because of those that hate you.
My son, my true and glorious God,
have you already been drawn toward the places
where you are to suffer?)[6]

Both the play and Milton's epic include an extra-biblical temptation of "learning" embodied within one of the given biblical temptations. Milton's Satan offers Christ the learning of Athens; Michel's Satan dresses as a learned doctor for the temptation on the pinnacle of the temple, flatters Christ for his knowledge—Michel's devil is impressed that Christ knows Latin and Hebrew!—and tries to persuade Christ to abuse his role as priest in giving the people a false example by challenging God to save him. (Satan's three disguises in Michel are those of a hermit, a doctor, and a king, in which garments he tempts Christ under the triple equation of his roles—prophet, priest, and king.)

Both Michel's and Milton's Satans offer Christ the kingdoms of the world because they believe Christ's victory will be a military rather than a spiritual one and because they believe that Jesus, as a poor man, will be tempted by an offer of the means to his supposed ends. Both Satans claim that they in fact are the real owners of the world.

Je suis seigneur de tout le monde
et seigneur de tous terrïens;
soubz ma puissante main je tiens,
par auctorité souveraine,
quasi toute nature humaine.
J'ay subjectz, vassaulx et soudars;
j'ay gens a moy de toutes par:
tous sont mes subjectz, vifs et mors.
Je possede tous lesthesors
qui sortirent jamaiz de mine
et, bref, je preside et domine
sur tout le monde, bas et hault.
Et, pour ce, pence combien vault
le bien que je te veuil donner.

(I am the lord of the whole world
and lord of all earthlings;
I hold under my powerful hand
with sovereign authority
(as it were) all human nature.
I have subjects, vassals and soldiers,
and my people are everywhere;
all are my subjects, living and dead.
I possess all treasures
that ever came from a mine
and, in short, I preside over and rule
the whole world, high and low.
And therefore think of the worth
of the good I wish to give you.)

                    (Michel, lines 3035–3048;
                        cf. *P. R.* IV, 155–169.)

Both works include similar catalogues of the Old Testament types
that foreshadow Christ's wandering in the wilderness (Michel, lines
2784–2803; *P. R.* I, 351–355 and Christ's dream, *P. R.* II, 260–278). Both
works show Satan in a physical drop after the final temptation.

Je suis vaincu, je ne puis riens;
en mon fait n'a point de recours.
Je m'en voys en enfer le cours
plonger au fons de la chaudiere.

(I am vanquished, I can do nothing;
there is no recourse in my case.
I exit along the route to hell
to plunge to the bottom of the kettle.)

                    (Michel, lines 3081–3084.)

Both works include extra-biblical scenes in heaven and hell, and both
works end the story of the temptations with a return by Jesus to
Mary—as does the prose treatment in the pseudo-Bonaventura's *Life
of Christ,* which probably lies behind this dramatic tradition.

The characterization of Satan is, as I have said, also similar in the
two authors, though Michel's Satan is much more of a medieval demon
and far more easily thwarted than Milton's. The subtlety of which

Michel's Satan is capable, however, displays itself in speeches such as
the following:

> Jheses, dy moy quoy te sert
> que ainsi te tiens en ce desert
> sans estre de Dieu appelé?
> Ton esp(e)ril te y a compellé
> pour faire austere penitence;
> mais as tu faict aucunne offence
> si grefve que, pour satisfaire,
> fault telle penitence faire
> et en si grande austerité?
> Nenny, car, a la verite,
> tu ne es ne larron murtrier
> ne sodomite ne putier,
> ydolatre ne faulx tesmoing;
> par quoy ja ne te fust besoing
> d'avoir tel jeune commencé,
> veu que tu n'as rien offencé
> vers Dieu, vers quelque ung ou quelque une.
> De quoy te peult servir ce jeune?
>
> (Jesus, tell me what use it is to you
> to abide here in this desert
> without having been called by God?
> Your spirit has driven you here
> to make an austere penance;
> but have you committed any sin
> so bad that, to redress it,
> you must do such penance
> and in such strict austerity?
> Of course not; for, in truth,
> you are neither a murderous thief
> nor a sodomite nor a whoremonger
> nor an idolater nor false witness.
> Why did you feel it necessary
> to start such a fast
> seeing that you have in no way offended
> either God or any man or woman?
> Of what use can this fast be to you?)
>
> (Michel, lines 2729–2746.)

This speech immediately precedes the temptation to turn stones into bread. Michel's Satan also uses flattery in a way similar to Milton's. As for the characterization of Michel's Jesus, he is what he is in Milton and in all of the mystery plays that deal with this theme—the quiet, long-suffering Christ who is capable of momentary anger perhaps, but who feels little need to argue with Satan's sophistries; the words of the Bible are sufficient refutation.

One of the most interesting parallels between the two works is in the treatment of the "identity motif." Most of the mystery plays dealing with the temptation follow those Bible commentaries that interpreted this episode as an attempt on Satan's part to discover Jesus's true identity. Both Michel and Milton, however, present Satans who are simultaneously aware and yet not really aware of who Jesus is. Both Satans are fully convinced that Jesus is the Messiah, but neither is sure exactly what Jesus' relationship to God might be.

> SATHAN: Bref, nous y sommes tous deceuz
> et nous fault conceder en somme
> qu'il est plus en soy que pur homme
> pour deux peremptoyres raisons.
> La priere est car nous sçavons
> que sa mere est vierge et entiere
> en fait, en dit et en maniere. . . .
> L'autre raison est que je nomme
> touchant ceste incarnacion:
> Jhesus, en sa devocion,
> quant il esleve son esp(e)ril
> en Dieu souverain, il ravit
> luy mesme voluntairement
> sa raison, son entendement,
> son ame et toute sa puissance
> et comprend la divine essence
> sans aucune ayde exterïoire. . . .
> LUCIFER: Qui est il donc?
> SATHAN: Je ne sçay quoy
> . . . Dieu nous celle
> la quidité da sa nature.
>
> (SATAN: In short, we are all deceived
> and in summation we must concede

that he is in himself more than purely a man
for two cogent reasons.
The first is that we know
his mother is a virgin and chaste
in deed, word and manner. . . .
The other reason that I give
concerning this incarnation is this:
Jesus, in his devotions,
when he lifts his spirit
to the sovereign God, ravishes
himself voluntarily,
his reason, his understanding,
his soul and all his power,
and comprehends the divine essence
without any exterior aid. . . .
LUCIFER: Who is he then?
SATAN: I do not know.
. . . God is hiding from us
the *quidditas* of his nature.)

(Michel, lines 3159–3165, 3173–
3182, 3189–3190, 3197–3198.)

Michel's Satan does not discover the nature of Christ's *quidditas,* nor,
I believe, does Milton's Satan—though that is currently a matter of
critical debate.

Finally, both works are part of a dramatic tradition that emphasizes
the exemplary nature of Christ's behavior during the temptations. In
the Chester "Temptation" play, for instance, the Expositor steps forward to explain the connection of Christ and the first Adam to the
audience; in both the York and *Ludus Coventriae* plays, Christ's last
words in this episode point up the action as a pattern for every man
to imitate. Milton's Christ expounds Scripture to the devil because, as
in these dramas, he is acting as an example. Michel's Jesus sums up
the meaning of what he has done in this manner:

Sathan, le dyable cauteleux,
faulx incitateur de tous maulx,
m'a tempté par troys grans assaulx.
Humainement ay resisté

a sa maulvaise volunté:
ne soient donc mes imitateurs
impuissans contre le tempteurs;
Dieu ne permect point de sa grace
que la temptacion se face
oultre le povoir singulier
de chascun en particulìer.

(Satan, the plotting devil,
false cause of all evil,
has tempted me in three great assaults.
Humanly I have resisted
his evil will:
therefore my imitators will not be
impotent against tempters;
God in his grace does not permit
that temptation be
beyond the individual power
of each particular person.)
                    (Michel, lines 3285–3295.)

Parker and others have supposed that *Paradise Regained* was origi-
nally written as a drama. (It is, after all, almost completely in dialogue.)
If so, it was a biblical drama in the tradition of Michel's *Mystère de la
Passion.*

Notes

Preface

1. (Oxford: The Clarendon Press, 1984).

2. *The Order of Things: An Archaeology of the Human Sciences* (London: Tavistock Publications, 1970 [French original, *Les mots et les choses*, 1966]), p. 17.

3. (Baltimore and London: Johns Hopkins Press, 1981).

4. Trans. Catherine Porter (London: Routledge and Kegan Paul, 1983 [trans. originally published 1982; French original, 1973]).

Chapter 1: Symbolic Characters . . .

1. *Spaccio* II, quoted in A. O. Lovejoy, *The Great Chain of Being: A Study in the History of an Idea* (New York, Evanston and London: Harper and Row, 1960 [original edition, 1936]), p. 86.

2. *Tractatus Logico-Philosophicus,* 4.0311, quoted in Susanne K. Langer, *Philosophy in a New Key: A Study in the Symbolism of Reason, Rite, and Art* (Cambridge, Mass.: Harvard University Press, 1969 [original edition, 1942]), p. 79.

3. *Sophrosyne: Self-Knowledge and Self-Restraint in Greek Literature* (Ithaca, N.Y.: Cornell University Press, 1966). My following remarks on the history of *sophrosyne* in classical literature are indebted to this study.

4. On the history of attitudes toward Ulysses see: W. B. Stanford, *The Ulysses Theme: A Study in the Adaptability of a Traditional Hero* (Oxford: Basil Blackwell, second edition, 1963 [original edition, 1954]); M. I. Finley, *The World of Odysseus* (London: Chatto and Windus, second edition, 1977 [original edition, 1956]); W. B. Stanford and J. V. Luce, *The Quest for Ulysses* (New York and Washington: Prager, 1974).

5. *European Literature and the Latin Middle Ages,* trans. Willard R. Trask (London: Routledge and Kegan Paul, 1953 [German original, 1948]), p. 173.

6. *Collected Shorter Poems, 1927–1957* (London: Faber and Faber, 1969 [original edition, 1966]), p. 147. The same attitude prevails in Homer, as E. M. W. Tillyard has said: "Homer is always aware of the two opposing values of honour through strife and the cruel sacking of cities, and of domestic and civil order. . . . But he accepts or puts up with it, and does not worry." (*The English Epic and its Background* [London: Chatto and Windus, 1954], p. 39).

7. *The Descent from Heaven: A Study in Epic Continuity* (New Haven and London: Yale University Press, 1963), p. 15.

8. On the development of the Christian hero see: *Concepts of the Hero in the Middle Ages and the Renaissance: Papers of the Fourth and Fifth Annual Conferences of the Center for Medieval and Early Renaissance Studies, State University of New York at Binghamton 2–3 May 1970, 1–2 May 1971,* eds. Norman T. Burns and Christopher J. Reagan (Albany: State University of New York Press, 1975). The paper

in this collection by Bernard F. Huppé speaks of "the antithesis between the heroic and the saintly as ideals" (p. 8) and the problems this presented for medieval writers. R. G. Bolger writes of Erasmus's condemnation of war as producing a new type of Christian hero, and John M. Steadman's paper stresses "the ambiguous and controversial relationship between the aesthetic aims of heroic poetry and its moral or religious ends" (p. 149). On John Milton's transformation of the epic hero see: Merritt Y. Hughes, "The Christ of *Paradise Regained* and the Renaissance Heroic Tradition," *Studies in Philology* 35 (1938), 254–277; Frank Kermode, "Milton's Hero," *Review of English Studies* N.S. 4 (1953), 317–330; and John M. Steadman, *Milton and the Renaissance Hero* (Oxford: Clarendon Press, 1967).

9. *The Oxford Book of Modern Verse 1892–1935* (Oxford: The Clarendon Press, 1936), p. xxxiv.

10. A. L. Rowse, *The Elizabethan Renaissance: The Cultural Achievement* (London: Sphere Books, 1974 [original edition, 1972]), p. 376.

11. *Elizabethan and Metaphysical Imagery: Renaissance Poetic and Twentieth-Century Critics* (Chicago and London: University of Chicago Press, 1947), p. 26.

12. *Ben Jonson,* ed. C. H. Herford, Percy and Evelyn Simpson; Volume 8 (Oxford: The Clarendon Press, 1947), 638–639.

13. See Winthrop Wetherbee, *Platonism and Poetry in the Twelfth Century: The Literary Influence of the School of Chartres* (Princeton, N.J.: Princeton University Press, 1972).

14. Students of literature working in this area owe most to the well-known studies of renaissance art theory by Erwin Panofsky, Edgar Wind, and E. H. Gombrich. I have also found the following books particularly useful: Don Cameron Allen, *Mysteriously Meant: The Rediscovery of Pagan Symbolism and Allegorical Interpretation in the Renaissance* (Baltimore, Md.: Johns Hopkins Press, 1970); Ernst Cassirer, *The Platonic Renaissance in England,* trans. James P. Pettegrove (Austin, Texas: University of Texas Press, 1953 [German original, 1932]) and *The Individual and the Cosmos in Renaissance Philosophy,* trans. Mario Domandi (Oxford: Basil Blackwell, 1952); G. L. Finney, *Musical Backgrounds for English Literature: 1580–1650* (New Brunswick, N.J.: Rutgers University Press, 1962); *Silent Poetry: Essays in numerological analysis,* ed. Alastair Fowler (London: Routledge and Kegan Paul, 1970); Alastair Fowler, *Triumphal Forms: Structural Patterns in Elizabethan Poetry* (Cambridge: Cambridge University Press, 1970); S. K. Heninger, Jr., *Touches of Sweet Harmony: Pythagorean Cosmology and Renaissance Poetics* (San Marino, Calif.: Huntington Library, 1974); John Hollander, *The Untuning of the Sky: Ideas of Music in English Poetry 1500–1700* (Princeton, N.J.: Princeton University Press, 1961); Maren-Sofie Røstvig, *The Hidden Sense and Other Essays* (Oslo: Universitetsforlaget; New York: Humanities Press, 1963); Jean Seznec, *The Survival of the Pagan Gods: The Mythological Tradition and its Place in Renaissance Humanism and Art,* trans. Barbara F. Sessions (Princeton, N.J.: Princeton University Press, 1972 [French original, 1940]); Leo Spitzer, *Classical and Christian Ideas of World Harmony: Prolegomena to an Interpretation of the Word "Stimung",* ed. Anna G. Hatcher (Baltimore, Md.: Johns Hopkins Press, 1963 [original in *Traditio,* 1944–1945]); D. P. Walker, *The Ancient Theology: Studies in Christian Platonism from the Fifteenth to the Eighteenth Century* (Ithaca, N.Y.: Cornell University Press, 1972) and *Spiritual*

and Demonic Magic From Ficino to Campanella (London: Alec Tiranti, 1967 [original edition, 1958]); and the works of Frances A. Yates.

15. I cite the first English translation: *Three Books of Occult Philosophy, written by Henry Cornelius Agrippa of Nettesheim, Counseller to Charles the Fifth, Emperor of Germany: and Judge of the Prerogative Court* (London, 1651). Thomas Vaughan described Agrippa as his "Author" and declared:

> Next to God I owe all that I have unto Him. Why should I be ashamed to confess it? He was, Reader, By Extraction, Noble. By Religion a Protestant. . . . For his Course of Life, a man famous in his person both for Actions of war, and peace. A Favorit to the greatest Princes of his Time, and the just wonder of all learned men. Lastly He was One that carried himself above the Miseries he was born to, and made fortune know, Man might be her Master. (*Anthroposophia Theomagica; or A Discourse of the Nature of Man and his state after death* [London, 1650], pp. 50–51.)

See also Vaughan's "To the Reader" in *Anima Magica Abscondita or A Discourse of the Universal Spirit of Nature* (London, 1650).

16. See Richard D. Jordan, *The Temple of Eternity: Thomas Traherne's Philosophy of Time* (Port Washington, N.Y. and London: Kennikat Press, 1972).

17 From the "Life of Agrippa," which was prefaced to the 1651 translation of *Three Books of Occult Philosophy* by the translator, John French.

18. See John MacQueen, *Allegory* (London: Methuen and Co., 1970), p. 7.

19. (New York: Oxford University Press, 1958 [original edition, 1936]), pp. 44–45. A similar view of the difference between allegory and symbol is put forward by J. Huizinga in *The Waning of the Middle Ages,* trans. F. Hopman (Harmondsworth, England: Penguin Books, 1976 [original edition, 1924]):

> Symbolism expresses a mysterious connexion between two ideas, allegory gives a visible form to the conception of such a connexion. Symbolism is a very profound function of the mind, allegory is a superficial one. It aids symbolic thought to express itself, but endangers it at the same time by substituting a figure for a living idea. The force of the symbol is easily lost in the allegory. (p. 197.)

Both views are products of the flowering of Symbolist poetry, and both reflect the general over-simplification and depreciation of allegory in the early twentieth century. Lewis himself suggests a more pluralistic view of allegory in *Studies in Medieval and Renaissance Literature* (Cambridge: Cambridge University Press, 1966), p. 160.

E. M. W. Tillyard seems to have been among the first modern critics to recognize the ineluctable modality of renaissance allegory:

> All but the simplest allegory (I mean when it has any literary value) tends to grow complicated and . . . we should think of it not as a cool rhetorical substitution but as allied to the medieval impulse to stratify existence, not, like the classical Greeks, choosing a fixed position and approximating everything to it, but recognizing several positions and passing to and fro between them. (*The English Epic and its Background,* p. 142.)

The notion of "polysemeous meaning" in relation to the symbol is also important in Northrop Frye's *Anatomy of Criticism: Four Essays* (Princeton, N.J.: Princeton University Press, 1957), but it is robbed of all usefulness when Frye radically redefines the word "symbol" to mean "any literary structure that can be isolated for critical attention" (p. 71). The older idea of renaissance allegory as a relatively simple, two-level form has survived and may be found in Angus Fletcher's lengthy study, *Allegory: The Theory of a Symbolic Mode* (Ithaca, N.Y.: Cornell University Press, 1964): "Allegories are based on parallels between two levels of being that correspond to each other, the one supposed by the reader, the other literally present in the fable" (p. 113). Barbara Seward believed that the symbol's "ability to imply indefinite levels" made it different from allegory (*The Symbolic Rose* [New York: Columbia University Press, 1960], pp. 3–4). The close relation between symbol and allegory was perceived by W. L. Renwick in his 1925 study *Edmund Spenser: An Essay on Renaissance Poetry*, and it has recently been elaborately worked out, with a focus on the polysemy of words themselves, by Maureen Quilligan in *The Language of Allegory: Defining the Genre* (Ithaca and London: Cornell University Press, 1979). Quilligan also points out the encyclopedic nature of allegory and the way in which the Bible serves as a "pretext" for all Christian allegory. Michael Murrin comments on Neoplatonic aspects of the symbolism in renaissance allegory in *The Veil of Allegory: Some Notes Toward a Theory of Allegorical Rhetoric in the English Renaissance* (Chicago: University of Chicago Press, 1969).

20. *Spenser's Allegory: The Anatomy of Imagination* (Princeton, N.J.: Princeton University Press, 1976), p. 61. In arguing against Graham Hough's distinction between ideas and the images used to clothe them, she notes that in the Renaissance "'ideas' and visible objects all belong to the same universe and are elements in the Providential scheme of Creation" (p. 28).

21. p. xiv, et passim.

22. John Erskine Hankins, for example, says:

Spenser's characters become real people for him as well as for his readers, though he had planned them originally as figures like those in a morality play, representing abstract ideas. At such moments he pictures them as human beings in human situations; his interest in personality supplants his interest in allegorical portrayals. (*Source and Meaning in Spenser's Allegory: A Study of the Faerie Queene* [Oxford: Clarendon Press, 1971], p. 18.)

Hankins cites Paul Alpers and Edwin Honig as in agreement with this theory of intermittent allegory. In the seventeenth century there is evidence of an opposite point of view: Henry Reynolds, in 1632, speaks of "some good judgements" that have wished Spenser, in *The Faerie Queene*, "had therein been a little freer of his fiction, and not so close rivetted to his Morall" (*Mythomystes*, p. 8.)

23. *Elizabethan and Metaphysical Imagery*, p. 77.

24. Cf. Paul Ricoeur on the multiple interpretations of parables in "Biblical Hermeneutics: The Specificity of Religious Language," *Semeia* 4 (1975), 134.

25. (New York: Columbia University Press, 1955), p. 11.

26. *The Transformations of Allegory* (London and Boston: Routledge and Kegan Paul, 1974), p. 53.

27. *S/Z,* trans. Richard Miller (London: Jonathan Cape, 1975 [French original, 1970]), p. 20.

28. *The Philosophy of Symbolic Forms; Volume Two: Mythical Thought,* trans. Ralph Manheim (New Haven: Yale University Press, 1955 [German original, 1925]), p. 36.

29. *Myths, Dreams and Mysteries: The Encounter Between Contemporary Faiths and Archaic Realities,* trans. Philip Mairet (London: Harvill Press, 1960 [French original, 1957]), p. 15.

30. *Images and Symbols: Studies in Religious Symbolism,* trans. Philip Mairet (London: Harvill Press, 1961 [French original, 1952]), p. 15. His italics.

31. A distinction made by Rhodes Dunlap, who supports "open" form in "The Allegorical Interpretation of Renaissance Literature," *PMLA* 82 (1967), 42.

32. Cf. Thomas P. Roche, Jr., *The Kindly Flame: A Study of the Third and Fourth Books of Spenser's Faerie Queene* (Princeton, N.J.: Princeton University Press, 1964): "It [allegory] postulates a verbal universe at every point correspondent with the physical world in which we live, that is, a Realistic view of language" (p. 7). Allegory generally fails to respond to modern literary theory because of this kind of realism; in addition, as Maureen Quilligan has said, "In dealing with allegorical narrative, a reading cannot escape the text's historical intentionality" (*Milton's Spenser: The Politics of Reading* [Ithaca, N.Y.: Cornell University Press, 1983], p. 26), her remark derives from Foucault.

33. *Philosophy in a New Key,* p. 284.

34. *Spenser and Literary Pictorialism* (Princeton, N.J.: Princeton University Press, 1972), p. 67. Robert Scholes and Robert Kellog, though they assume the old dualism of a physical/abstract split in allegory, offer a similar defense of the importance of the phenomenal in allegory:

> Late medieval and Renaissance artists obviously enjoyed representing the social and physical types of which they were becoming empirically aware and at the same time illustrating through these representational images the essences and universals of abstract ethical and theological thought. (*The Nature of Narrative* [New York: Oxford University Press, 1966], p. 143.)

35. *Allegorical Imagery: Some Mediaeval Books and Their Posterity* (Princeton, N.J.: Princeton University Press, 1966), p. 37.

36. Roland Barthes, in one of his more traditionalist moments, said:

> It is under the pressure of History and Tradition that the possible modes of writing for a given writer are established.... Writing still remains full of the recollection of previous usages, for language is never innocent: words have a second-order memory which mysteriously persists in the midst of new meanings. (*Writing Degree Zero,* trans. Annette Lavers and Colin Smith [London: Jonathan Cape, 1967 (French original, 1953)], p. 22.)

37. "How Myths Die," *New Literary History* 5 (1974 [French original, 1971]), 269.

38. "The Metaphoric Process as Cognition, Imagination, and Feeling," *Critical Inquiry* 5 (1978), 146.

39. *S/Z,* p. 67. Cf. Martin Price, "The Other Self: Thoughts about Character

in the Novel" in *Imagined Worlds: Essays on some English Novels and Novelists in Honour of John Butt,* eds. Maynard Mack and Ian Gregor (London: Methuen & Co., 1968), pp. 279–299.

Chapter 2: Spencer's Image of Temperance

1. *Orlando Furioso (The Frenzy of Orlando): A Romantic Epic by Ludovico Ariosto,* Part One, trans. Barbara Reynolds (Harmondsworth: Penguin Books, 1975), p. 257.

2. *Philosophy in a New Key: A Study in the Symbolism of Reason, Rite, and Art* (Cambridge, Mass.: Harvard University Press, 1969; original edition, 1942), p. 203.

3. *The Allegorical Temper: Vision and Reality in Book II of Spenser's Faerie Queene* (New Haven: Yale University Press, 1957), pp. 18 et seq. Maureen Quilligan has since claimed that Guyon is tempted "by curiosity if by nothing else," though she offers no evidence for this. (*Milton's Spenser: The Politics of Reading* [Ithaca, N.Y.: Cornell University Press, 1983], p. 55.)

4. See Ernest Sirluck, "Milton Revises *The Faerie Queene,*" *Modern Philology* 48 (1950), 90–96. Sirluck's interpretation of the causes for Milton's mistake depends upon a reading of the Palmer different from my own, as does the interpretation offered by Karen L. Edwards, "On Guile and Guyon in *Paradise Lost* and *The Faerie Queene,*" *Philological Quarterly* 64 (1985), 83–97.

5. *Complete Prose Works of John Milton:* Volume II, 1643–1648 (New Haven: Yale University Press, 1959), pp. 515–516.

6. For the text of *The Faerie Queene,* I use the J. C. Smith edition as reproduced in Edmund Spenser, *The Faerie Queene,* ed. A. C. Hamilton (London and New York: Longman, 1977). I modernize u/v and sometimes i/y and i/j.

7. In this I am in general agreement with Roger G. Swearingen, "Guyon's Faint," *Studies in Philology* 74 (1977), 165–185. See also Carl Robinson Sonn, "Sir Guyon in the Cave of Mammon," *Studies in English Literature* 1 (1961), 17–30. For a view of Guyon as divesting himself of pride in the Cave see Peter D. Stambler, "The Development of Guyon's Christian Temperance," *ELR* 7 (1977), 67. All recent discussions of Guyon in the Cave are indebted to Frank Kermode's "The Cave of Mammon" in *Elizabethan Poetry,* Stratford-Upon-Avon Studies 2 (London: Edward Arnold, 1960), pp. 151–173.

8. *Infernal Triad: The Flesh, the World, and the Devil in Spenser and Milton* (Princeton: Princeton University Press, 1974), p. 76.

9. Nelson, *The Poetry of Edmund Spenser: A Study* (New York: Columbia University Press, 1963), p. 196; Evans, "The Fall of Guyon," *ELH* 28 (1961), 218.

10. Sonn much exaggerates Guyon's situation when he writes: "Stygian laws . . . afford Guyon the alternatives of yielding to Mammon, and dying in the 'greedy gripe' of the fiend; or not, and dying of hunger and the want of sleep" (p. 26). This ignores the law cited in stanza 66, that no human could be kept below ground longer than three days by Mammon. The literal importance of Guyon's hunger is noted by Quilligan in *Milton's Spenser* and by Stephen Greenblatt, *Renaissance Self-Fashioning: From More to Shakespeare* (Chicago: University of Chicago Press, 1980), p. 173. Thomas E. Maresca, while recognizing the importance of the human body in Book II, still moralizes the faint as the result of "lingering too long in the contemplation of material things" (*Three English Epics: Studies of Troilus*

and Criseyde, The Faerie Queen, and Paradise Lost [Lincoln: University of Nebraska Press, 1979], p. 37.

11. *Source and Meaning in Spenser's Allegory: A Study of The Faerie Queene* (Oxford: Clarendon Press, 1971), p. 29.

12. This is discussed at greater length in the chapter on *Paradise Regained*, below. The heavy use of biblical echoes in Book II has been examined by Peter Stambler, "The Development of Christian Temperance in Book II of *The Faerie Queene*" (Syracuse University Ph.D. thesis, 1974).

13. I owe this suggestion to A. J. Magill, "Spenser's Guyon and the Mediocrity of the Elizabethan Settlement," *Studies in Philology* 67 (1970), 170; Magill, however, sees the name only as an anagram of that of Bishop Young of Rochester. I should add here that, because of the kind of symbolism involved, identifications such as this in no way exclude other meanings; Spenser may well have chosen to use this anagram rather than call his hero Youth because of the verbal association of "Guyon" with the river Gihon (Alastair Fowler, "The River Guyon," *Modern Language Notes* 70 [1960], 289–292) and because of associations with romance heroes named Guion, particularly the hero of that name in the *Melusine* of Jean D'Arras, who is a sixteen-year-old beardless youth.

14. *Orlando Furioso* I, 1 (p. 117).

15. "'Religious Reuerence Doth Buriall Teene': Christian and Pagan in *The Faerie Queene*, II, i–ii," *Review of English Studies* (n.s.) 30 (1979), 142.

16. This reaction, which anticipates his faint at the end of the Cave of Mammon episode, is not at all an unchristian turning aside "from the sight of the dead Amavia" as Isabel G. MacCaffrey suggested in *Spenser's Allegory: The Anatomy of Imagination* (Princeton, N.J.: Princeton University Press, 1976), p. 232; literally, Guyon moves toward Amavia rather than turning away from her in the narrative action, and figuratively, he shares her death through a catharsis.

17. *A Discourse of Civill Life: Containing the Ethike part of Morall Philosophie* (London, 1606).

18. *Elizabethan Revenge Tragedy, 1587–1642* (Princeton, N.J.: Princeton University Press, 1940), p. 11.

19. A. D. S. Fowler, "The Image of Mortality: *The Faerie Queene*, II, i–ii," *Huntington Library Quarterly* 24 (1961), 107.

20. In addition, Phaedra's stabbing of herself over the body of the dead Hippolytus in Seneca's play may be a precedent for the staging of the death of Amavia in Spenser's poem.

21. For a different view of the relationship between Hamlet and Guyon, see Abbie Findlay Potts, *Shakespeare and the Faerie Queene* (Ithaca, N.Y.: Cornell University Press, 1958), pp. 128–129.

22. (Dublin, 1633), p. 4.

23. W. B. Stanford, *The Ulysses Theme: A Study in the Adaptability of a Traditional Hero* (Oxford: Basil Blackwell, 1963; original edition, 1954), p. 125. Red Crosse and Una in Book I have recently been seen as related to the "good" Ulysses by Thomas H. Cain, *Praise in the Faerie Queene* (Lincoln: University of Nebraska Press, 1978), pp. 82–83.

24. An exception to this might be the pummelling Guyon receives from Furor after Guyon "overthrew himselfe unwares" in iv: 8; but here again the poem

contains a direct statement that Guyon has made a mistake, and an immediate correction of it. The Cave of Mammon episode contains neither.

25. *On the Cave of the Nymphs in the Thirteenth Book of the Odyssey,* trans. Thomas Taylor (London: John M. Watkins, 1917), p. 11.

26. Spenser's joining of Pilate with Tantalus has troubled recent critics, who have declared themselves unaware of a tradition linking Pilate with avarice; yet Arnold Williams as long ago as 1950 published a book in which he demonstrated just such an association: *The Characterization of Pilate in the Towneley Plays* (East Lansing, Michigan: Michigan State University Press). The Pilate of this tradition stole money from the temple treasury, played dice for Christ's robe and, when he lost, appropriated it anyway, obtained a field from a squire by tricking him into handing over the deed, and took bribes before his judgment of Christ (see Williams, esp. pp. 13, 29, and 44). Tantalus in a garden is a symbol of *vanitas* according to Erasmus's *Adagia* (cited in James Nohrnberg, *The Analogy of The Faerie Queene* [Princeton, N.J.: Princeton University Press, 1976], p. 698).

27. In comparisons such as this, differences (when not simply discontinuities) can be as important as similarities: Ulysses outside the Cave of the Nymphs sits down with Minerva beside a sacred olive tree; Guyon, in the depths of the Cave of Mammon, refuses to sit down on a bench near a diabolic apple tree—Mammon is a false Wisdom.

28. *The Works of Edmund Spenser: a Variorum Edition,* ed. Edwin Greenlaw, *The Faerie Queene, Book II* (Baltimore, Md.: Johns Hopkins, 1933), p. 366.

29. *Variorum,* p. 301.

30. Philippa Tristram has epitomized the main elements of the medieval form of this tradition in *Figures of Life and Death in Medieval English Literature* (London: Paul Elek, 1976).

31. The common identification of the Palmer as Reason seems to me to be so reductive as to be almost wrong. When Guyon is separated from the Palmer, he is not—as has been supposed—separated from reason; indeed, he gives some of his most impressive displays of reason then. When he must face Phaedria on his own, Guyon is, according to the narrator, "wise, and warie of her will" (vi: 26); and in that same Canto, when he is accused of cowardice by Atin, Guyon without his Palmer is able to control himself "with strong reason" (40). J. C. Maxwell's suggestion that Guyon should not have stepped so hastily into Phaedria's boat without waiting for the Palmer to stop him ("Guyon, Phaedria, and the Palmer," *Review of English Studies,* [n.s.] 5 [1954], 388–390) is rather discounted by the fact that, far from advising Guyon to leave the boat, the Palmer is forced by Phaedria to stay out. Guyon's discussions with Mammon are the most extended examples of Guyon's ability to meet temptation with reason in the book; and there is a grand piece of irony when, at the one point in the episode when Guyon's passions begin to get out of control, Mammon himself steps in to play the role of the Palmer "And counseld him abstaine from perilous fight" (vii: 42). On the other hand, the powers of the Palmer exceed anything that might be called reason. He can interpret mysterious symbols and perceive the true natures of non-human characters; he receives guidance in finding Guyon from an angel; he has a staff with which he

can calm the waves of the sea and subdue monsters, a staff made of the same wood as *"Caduceus* the rod of *Mercury"* (xii: 41). As the rod of Mercury was a symbol of Hermetic wisdom, it is possible that the Palmer represents something higher than even the wisdom of age and experience, and is in some ways an anticipation of Shakespeare's Prospero. A similar charge of over-reductiveness also applies to other interpretations of the Palmer as prudence (Upton's view) and as sobriety (John Hughes).

32. Guyon is described to the Palmer as "thy pupill" by the Angel in viii: 7; the Palmer's role as a teacher is specifically described in iv: 2.

33. Samuel C. Chew, *The Pilgrimage of Life* (New Haven: Yale University Press, 1962), p. 164. The use of "avatars" and "antitypes," characters who parallel and contrast with the main characters in Spenser, is discussed in Ronald Arthur Horden, *The Unity of the Faerie Queene* (Athens: University of Georgia Press, 1978).

34. This manipulation of reader psychology in Canto xii is explored in Arlene N. Okerlund, "Spenser's Wanton Maidens: Reader Psychology and the Bower of Bliss," *PMLA* 88 (1973), 62–68. In attempting to apply a modern psychology to this event, however, Stephen Greenblatt, in *Renaissance Self-Fashioning,* misses Spenser's point almost completely.

35. Rosemond Tuve has said, "If large portions of a work have to be covered with blotting paper while we read our meaning in what is left, we are abusing instead of using the images" (*Allegorical Imagery: Some Medieval Books and Their Posterity* [Princeton, N.J.: Princeton University Press, 1966], p. 234).

36. See Brian Crossley and Paul Edwards, "Spenser's Bawdy: A Note on *The Fairy Queen* 2.6," *Papers on Language and Literature* 9 (1973), 314–319.

37. I cannot share John Hollander's view that the musical "mingling" that goes on here is manifestly unwholesome. In another context this stanza might stand as an image of man's harmony with nature or of the consonance of all categories of music. Only the context leads one to suspect that such things as the "base murmure" of the water have moral connotations. ("Spenser and the Mingled Measure," *English Literary Renaissance* 1 [1971], 226–238).

38. This is not meant to suggest any inconsistency in Spenser's characterization of Guyon. His behavior in Book III is not out of keeping with that of Book II, but he appears a lesser figure because he comes in contact with an idea that is superior to his youth, a symbol of female love beyond anything he has yet experienced. He, like his virginal female counterpart Belphoebe (who also avoids fighting in Book II), "had not yet felt *Cupides* wanton rage" (ix: 18), a remark made of Guyon's *alter-psyche* Alma. There is nothing to indicate at the beginning of Book III that temperance is a lesser virtue; youth simply proves to be young.

39. Trans. Mariella Cavalchini and Irene Samuel (Oxford: Clarendon Press, 1973), p. 5.

40. *Allegorical Imagery,* p. 106. On the interpretation of Spenser as the building of a simultaneous whole, see Humphrey Tonkin, "Some Notes on Myth and Allegory in the *Faerie Queene,"* *Modern Philology* 70 (1973), 291–301. For a thorough examination of how the analogies between books work to establish this whole, see the study by James Nohrnberg, cited in note 26 above.

41. *Elizabethan Critical Essays,* ed. G. Gregory Smith (Oxford: Oxford University Press, 1904), vol. 2, p. 202.

Chapter 3: "Harmony Was She"

1. John Donne, *The Sermons of John Donne,* ed. George R. Potter and Evelyn M. Simpson, IV (Berkeley and Los Angeles: University of California Press, 1959), 98; cf. *Sermons* VII (1954), 80.

2. On Donne's employing a single death as a universal type, compare the following:

> We may better discern our selves *in singulis,* then *in omnibus;* better by taking ourselves in pieces, then altogether, we understand the frame of mans body, better when we see him naked, than apparrelled, howsoever; and better by seeing him cut up, than by seeing him do any exercise alive; one desection, one Anatomy teaches more of that, than the marching, or drilling of a whole army of living men. (*Sermons* I [1953], 273)

All students of Donne's *Anniversaries* owe a great debt to Barbara Kiefer Lewalski's *Donne's Anniversaries and the Poetry of Praise: The Creation of a Symbolic Mode* (Princeton: Princeton University Press, 1973). The following study shares that indebtedness while offering an implicit counter-argument against one of her main claims: that Elizabeth Drury in Donne's *Anniversaries* is not used as a Neoplatonic symbol.

3. *De Veritate,* trans. Meyrick H. Carré (Bristol: University of Bristol, 1937), pp. 327, 330.

4. Trans. E. R. Dodds (Oxford: Clarendon Press [second edition], 1963), pp. 24–25.

5. Ed. and trans. Michael J. B. Allen (Berkeley and Los Angeles: University of California Press, 1975), pp. 88, 94.

6. *The Philosophie, Commonlie Called, The Morals* (London), p. 1030; sig. Rrrr 5, v.

7. *Marsilio Ficino's Commentary on Plato's Symposium,* trans. Sears Reynolds Jayne (Columbia: University of Missouri Press, 1944), pp. 126–127.

8. ("Englished by Ia. San. Gent. . . . Imprinted at London. . . . 1575." Agrippa's catalogue is based on a similar one in Macrobius's *Commentary on the Dream of Scipio.*

9. *A Woorke Concerning the Trewnesse of the Christian Religion,* trans. Sir Philip Sidney and Arthur Golding (London, 1587), p. 264; sig. R 4, v.

10. It also characterizes his position in other works. In one of his last sermons, preached on Whitsunday, 1628, at St. Paul's, Donne said:

> And yet, here in this world, knowledge is but as the earth, and ignorance as the Sea; there is more sea then earth, more ignorance then knowledge; and as if the sea do gaine in one place, it loses in another, so is it with knowledge too; if new things be found out, as many, and as good, that were knowne before, are forgotten and lost. What Anatomist knowes the body of man thorowly, or what Casuist the soule? (*Sermons* VIII [1956], 255)

11. For Donne's *Anniversaries* and their associated poems I quote the edition of Frank Manley (Baltimore: Johns Hopkins Press, 1963). I have in most instances modernized the use of "u" and "v" and of "i" and "j".

12. Robert S. Jackson, *John Donne's Christian Vocation* (Evanston: Northwestern University Press, 1970), p. 119.

13. It is also seen, by Ficino for example, as the *spiritus mundi*, binding the *anima* to the *corpus mundi*. (See D. P. Walker, *Spiritual and Demonic Magic from Ficino to Campanella* [London: The Warburg Institute, University of London, 1958], pp. 12–13.) There are suggestions in Donne's poems that the soul, or at least its memory, has left something of this spirit behind, saving the world from immediate collapse. Laurence Stapleton links this "Balme" and spirit with the medical theories of Paracelsus ("The Theme of Virtue in Donne's Verse Epistles," *Studies in Philology* 55 [1958], 187–200), though Stapleton rightly sees this Paracelsian imagery being employed by Donne to give concreteness to "the underlying Platonic and Neo-Platonic ideas" (p. 197).

14. The earlier reference to the apotheosis of a queen (line 7) and the subsequent reference to the death of a prince (lines 43–46), combined with the emphasis on the significance of the unstated name, do suggest a relationship between the names of Elizabeth I and Elizabeth Drury, though this is not, I think, one of the most important elements of the symbolic complex. Nor, in spite of its support to a Neoplatonic reading, do I see any need to find a reference to the Tetragrammaton in these lines, as does Frank Manley.

15. As the world is the whole frame of the world, God hath put into it a reproofe, a rebuke, lest it should seem eternall, which is, a sensible decay and age in the whole frame of the world, and every piece thereof. The seasons of the yeare irregular and distempered; the Sun fainter, and languishing; men lesse in stature, and shorter-lived. No addition, but only every yeare, new sorts, new species of wormes, and flies, and sicknesses, which argue more and more putrefaction of which they are engendred. And the Angels of heaven, which did so familiarly converse with men in the beginning of the world, though they may not be doubted to perform to us still their ministeriall assistances, yet they seem so far to have deserted this world, as that they do not appeare to us, as they did to those our Fathers. (*Sermons* VI [1953], 323)

16. Pythagoras, particularly, was himself a "quiet hero":

In all his words and actions, he discovered an inimitable quiet and serenity, not being subdued at any time by anger, or laughter, or emulation, or contention, or any other perturbation or precipitation of conduct; but he dwelt at Samos like some beneficent daemon. (*Iamblichus' Life of Pythagoras,* trans. Thomas Taylor [London: John M. Watkins, 1965], p. 5)

17. *The Poems of Sir John Davies,* ed. Robert Krueger (Oxford: Clarendon Press, 1975), p. 13.

18. That this idea of the ark had a venerable tradition with which Donne's readers would have been familiar is amply demonstrated by Don Cameron Allen in *The Legend of Noah: Renaissance Rationalism in Art, Science and Letters* (Urbana: University of Illinois Press, 1949).

19. *Essays in Divinity,* ed. Evelyn M. Simpson (Oxford: Clarendon Press, 1952), p. 10.

20. "A Note on Donne and Aquinas," *Modern Language Review* 48, 181.

21. *Three Books of Occult Philosophy,* trans. "J. F." (London, 1651), p. 460; sig. Gg, 6v.

22. See contra O. B. Hardison, Jr., *The Enduring Monument: A Study of the Idea of Praise in Renaissance Literary Theory and Practice* (Chapel Hill: University of North Carolina Press, 1962), pp. 163–186. Hardison argues that the primary organization is analytic.

23. Ronald S. Crane, "Anglican Apologetics and The Idea of Progress, 1699–1745," *Modern Philology* 31 (1934), 274–275.

24. *The Works of George Herbert,* ed. F. E. Hutchinson (Oxford: Clarendon Press, 1941), p. 43.

25. As Donne himself says in a sermon, quoting Aquinas, "*Ordo semper dicitur ratione principii: Order alwayes presumes a head.* ... But *the body* speaks not, the *head* does" (IV, 198–199).

26. *The Poetry of Meditation: A Study in English Religious Literature of the Seventeenth Century* (New Haven: Yale University Press, 1962 [original edition, 1954]), p. 242.

27. *Classical and Christian Ideas of World Harmony* (Baltimore: Johns Hopkins Press, 1963 [originally published in *Traditio,* 1944–1945]), pp. 10–11.

28. James Hutton, "Some English Poems in Praise of Music," *English Miscellany* 2 (1951), 8.

29. *Touches of Sweet Harmony: Pythagorean Cosmology and Renaissance Poetics* (San Marino: Huntington Library, 1974), pp. 187–189.

30. *Martianus Capella and the Seven Liberal Arts, Vol. II: The Marriage of Philology and Mercury,* trans. William Harris Stahl and Richard Johnson with E. L. Burge (New York: Columbia University Press, 1977), p. 349.

31. Donne has precedent for the identification of his heroine as both a preservative and the Virgin Mary in some praise given to Queen Elizabeth by John Davies of Hereford:

> Unto a *Mother-maide* we all are bound,
> For bringing forth our *Soule's* preservative;
> Who, for the same, is Queene in *Heaven* Crownd;
> And, sith thou bring'st our *Corpes* conservative,
> We must crown thee in *Earth,* or els, we should
> Do otherwise then *Saints* & *Angels* would.
> (From *The Complete Works of John Davies of Hereford,* Vol. 1, ed. Alexander B. Grosart [Edinburgh University Press: Chertsey Worthies' Library, 1878], *Microcosmos,* p. 5.

32. Hiram Haydn, *The Counter Renaissance* (New York: Charles Scribner's Sons, 1950), p. 13. Haydn does not offer this as a negative criticism.

33. A statement like this inevitably raises the question of whether the Drurys could have been expected to follow the complex symbolic developments and transformations Donne employs in these poems, or whether they would have shared the view of Ben Jonson and some of Donne's lady friends who, for very different

reasons, thought the presentation of the "she" of the poems to be excessive. At the distance of nearly four centuries, however, the Drurys must be given the benefit of the doubt, if for no other reason than that they had the poet readily available for any explanations of the poem they might need.

34. *L. A. Seneca the Philosopher, His Booke of Consolation to Marcia Translated into an English Poem* (London), p. 40.

Chapter 4: "Temperance Invincible"

1. *The Complete Poetical Works of John Milton,* ed. Douglas Bush (Boston: Houghton Mifflin, 1965). All citations of Milton's poetry are from this edition.

2. A major exception is John M. Steadman's *Milton and the Renaissance Hero* (Oxford: Clarendon Press, 1967).

3. For a summary of opinion on *Paradise Regained,* see Arthur E. Barker, "Calm Regained Through Passion Spent: The Conclusions of the Miltonic Effort," in *The Prison and the Pinnacle: Papers to Commemorate the Tercentenary of "Paradise Regained" and "Samson Agonistes" 1671–1971,* ed. Balachandra Rajan (London: Routledge and Kegan Paul, 1973), pp. 3–48. Walter MacKellar, in the introduction to the *Variorum Commentary on the Poems of John Milton.* vol. 4, *Paradise Regained* (London: Routledge and Kegan Paul, 1975) points out passages in *Paradise Regained* that show Christ to have knowledge of his own divinity (see pp. 36–37); none the less, MacKellar maintains that in spite of these repeated assertions of divinity, "Christ in his divine nature cannot be tempted" and thus "it is Christ the *man,* meeting trials on a strictly human level, whom we are to witness" (p. 35). MacKellar does not resolve this apparent contradiction. After the original version of the present chapter was published in *Milton Studies* for 1976, other studies arguing for a reading of *Paradise Regained* as a continuation of *Paradise Lost* appeared, including those by Joan Webber in *Milton and His Epic Tradition* (Seattle: University of Washington Press, 1979), and by Joseph Anthony Wittreich, Jr. in *Visionary Poetics: Milton's Tradition and His Legacy* (San Marino, California: Huntington Library, 1979).

4. Jackson I. Cope, *"Paradise Regained*: Inner Ritual," in *Milton Studies* I, ed. James D. Simmonds (Pittsburgh: University of Pittsburgh Press, 1969), pp. 51–65; Irene Samuel, "The Regaining of Paradise," in *The Prison and the Pinnacle,* pp. 111–134. Thomas O. Sloane reads the poem as a failed debate in which Satan "tries unsuccessfully to turn the action into a debate" but Christ refuses. (*Donne, Milton, and The End of Humanist Rhetoric* [Berkeley: University of California Press, 1985], pp. 249–278.)

5. The classic article on the typology of *Paradise Regained* is that of Northrop Frye ("The Typology of *Paradise Regained," Modern Philology* 53 [1956], 227–238). Because his purposes are different from mine, he refers only briefly to the Adam-Christ relationship. Barbara Kiefer Lewalski discusses the typology in *Milton's Brief Epic: The Genre, Meaning, and Art of "Paradise Regained"* (Providence: Brown University Press, 1966), pp. 164–182 et passim. She feels, however, that emphasis is drawn away from the Adam-Christ figure to point up the Job-Christ typology. But since Job, like Christ, was seen as a reversal of Adam, the references to Job could be taken as a means to reinforce the importance of the original typology.

6. *Luther's Works,* ed. Hilton C. Oswald (St. Louis: Concordia Publishing House, 1973), vol. 28, p. 113.

7. The other commentator was Calton. Both base their judgments on Book I, lines 163–167. They are cited in Henry J. Todd's edition of *The Poetical Works of John Milton* (London, 1809; reprinted, New York, 1970), vol. 5, pp. 26–27. Recently, Louis L. Martz has again presented the poem as "the self-discovery of the hero," while ignoring the passages that show Christ to be illuminated from the first (*Poet of Exile: A Study of Milton's Poetry* [New Haven and London: Yale University Press, 1980], p. 252). A similar view of Christ as the ignorant "would-be redeemer" is offered by George deForest Lord in "Folklore and Myth in *Paradise Regain'd*" (*Poetic Traditions of the English Renaissance,* ed. Maynard Mack and George deForest Lord [New Haven: Yale University Press, 1982], p. 230); however, Lord does see him as an Odysseus figure and "the Ultimately heroic antihero" (p. 248). Andrew Milner sees the poem as dealing with Christ's "personal redemption" and the hero's "self-discovery" delayed until the temptation on the pinnacle (*John Milton and the English Revolution: A Study in the Sociology of Literature* [London: Macmillan, 1981], pp. 167, 178). On the other hand, Sanford Budick has shown that "if Christ may be said to learn or confirm anything, it is that he has nothing to learn because he somehow is or represents the knowledge he would gain" (*The Dividing Muse: Images of Sacred Disjunction in Milton's Poetry* [New Haven: Yale University Press, 1985], p. 130).

8. *"Paradise Regained": The Tradition and the Poem* (1947; reprinted, New York: Russell and Russell, 1962).

9. *Complete Prose Works of John Milton,* Don M. Wolfe, general editor (New Haven: Yale University Press, 1953–   ), vol. 6, ed. Maurice Kelley (1973), pp. 228–229.

10. *A Harmony of the Gospels Matthew, Mark and Luke,* trans. A. W. Morrison (Edinburgh: St. Andrew Press, 1972), vol. 1, p. 135.

11. *Prayers and Other Pieces of Thomas Becon,* ed. Rev. John Ayre (Cambridge: Parker Society, 1844), p. 505. The baptism would also have been important for Milton's poem because baptism was a type of the entrance into paradise. On the place of the Holy Spirit in *Paradise Regained,* see Georgia B. Christopher, *Milton and the Science of the Saints* (Princeton: Princeton University Press, 1982).

12. This change was probably based, as Dr. Newton pointed out in the eighteenth century, on John, chapter 1.

13. (London: Faber and Faber, 1977), p. 416.

14. I cite the facsimile of the 1656 edition, ed. Paul J. Korshin (Gainesville, Fla.: Scholar's Facsimiles and Reprints, 1970).

15. The many definitions that "enthusiasm" has had a. ° surveyed by Susie I. Tucker in *Enthusiasm: A Study in Semantic Change* (Cambridge: Cambridge University Press, 1972).

16. Augustan Reprint Society Publication Number 118, ed. M. V. De Porte (Los Angeles: University of California Press, 1966), p. 1.

17. Ed. Alexander Campbell Fraser, 2nd ed. (New York: Dover, 1959), vol. 2, p. 430.

18. 3rd ed. (London, 1683), p. 38.

19. *The Christen Knighte* in Becon's *Works,* Vol. 3, ed. John Ayre (Cambridge:

Parker Society, 1844), p. 628. The pattern of the debate between Christ and Satan in Milton's poem can also be seen as based on the methods of the Catholic Inquisition, the "demonic theater" of which has been described by Stephen Greenblatt in *Renaissance Self-Fashioning: From More to Shakespeare* (Chicago: University of Chicago Press, 1980).

20. In this I am in agreement with Irene Samuel, "The Regaining of Paradise."

21. For a view that this "also" makes the lines *more* effective dramatically, see Lee Sheridan Cox, "Food-Word Imagery in *Paradise Regained*," *ELH* 28 (1961), 225–243.

22. *Harmony of the Gospels,* vol. 1, p. 135.

23. I am aware of the effort that has been made to group the events of this poem under the "triple equation" of biblical temptations. While Milton may have intended such a grouping to be made, it is more important to observe that he, like some of the Church Fathers, did not feel confined to the belief that Satan offered only those three temptations given in the Bible. Noting each of Satan's attempts separately produces the list I give here. Since I first published this list in *Milton Studies,* it has served as a basis for studies of *Paradise Regained* by Anthony Low ("Milton, *Paradise Regained,* and Georgic," *PMLA* 98 [1983], 152–169), and by Mary Wilson Carpenter ("Milton's Secret Garden: Structural Correspondences Between Michael's Prophecy and *Paradise Regained,*" *Milton Studies* 14 [1980], 153–182).

24. Ed. L. M. Rigollot (Paris and Brussels, 1878), pt. 1, vol. 1, pp. 195–196.

25. *On Christian Doctrine,* II, 16, in *Great Books of the Western World* (Chicago: Encyclopaedia Britannica, 1952), 18: 644–645.

26. Ed. Frances A. Foster (London: Early English Text Society, 1926), pp. 152–153.

27. (London, 1582), fol. 150v; sig. Cc iiii, v.

28. *The Great Exemplar,* in *The Whole Works of the Right Rev. Jeremy Taylor,* ed. Rev. Charles Page Eden (London, 1847), vol. 2, p. 198.

29. "The Quip" in *The Works of George Herbert,* ed. F. E. Hutchinson (Oxford: Clarendon Press, 1941), p. 111.

30. "The Reader's Attitude in *Paradise Regained,*" *PMLA* 85 (1970), 501.

31. The closest parallel in the drama to *Paradise Regained* that I know is the Temptation play in Jean Michel's *Le Mystère de la Passion,* a French play, which, unlike the English mystery plays, was in print (and in many editions) when Milton wrote. It has never, to my knowledge, been noted by previous Milton scholars, and I include at the end of this book an appendix describing it and pointing out its similarities to Milton's epic. An important English precedent that has been noticed but neglected is John Bale's *The Temptation of Our Lord,* the protestant emphasis of which would have made it attractive to Milton. "Baleus Prolocutor" in his prologue makes the same point about learning and knowledge as does Milton's Christ:

> After his baptism, Christ was God's son declared
> By the Father's voice, as ye before have heard;
> Which signifieth to us that we, once baptised,
> Are the sons of God by His gift and reward.

And, because that we should have Christ in regard,
He have unto him the mighty authority
Of his heavenly word, our only teacher to be.

> (*The Dramatic Writings of John Bale,* ed. John S.
> Farmer [London: Early English Drama Society,
> 1907], p. 153.)

Bale's play emphasizes the proper and improper use of "The Scriptures of God, which are the mighty weapon / That Christ left them here, their souls from hell to save" (p. 170), and Bale's devil also has "scripture at hand" though he "wrast it all amiss" (pp. 160–161).

32. Among others are Guyon's and Christ's shared imperviousness to the temptations of lust, their rejection of gifts because of the nature of the giver (*Paradise Regained* II, 321–322) and of money as a way to honor, their desire to "learn and know" (I, 203), and—not minor—the misinterpretation other characters make of their acts of temperance. Cf. also Milton's "swarm of flies in vintage time, / About the wine-press" (IV, 15–16) and Spenser's "swarme of Gnats at eventide / Out of the fennes of Allan" (*Faerie Queene* II, ix. 16—though there are earlier precedents for both) and the parallel use of the Anteas myth in *Paradise Regained* IV and *Faerie Queene* II, xi. The forces of Satan will, according to *Paradise Regained* IV, 629–630, "beg to hide them in a herd of swine," a slanting of the bible story which may reflect Grill's desire to remain a pig in *Faerie Queene* II, xii.

Chapter 5: Unconquered Bloom

1. (Harmondsworth: Penguin Books, 1973 reprint), p. 213. I cite the Penguin edition throughout.

2. (London: Faber and Faber, 1975; original edition, 1939), p. 20.

3. *Literary Origins of Surrealism: A New Mysticism in French Poetry* (London: University of London Press, 1967; original edition, 1947), p. 100.

4. The only extended comparison of Joyce and Spenser that I know of is Edwin Honig's "Hobgoblin or Apollo," *Kenyon Review* 10 (1948), 664–681. My own comparison generally covers different areas than did Honig's, though on two points I am in disagreement with him: I do not believe that "the important thing to note about both works is that the use of classical myth is not central to the meaning of either of them" (p. 666), and I do not agree that Spenser's characters become naturalistic by breaking away from their abstract roles.

5. *Axel's Castle: A Study in the Imaginative Literature of 1870–1930* (London: Collins, 1969; original edition, 1931), p. 165.

6. (New York: Vintage Books, 1952 reprint). Michael Groden, in *Ulysses in Progress* (Princeton, N.J.: Princeton University Press, 1977), has identified the opposing poles of *Ulysses* criticism as represented on the one side by Gilbert and on the other by S. L. Goldberg's *The Classical Temper: A Study of James Joyce's Ulysses* (New York: Barnes and Noble, 1961), with Gilbert primarily interested in symbols and analogies, Goldberg in the drama of human experience à la Leavis. Given Joyce's collaboration with Gilbert, one might say that the two extremes are really Joyce and Goldberg. But, as in the case of most such opposition, the truth rests

in the middle. Both the realistic and symbolic aspects are equally important to the novel and most often are to be found in exactly the same things, though, as Groden points out, the symbols become more important to Joyce from 1919 onward, and most of Goldberg's positive examples come from parts of *Ulysses* written before that date. Goldberg, in making a distinction between the dramatized and the symbolized, is making a split Joyce himself would not have recognized; and his bias leads him to make some rather strange statements about Joyce and his novel: that Joyce "came to see Art as a symbol of moral and social vitality" (p. 34—in spite of all the author said to the contrary); that "Joyce never believed that art represents ideas that can be extraneously formulated" (p. 62—yet Joyce spent a good deal of time formulating the ideas of *Ulysses* for friends and critics); and that though the novel is a symbolic one it is "rather more obviously—a representational novel" (p. 107—though it was not obviously representational to most of the first reviewers). Goldberg's well-known analysis of Stephen's aesthetic theory in *Scylla and Charybdis* clings almost exclusively to the "Rocks" of Joyce's schema entry for this episode: Aristotle. A very even-tempered attempt to formulate a balanced reading, which would include the Whirlpool of Plato, is made by Robert Kellogg in *James Joyce's Ulysses: Critical Essays*, ed. Clive Hart and David Hayman (Berkeley: University of California Press, 1974), pp. 147–179.

7. *James Joyce and the Making of "Ulysses" and other writings* (London: Oxford University Press, 1972).

8. The testing of Joyce's schema has been most thoroughly undertaken by Richard Ellman in *Ulysses on the Liffey* (London: Faber and Faber, 1972; corrected edition, 1974).

9. A point similar to this has been made by Richard M. Kain in Marvin Magalaner and Kain, *Joyce: The Man, the Work, the Reputation* (London: John Calder, 1957), p. 203.

10. Contrary to the views of some aesthetic purists, however, he does have some; *Ulysses* clearly takes a stand against physical violence, as well as against such lesser evils as contraception.

11. *Ulysses on the Liffey*, p. 2.

12. Clive Hart, *James Joyce's Ulysses* (Sydney: Sydney University Press, 1968), p. 39.

13. *Dublin's Joyce* (London: Chatto and Windus, 1955), p. 189.

14. Quoted in Ellman, *Ulysses on the Liffey*, p. xvii.

15. It is interesting that Stephen's spirituality also seems to include his sexuality, and it is implied that Stephen might be a more complete Boylan symbolically.

16. *James Joyce* (New York: Oxford University Press, 1977 reprint; original edition 1959), p. 379.

17. That contemporary works of popular science had also adopted the catechism form in no way qualifies the fact that the form is one the novel would lead us to associate with the inverted theologian Stephen.

18. *Great Books of the Western World* (Chicago: Encyclopaedia Britannica, 1952), 53: 673.

19. This Yeatsian "universal memory" was invoked by Joyce in a discussion with Frank Budgen. "Further Recollections" (1955) reprinted in *James Joyce and the Making of "Ulysses" and other writings*, p. 361.

20. "Metaphor and the Cultivation of Intimacy," *Critical Inquiry* 5 (1978), 10.

21. *Ulysses: The Mechanics of Meaning* (Englewood Cliffs, N. J.: Prentice-Hall, 1970), pp. 55, 61.

22. This begs the vexed question of whether the ordinary reader is capable of retaining Joyce's and Spenser's vast networks in mind while engaged in the reading process. Perhaps no single human consciousness does have this power; perhaps the connections are retained below the conscious level and rise to the surface as context and memory demand; perhaps both writers addressed themselves to something larger than the unaided consciousness of a single mind.

23. *James Joyce*, pp. 370–371.

24. Ellmann, *Ulysses on the Liffey*, p. 30.

25. "Cyclops," *James Joyce's Ulysses: Critical Essays*, p. 251.

26. Howarth, *The Irish Writers 1880–1940: Literature Under Parnell's Star* (London: Rockliff, 1958), p. 260; Hühner, *Transactions* 5: 226. Hühner also notes that the Lord Mayor of Belfast in 1904 was a Jew, Sir Otto Jaffe, a fact that may lie behind Bloom's own political dreams.

27. Ed. A. C. Hamilton (London: Longman, 1977).

28. *Natural Symbols: Explorations in Cosmology* (London: Barrie and Jenkins, 1973; original edition, 1970), pp. 17, 12.

29. *James Joyce and the Making of "Ulysses" and other writings*, p. 21. Lindsey Tucker's *Stephen and Bloom at Life's Feast: Alimentary Symbolism and the Creative Process in James Joyce's "Ulysses"* (Columbus: Ohio State University Press, 1984) nowhere mentions Fletcher or Spenser or, indeed, any of the literary background of this symbolism. The use of this kind of symbolism in Dante's *Inferno* is discussed in Robert M. Durling, "Deceit and Digestion in the Belly of Hell," in *Allegory and Representation: Selected Papers from the English Institute, 1979–80*, ed. Stephen Greenblatt (Baltimore: Johns Hopkins University Press, 1981), pp. 61–93.

30. (London: Jonathan Cape, 1956; original edition, 1944), p. 32.

31. It also supplies a symbolic explanation of why Molly doubts she had a mother. Gea was produced from Chaos.

32. H. J. Rose, *A Handbook of Greek Mythology* (New York: E. P. Dutton and Co., 1959; original edition, 1928), p. 20.

33. As with most things in the novel, there is more than one reason for the inclusion of this conversation; another may be to imply a connection to *Paradise Lost*, with its discussion of cosmology between Raphael and Adam in Eve's absence.

34. James H. Maddox, Jr., *Joyce's Ulysses and the Assault upon Character* (Hassocks, Sussex: The Harvester Press; first published by Rutgers University Press, 1978), p. 11.

35. The charge laid against Spenser by Ben Jonson, that he wrote an English that no Englishman had ever used, would apply equally well to Joyce, who became even more Spenserian in *Finnegans Wake* (e.g., cf. Spenser's twenty-four stanza catalogue of English and Irish rivers in *FQ.* IV, xi with chapter 8 of *Finnegans Wake*).

36. (London: Calder and Boyars, 1970 reprint; original edition, 1938), p. 76.

37. (London: Calder and Boyars, 1970 reprint; original edition, 1953), pp. 30–31.

Notes to the Appendix

1. Primarily by Elizabeth Pope, *"Paradise Regained": The Tradition and the Poem* (1947; reprinted, New York: Russell & Russell, 1962).

2. See Barbara Kiefer Lewalski, *Milton's Brief Epic* (Providence, Rhode Island: Brown University Press, 1966).

3. "Milton and the Mysteries," *Studies in Philology*, 17, 147–169.

4. The British Museum possesses copies from 1490, 1490(?), 1500(?), 1532(?), 1539, and 1541–2. There is a modern edition by Omer Jodogne (Editions J. Duculor S.A.: Gembloux, Belgium, 1959). I cite the Jodogne edition in this appendix. Michel's play is itself based on the much briefer Gréban mystery play (unpublished until recent times). Michel has expanded radically the speeches of Gréban's Satan and has produced a work much closer to Milton than was his original.

5. It is not cited in the major treatments of Milton's analogues for *Paradise Regained* (i.e., Pope, Lewalski, and Watson Kirkconnell's *Awake the Courteous Echo* [Toronto: University of Toronto Press, 1973]). Nor is it mentioned in Walter MacKellar's *Variorum Commentary on the Poems of John Milton: Volume Four. Paradise Regained* (London: Routledge & Kegan Paul, 1975). Nor, unless I have overlooked something, is it referred to by early or modern editors of Milton, or in the critical studies of *Paradise Regained* that I have perused.

6. Michel, lines 3252–3254, 3273–3278; cf. *Paradise Regained* II, 66–104.

Bibliography

Primary Sources

Agrippa, Henry Cornelius. *Of the Vanitie and Uncertaintie of Artes and Sciences.* Trans. Ia. San. London, England, 1575.

Agrippa, Henry Cornelius. *Three Books of Occult Philosophy.* Trans. J. F. London, England, 1651.

Ariosto, Lodovico. *Orlando Furioso (The Frenzy of Orlando),* Part One. Trans. Barbara Reynolds. Harmondsworth, England: Penguin Books, 1975.

Augustine, St. *On Christian Doctrine* in *Great Books of the Western World.* Vol. 18. Chicago, Illinois: Encyclopaedia Britannica, 1952.

Bale, John. "The Temptation of Our Lord" in *The Dramatic Writings of John Bale.* Ed. John S. Farmer. London, England: Early English Drama Society, 1907.

Bateman, Stephen. *Batman uppon Bartholome, his Booke De Proprietatibus Rerum.* Trans. John Trevisa. London, England, 1582.

Beckett, Samuel. *Murphy.* London, England: Calder and Boyars, 1970 (original edition, 1938).

Beckett, Samuel. *Watt.* London, England: Calder and Boyars, 1970 (original edition, 1953).

Becon, Thomas. *Prayers and Other Pieces of Thomas Becon.* Ed. Rev. John Ayre. Cambridge, England: Parker Society, 1844.

Becon, Thomas. Works, Vol. III. Ed. Rev. John Ayre. Cambridge, England: Parker Society, 1844.

Bryskett, Lodowick. *A Discourse of Civill Life: Containing the Ethike part of Morall Philosophie.* London, England, 1606.

Calvin, John. *A Harmony of the Gospels Matthew, Mark and Luke.* Trans. A. W. Morrison. Edinburgh, Scotland: St. Andrew Press, 1972.

Casaubon, Meric. *A Treatise concerning Enthusiasme, as it is an effect of Nature; but is mistaken by many for either Divine Inspiration or Diabolical Possession.* Ed. Paul J. Korshin. Gainesville, Florida: Scholars' Facsimiles and Reprints, 1970 (original edition, 1655).

Davies, John, of Hereford. *The Complete Works of John Davies of Hereford.* Vol. 1. Ed. Alexander B. Grosart. Edinburgh, Scotland: Edinburgh University Press: Chertsey Worthies' Library, 1878.

Davies, Sir John. *The Poems of Sir John Davies.* Ed. Robert Krueger. Oxford, England: Clarendon Press, 1975.

Donne, John. *Essays in Divinity.* Ed. Evelyn M. Simpson. Oxford, England: Clarendon Press, 1952.

Donne, John. *The Sermons of John Donne.* Eds. George R. Potter and Evelyn M. Simpson. Berkeley and Los Angeles, California: University of California Press, 1953–1962.

Donne, John. *John Donne: The Anniversaries.* Ed. Frank Manley. Baltimore, Maryland: Johns Hopkins Press, 1963.

Ficino, Marsilio. *Marsilio Ficino's Commentary on Plato's Symposium*. Trans. Sears Reynolds Jayne. Columbia, Missouri: University of Missouri Press, 1944.

Ficino, Marsilio. *The Philebus Commentary*. Trans. Michael J. B. Allen. Berkeley and Los Angeles, California: University of California Press, 1975.

Foster, Frances A., ed. *A Stanzaic Life of Christ*. London, England: Early English Text Society (no. 166), 1926.

Harington, Sir John. "Preface to the Translation of *Orlando Furioso*" in *Elizabethan Critical Essays*. Vol. 2. Ed. G. Gregory Smith. London, England: Oxford University Press, 1904, pp. 194–222.

Herbert, Edward Lord. *De Veritate*. Trans. Meyrick H. Carré. Bristol, England: University of Bristol, 1937.

Herbert, George. *The Works of George Herbert*. Ed. F. E. Hutchinson. Oxford, England: Clarendon Press, 1941.

Hickes, George. *The Spirit of Enthusiasm Exorcised*. London, England, 1683 (3rd edition).

Homer. *The Iliad of Homer*. Trans. Richmond Lattimore. Chicago, Illinois: The University of Chicago Press, 1951.

Homer. *The Odyssey of Homer*. Trans. Richmond Lattimore. New York, New York: Harper and Row, 1967.

Iamblichus. *Iamblichus' Life of Pythagoras*. Trans. Thomas Taylor. London, England: John M. Watkins, 1965.

Ingpen, William. *The Secret of Numbers*. London, England, 1624.

James, William. *Principles of Psychology* in *Great Books of the Western World*. Vol. 53. Chicago, Illinois: Encyclopaedia Britannica, 1952.

Jonson, Ben. *Ben Jonson*. Eds. C. H. Herford, Percy and Evelyn Simpson. Oxford, England: Clarendon Press, 1947. Vol. VIII.

Joyce, James. *Ulysses*. Harmondsworth, England: Penguin Books, 1973 (original edition, 1922).

Joyce, James. *Finnegans Wake*. London, England: Faber and Faber, 1975 (original edition, 1939).

Joyce, James. *Stephen Hero*. London, England: Jonathan Cape, 1956 (original edition, 1944).

Locke, John. *An Essay Concerning Human Understanding*. Ed. Alexander Campbell Fraser. New York, New York: Dover Publications, 1959.

Ludolphus de Saxonia. *Vita Jesu Christi*. Ed. L. M. Rigollot. Paris, France and Brussels, Belgium: V. Palmé, 1878.

Luther, Martin. *Luther's Works*. Vol. 28. Ed. Hilton C. Oswald. St. Louis, Missouri: Concordia Publishing House, 1973.

Martianus Capella. *Martianus Capella and the Seven Liberal Arts, Vol. II: The Marriage of Philology and Mercury*. Trans. William Harris Stahl and Richard Johnson with E. L. Burge. New York, New York: Columbia University Press, 1977.

Michel, Jean. *Le Mystère de la Passion*. Ed. Omer Jodogne. Gembloux, Belgium: Editions J. Duculor S.A., 1959.

Milton, John. *The Complete Poetical Works of John Milton*. Ed. Douglas Bush. Boston, Massachusetts: Houghton Mifflin, 1965.

Milton, John. *The Poetical Works of John Milton*. Vol. 5. Ed. Henry J. Todd. London, England, 1809 (reprinted 1970).

Milton, John. *Complete Prose Works of John Milton.* Gen. ed. Don M. Wolfe. New Haven, Connecticut: Yale University Press, 1953–

More, Henry. *Enthusiasmus Triumphatus, 1662.* Ed. M. V. De Porte. Los Angeles, California: Augustan Reprint Society Publication Number 118, University of California Press, 1966.

Mornay, Philip de. *A Woorke Concerning the Trewnesse of the Christian Religion.* Trans. Sir Philip Sidney and Arthur Golding. London, England, 1587.

Plutarch. *The Philosophie, Commonlie Called, The Morals.* Trans. Philemon Holland. London, England, 1603.

Porphyry. *On the Cave of the Nymphs in the Thirteenth Book of the Odyssey.* Trans. Thomas Taylor. London, England: John M. Watkins, 1917.

Proclus. *The Elements of Theology.* Trans. E. R. Dodds. Oxford, England: Clarendon Press, 1963 (2nd edition).

Reynolds, Henry. *Mythomystes.* London, England, 1632.

Seneca. *Seneca his Tenne Tragedies.* Ed. T. Newton. London, England, 1581.

Seneca. L. A. *Seneca the Philosopher, His Booke of Consolation to Marcia Translated into an English Poem.* Trans. Ralph Freeman. London, England, 1635.

Spenser, Edmund. *A View of the State of Ireland.* Dublin, Ireland, 1633.

Spenser, Edmund. *The Works of Edmund Spenser: a Variorum Edition: The Faerie Queene. Book II.* Ed. Edwin Greenlaw. Baltimore, Maryland: Johns Hopkins Press, 1933.

Spenser, Edmund. *The Faerie Queene.* Eds. J. C. Smith and A. C. Hamilton. London, England and New York, New York: Longman, 1977.

Tasso, Torquato. *Discourses on the Heroic Poem.* Trans. Mariella Cavalchini and Irene Samuel. Oxford, England: Clarendon Press, 1973.

Taylor, Jeremy. *The Great Exemplar* in *The Whole Works of the Right Rev. Jeremy Taylor.* Vol. 2. London, England: Longman, etc., 1847.

Vaughan, Thomas. *Anthroposophia Theomagica; or A Discourse of the Nature of Man and his state after death.* London, England, 1650.

Vaughan, Thomas. *Anima Magica Abscondita or A Discourse of the Universal Spirit of Nature.* London, England, 1650.

Virgil. *The Eclogues, Georgics and Aeneid of Virgil.* Trans. C. Day Lewis. Oxford, England: Oxford University Press, 1966.

Secondary Sources

Allen, Don Cameron. *The Legend of Noah: Renaissance Rationalism in Art, Science and Letters.* Urbana, Illinois: University of Illinois Press, 1949.

Allen, Don Cameron. *Mysteriously Meant: The Rediscovery of Pagan Symbolism and Allegorical Interpretation in the Renaissance.* Baltimore, Maryland: Johns Hopkins Press, 1970.

Auden, W. H. *Collected Shorter Poems, 1927–1957.* London, England: Faber and Faber, 1969 (original edition, 1966).

Balakian, Anna. *Literary Origins of Surrealism: A New Mysticism in French Poetry.* London, England: University of London Press, 1967 (original edition, 1947).

Barker, Arthur E. "Calm Regained Through Passion Spent: The Conclusions of the Miltonic Effort" in *The Prison and the Pinnacle: Papers to Commemorate the*

Tercentenary of "Paradise Regained" and "Samson Agonistes" 1671–1971. Ed. Balachandra Rajan. London, England: Routledge and Kegan Paul, 1973, pp. 3–48.

Barthes, Roland. *Writing Degree Zero.* Trans. Annette Lavers and Colin Smith.
London, England: Jonathan Cape, 1967 (French original, 1953).

Barthes, Roland. *S/Z.* Trans. Richard Miller. London, England: Jonathan Cape,
1975 (French original, 1970).

Bender, John B. *Spenser and Literary Pictorialism.* Princeton, New Jersey: Princeton
University Press, 1972.

Berger, Harry, Jr. *The Allegorical Temper: Vision and Reality in Book II of Spenser's
"Faerie Queene."* New Haven, Connecticut: Yale University Press, 1957.

Bowers, Fredson Thayer. *Elizabethan Revenge Tragedy, 1587–1642.* Princeton, New
Jersey: Princeton University Press, 1940.

Budgen, Frank. *James Joyce and the Making of "Ulysses" and other writings.* London,
England: Oxford University Press, 1972.

Budick, Sanford. *The Dividing Muse: Images of Sacred Disjunction in Milton's Poetry.*
New Haven, Connecticut: Yale University Press, 1985.

Burns, Norman T. and Christopher J. Reagan, eds. *Concepts of the Hero in the
Middle Ages and the Renaissance: Papers of the Fourth and Fifth Annual Conferences
of the Center for Medieval and Early Renaissance Studies, State University of New
York at Binghamton 2–3 May 1970, 1–2 May 1971.* Albany, New York: State
University of New York Press, 1975.

Cain, Thomas H. *Praise in the Faerie Queene.* Lincoln, Nebraska: University of
Nebraska Press, 1978.

Carpenter, Mary Wilson. "Milton's Secret Garden: Structural Correspondences
Between Michael's Prophecy and *Paradise Regained*" in *Milton Studies XIV.* Ed.
James B. Simmonds. Pittsburgh, Pennsylvania: University of Pittsburgh Press,
1980, pp. 153–182.

Cassirer, Ernst. *The Philosophy of Symbolic Forms; Volume Two: Mythical Thought.*
Trans. Ralph Manheim. New Haven, Connecticut: Yale University Press, 1955
(German original, 1925).

Cassirer, Ernst. *The Individual and the Cosmos in Renaissance Philosophy.* Trans.
Mario Domandi. Oxford, England: Basil Blackwell, 1963 (German original,
1927).

Cassirer, Ernst. *The Platonic Renaissance in England.* Trans. James P. Pettegrove.
Austin, Texas: University of Texas Press, 1953 (German original, 1932).

Chew, Samuel C. *The Pilgrimage of Life.* New Haven, Connecticut: Yale University
Press, 1962.

Christopher, Georgia B. *Milton and the Science of the Saints.* Princeton, New Jersey:
Princeton University Press, 1982.

Clifford, Gay. *The Transformations of Allegory.* London, England and Boston, Massachusetts: Routledge and Kegan Paul, 1974.

Cohen, Ted. "Metaphor and the Cultivation of Intimacy." *Critical Inquiry,* 5 (1978),
3–12.

Colie, Rosalie L. *Paradoxia Epidemica: The Renaissance Tradition of Paradox.* Princeton, New Jersey: Princeton University Press, 1966.

Cope, Jackson I. "*Paradise Regained*: Inner Ritual" in *Milton Studies I.* Ed. James D.

Simmonds. Pittsburgh, Pennsylvania: University of Pittsburgh Press, 1969, pp. 51–65.

Cox, Lee Sheridan. "Food-Word Imagery in *Paradise Regained*." *ELH*, 28 (1961), 225–243.

Crane, Ronald S. "Anglican Apologetics and The Idea of Progress, 1699–1745." *Modern Philology*, 31 (1934), 349–382.

Crossley, Brian and Paul Edwards. "Spenser's Bawdy: A Note on *The Fairy Queen* 2.6." *Papers on Language and Literature*, 9 (1973), 314–319.

Cullen, Patrick. *Infernal Triad: The Flesh, the World, and the Devil in Spenser and Milton*. Princeton, New Jersey: Princeton University Press, 1974.

Curtius, Ernst Robert. *European Literature and the Latin Middle Ages*. Trans. Willard R. Trask. London, England: Routledge and Kegan Paul, 1953 (German original, 1948).

Docherty, Thomas. *Reading (Absent) Character: Towards a Theory of Characterization in Fiction*. Oxford, England: The Clarendon Press, 1983.

Douglas, Mary. *Purity and Danger: An Analysis of Concepts of Pollution and Taboo*. London, England: Routledge and Kegan Paul, 1966.

Douglas, Mary. *Natural Symbols: Explorations in Cosmology*. London, England: Barrie and Jenkins, 1973 (original edition, 1970).

Dunlap, Rhodes. "The Allegorical Interpretation of Renaissance Literature." *PMLA*, 82 (1967), 39–43.

Durling, Robert M. "Deceit and Digestion in the Belly of Hell" in *Allegory and Representation: Selected Papers from the English Institute, 1979–80*. Ed. Stephen Jay Greenblatt. Baltimore, Maryland: Johns Hopkins Press, 1981, pp. 61–93.

Edwards, Karen L. "On Guile and Guyon in *Paradise Lost* and *The Faerie Queene*." *Philological Quarterly*, 64 (1985), 83–97.

Eliade, Mircea. *Images and Symbols: Studies in Religious Symbolism*. Trans. Philip Mairet. London, England: Harvill Press, 1961 (French original, 1952).

Eliade, Mircea. *Myths, Dreams and Mysteries: The Encounter Between Contemporary Faiths and Archaic Realities*. Trans. Philip Mairet. London, England: Harvill Press, 1960 (French original, 1957).

Ellmann, Richard. *James Joyce*. New York, New York: Oxford University Press, 1977 (original edition, 1959).

Ellmann, Richard. *Ulysses on the Liffey*. London, England: Faber and Faber, 1972 (corrected edition, 1974).

Evans, Maurice. "The Fall of Guyon." *ELH*, 28 (1961), 215–224.

Finley, M. I. *The World of Odysseus*. London, England: Chatto and Windus, 1977 (second edition; original edition, 1956).

Finney, G. L. *Musical Backgrounds for English Literature: 1580–1650*. New Brunswick, New Jersey: Rutgers University Press, 1962.

Fletcher, Angus. *Allegory: The Theory of a Symbolic Mode*. Ithaca, New York: Cornell University Press, 1964.

Foucault, Michel. *The Order of Things: An Archaeology of the Human Sciences*. London, England: Tavistock Publications, 1970 (French original, 1966).

Fowler, Alastair. "The River Guyon." *Modern Language Notes*, 75 (1960), 289–292.

Fowler, Alastair. "The Image of Mortality: *The Faerie Queene*, II, i–ii." *Huntington Library Quarterly*, 24 (1961), 91–110.

Fowler, Alastair. *Triumphal Forms: Structural Patterns in Elizabethan Poetry.* Cambridge, England: Cambridge University Press, 1970.

Fowler, Alastair, ed. *Silent Poetry: Essays in numerological analysis.* London, England: Routledge and Kegan Paul, 1970.

Frye, Northrop. "The Typology of *Paradise Regained.*" *Modern Philology,* 53 (1956), 227–238.

Frye, Northrop. *Anatomy of Criticism: Four Essays.* Princeton, New Jersey: Princeton University Press, 1957.

Gilbert, Allan H. "Milton and the Mysteries." *Studies in Philology,* 17 (1920), 147–169.

Gilbert, Stuart. *James Joyce's Ulysses: A Study.* New York, New York: Vintage Books, 1952 (original edition, 1930).

Goldberg, Jonathan. *Endlesse Worke: Spenser and the Structures of Discourse.* Baltimore, Maryland and London, England: Johns Hopkins Press, 1981.

Goldberg, S. L. *The Classical Temper: A Study of James Joyce's Ulysses.* New York, New York: Barnes and Noble, 1961.

Gombrich, E. H. *Symbolic Images.* London, England: Phaidon, 1972.

Greenblatt, Stephen. *Renaissance Self-Fashioning: From More to Shakespeare.* Chicago, Illinois: University of Chicago Press, 1980.

Greene, Thomas. *The Descent From Heaven: A Study in Epic Continuity.* New Haven, Connecticut and London, England: Yale University Press, 1963.

Groden, Michael. *Ulysses in Progress.* Princeton, New Jersey: Princeton University Press, 1977.

Hankins, John Erskine. *Source and Meaning in Spenser's Allegory: A Study of the Faerie Queene.* Oxford, England: Clarendon Press, 1971.

Hardison, O. B., Jr. *The Enduring Monument: A Study of the Idea of Praise in Renaissance Literary Theory and Practice.* Chapel Hill, North Carolina: University of North Carolina Press, 1962.

Hart, Clive. *James Joyce's Ulysses.* Sydney, Australia: Sydney University Press, 1968.

Hart, Clive and David Hayman, eds. *James Joyce's Ulysses: Critical Essays.* Berkeley, California: University of California Press, 1974.

Haydn, Hiram. *The Counter Renaissance.* New York, New York: Charles Scribner's Sons, 1950.

Hayman, David. *Ulysses: The Mechanics of Meaning.* Englewood Cliffs, New Jersey: Prentice-Hall, 1970.

Heninger, S. K., Jr. *Touches of Sweet Harmony: Pythagorean Cosmology and Renaissance Poetics.* San Marino, California: Huntington Library, 1974.

Hill, Christopher. *Milton and the English Revolution.* London, England: Faber and Faber, 1977.

Hollander, John. *The Untuning of the Sky: Ideas of Music in English Poetry 1500–1700.* Princeton, New Jersey: Princeton University Press, 1961.

Hollander, John. "Spenser and the Mingled Measure." *English Literary Renaissance,* 1 (1971), 226–238.

Honig, Edwin. "Hobgoblin or Apollo." *Kenyon Review,* 10 (1948), 664–681.

Horton, Ronald Arthur. *The Unity of the Faerie Queene.* Athens, Georgia: University of Georgia Press, 1978.

Howarth, Herbert. *The Irish Writers 1880–1940: Literature Under Parnell's Star.* London, England: Rockliff, 1958.

Hughes, Merritt Y. "The Christ of *Paradise Regained* and the Renaissance Heroic Tradition." *Studies in Philology,* 35 (1938), 254–277.

Huizinga, J. *The Waning of the Middle Ages.* Trans. F. Hopman. Harmondsworth, England: Penguin Books, 1976 (original edition, 1924).

Hutton, James. "Some English Poems in Praise of Music." *English Miscellany,* 2 (1951), 1–64.

Hühner, Leon. "The Jews of Ireland: An Historical Sketch." *Transactions of the Jewish Historical Society of England,* 5 (for 1902–1905) (1908), 226–242.

Hyman, Lawrence W. "The Reader's Attitude in *Paradise Regained.*" *PMLA,* 85 (1970), 496–503.

Hynes, Sam L. "A Note on Donne and Aquinas." *Modern Language Review,* 48 (1953), 179–181.

Jackson, Robert S. *John Donne's Christian Vocation.* Evanston, Illinois: Northwestern University Press, 1970.

Jordan, Richard D. *The Temple of Eternity: Thomas Traherne's Philosophy of Time.* Port Washington, New York and London, England: Kennikat Press, 1972.

Jordan, Richard D. "*Paradise Regained* and the Second Adam" in *Milton Studies IX.* Ed. James D. Simmonds. Pittsburgh, Pennsylvania: University of Pittsburgh Press, 1976, pp. 261–275.

Kaske, Carol V. " 'Religious Reuerence doth Buriall Teene': Christian and Pagan in *The Faerie Queene,* II, i–ii." *Review of English Studies,* 30 (n.s.) (1979), 129–143.

Kenner, Hugh. *Dublin's Joyce.* London, England: Chatto and Windus, 1955.

Kermode, Frank. "Milton's Hero." *Review of English Studies,* 4 (n.s.) (1953), 317–330.

Kermode, Frank. "The Cave of Mammon" in *Elizabethan Poetry,* (Stratford-Upon-Avon Studies 2). London, England: Edward Arnold, 1960.

Kirkconnell, Watson. *Awake the Courteous Echo: The Themes and Prosody of "Comus," "Lycidas" and "Paradise Regained" in World Literature with Translations of the Major Analogues.* Toronto, Canada: University of Toronto Press, 1973.

Langer, Susanne K. *Philosophy in a New Key: A Study in the Symbolism of Reason, Rite, and Art.* Cambridge, Massachusetts: Harvard University Press, 1969 (original edition, 1942).

Lewalski, Barbara Kiefer. *Milton's Brief Epic: The Genre, Meaning, and Art of "Paradise Regained."* Providence, Rhode Island: Brown University Press, 1966.

Lewalski, Barbara Kiefer. *Donne's Anniversaries and the Poetry of Praise: The Creation of a Symbolic Mode.* Princeton, New Jersey: Princeton University Press, 1973.

Lewis, C. S. *The Allegory of Love.* New York, New York: Oxford University Press, 1958 (original edition, 1936).

Lewis, C. S. *Studies in Medieval and Renaissance Literature.* Cambridge, England: Cambridge University Press, 1966.

Lévi-Strauss, Claude. "How Myths Die." *New Literary History,* 5 (1974 [French original, 1971]), 269–281.

Lord, George deForest. "Folklore and Myth in *Paradise Regain'd*" in *Poetic Tra-*

ditions of the English Renaissance. Eds. Maynard Mack and George deForest Lord. New Haven, Connecticut: Yale University Press, 1982, pp. 229–249.

Lovejoy, Arthur O. *The Great Chain of Being: A Study in the History of an Idea.* New York, New York: Harper and Row, 1960 (original edition, 1936).

Low, Anthony. "Milton, *Paradise Regained,* and Georgic." *PMLA,* 98 (1983), 152–169.

MacCaffrey, Isabel. *Spenser's Allegory: The Anatomy of Imagination.* Princeton, New Jersey: Princeton University Press, 1976.

MacKellar, Walter. *Variorum Commentary on the Poems of John Milton:* Vol. 4; *Paradise Regained.* London, England: Routledge and Kegan Paul, 1975.

MacQueen, John. *Allegory.* London, England: Methuen and Company, 1970.

Maddox, James H., Jr. *Joyce's Ulysses and the Assault upon Character.* Hassocks, Sussex, England: The Harvester Press, 1978.

Magalaner, Marvin and Richard M. Kain. *Joyce: The Man, the Work, the Reputation.* London, England: John Calder, 1957.

Magill, A. J. "Spenser's Guyon and the Mediocrity of the Elizabethan Settlement." *Studies in Philology,* 67 (1970), 167–177.

Maresca, Thomas E. *Three English Epics: Studies of Troilus and Criseyde, The Faerie Queene, and Paradise Lost.* Lincoln, Nebraska: University of Nebraska Press, 1979.

Martz, Louis L. *The Poetry of Meditation: A Study in English Religious Literature of the Seventeenth Century.* New Haven, Connecticut and London, England: Yale University Press, 1962 (original edition, 1954).

Martz, Louis L. *Poet of Exile: A Study of Milton's Poetry.* New Haven, Connecticut and London, England: Yale University Press, 1980.

Maxwell, J. C. "Guyon, Phaedria, and the Palmer." *Review of English Studies,* 5 (n.s.) (1954), 388–390.

Milner, Andrew. *John Milton and the English Revolution: A Study in the Sociology of Literature.* London, England: Macmillan, 1981.

Murrin, Michael. *The Veil of Allegory: Some Notes Toward a Theory of Allegorical Rhetoric in the English Renaissance.* Chicago, Illinois: University of Chicago Press, 1969.

Nelson, William. *The Poetry of Edmund Spenser: A Study.* New York, New York: Columbia University Press, 1963.

Norhnberg, James. *The Analogy of The Faerie Queene.* Princeton, New Jersey: Princeton University Press, 1976.

North, Helen. *Sophrosyne: Self-Knowledge and Self-Restraint in Greek Literature.* Ithaca, New York: Cornell University Press, 1966.

Okerlund, Arlene N. "Spenser's Wanton Maidens: Reader Psychology and the Bower of Bliss." *PMLA,* 88 (1973), 62–68.

Panofsky, Erwin. *Studies in Iconology: Humanistic Themes in the Art of the Renaissance.* New York, New York: Oxford University Press, 1939 (German original, 1924).

Panofsky, Erwin. *Idea: A Concept in Art Theory.* Trans. Joseph J. S. Peake. Columbia, South Carolina: University of South Carolina Press, 1968.

Pope, Elizabeth M. *"Paradise Regained": The Tradition and the Poem.* New York, New York: Russell and Russell, 1962 (original edition, 1947).

Potts, Abbie Findlay. *Shakespeare and the Faerie Queene*. Ithaca, New York: Cornell University Press, 1958.

Price, Martin. "The Other Self: Thoughts about Character in the Novel" in *Imagined Worlds: Essays on some English Novels and Novelists in Honour of John Butt*. Eds. Maynard Mack and Ian Gregor. London, England: Methuen & Company, 1968.

Quilligan, Maureen. *The Language of Allegory: Defining the Genre*. Ithaca, New York and London, England: Cornell University Press, 1979.

Quilligan, Maureen. *Milton's Spenser: The Politics of Reading*. Ithaca, New York: Cornell University Press, 1983.

Renwick, W. L. *Edmund Spenser: An Essay on Renaissance Poetry*. London, England: Edward Arnold, 1961 (original edition, 1925).

Ricoeur, Paul. "Biblical Hermeneutics." *Semeia*, 4 (1975), 29–148.

Ricoeur, Paul. "The Metaphoric Process as Cognition, Imagination, and Feeling." *Critical Inquiry*, 5 (1978), 143–159.

Roche, Thomas P., Jr. *The Kindly Flame: A Study of the Third and Fourth Books of Spenser's Faerie Queene*. Princeton, New Jersey: Princeton University Press, 1964.

Rose, H. J. *A Handbook of Greek Mythology*. New York, New York: E. P. Dutton and Company, 1959 (original edition, 1928).

Rowse, A. L. *The Elizabethan Renaissance. The Cultural Achievement*. London, England: Sphere Books, 1974 (original edition, 1972).

Røstvig, Maren-Sofie. *The Hidden Sense and Other Essays*. Oslo and New York, New York: Universitetsforlaget and Humanities Press, 1963.

Samuel, Irene. "The Regaining of Paradise" in *The Prison and the Pinnacle: Papers to Commemorate the Tercentenary of "Paradise Regained" and "Samson Agonistes" 1671–1971*. Ed. Balachandra Rajan. London, England: Routledge and Kegan Paul, 1973.

Scholes, Robert and Robert Kellogg. *The Nature of Narrative*. New York, New York: Oxford University Press, 1966.

Seward, Barbara. *The Symbolic Rose*. New York, New York: Columbia University Press, 1960.

Seznec, Jean. *The Survival of the Pagan Gods: The Mythological Tradition and its Place in Renaissance Humanism and Art*. Trans. Barbara F. Sessions. Princeton, New Jersey: Princeton University Press, 1972 (French original, 1940).

Sirluck, Ernest. "Milton Revises *The Faerie Queene*." *Modern Philology*, 48 (1950), 90–96.

Skeat, Walter W. *A Concise Etymological Dictionary of the English Language*. New York, New York: Capricorn Books, 1963 (original edition, 1882).

Sloane, Thomas O. *Donne, Milton, and The End of Humanist Rhetoric*. Berkeley, California: University of California Press, 1985.

Sonn, Carl Robinson. "Sir Guyon in the Cave of Mammon." *Studies in English Literature*, 1 (1961), 17–30.

Spitzer, Leo. *Classical and Christian Ideas of World Harmony: Prolegomena to an Interpretation of the Word "Stimmung."* Ed. Anna G. Hatcher. Baltimore, Maryland: Johns Hopkins Press, 1963 (original published in *Traditio*, 1944–1945).

Stambler, Peter D. "The Development of Christian Temperance in Book II of *The Faerie Queene*." Syracuse, New York: Syracuse University Ph.D. thesis, 1974.

Stambler, Peter D. "The Development of Guyon's Christian Temperance." *English Literary Renaissance,* 7 (1977), 51–89.

Stanford, W. B. *The Ulysses Theme: A Study in the Adaptability of a Traditional Hero.* Oxford, England: Basil Blackwell, 1963 (second edition; original edition, 1954).

Stanford, W. B. and J. V. Luce. *The Quest for Ulysses.* New York, New York and Washington, D.C.: Praeger, 1974.

Stapleton, Laurence. "The Theme of Virtue in Donne's Verse Epistles." *Studies in Philology,* 55 (1958), 187–200.

Steadman, John M. *Milton and the Renaissance Hero.* Oxford, England: Clarendon Press, 1967.

Swearingen, Roger G. "Guyon's Faint." *Studies in Philology,* 74 (1977), 165–185.

Tillyard, E. M. W. *The Elizabethan World Picture.* London, England: Chatto and Windus, 1943.

Tillyard, E. M. W. *The English Epic and its Background.* New York, New York: Oxford University Press, 1954.

Tindall, William York. *The Literary Symbol.* New York, New York: Columbia University Press, 1955.

Todorov, Tzvetan. *Symbolism and Interpretation.* Trans. Catherine Porter. London, England: Routledge and Kegan Paul, 1983 (French original, 1973).

Tonkin, Humphrey. "Some Notes on Myth and Allegory in the *Faerie Queene.*" *Modern Philology,* 70 (1973), 291–301.

Tristram, Philippa. *Figures of Life and Death in Medieval English Literature.* London, England: Paul Elek, 1976.

Tucker, Lindsey. *Stephen and Bloom at Life's Feast: Alimentary Symbolism and the Creative Process in James Joyce's "Ulysses."* Columbus, Ohio: Ohio State University Press, 1984.

Tucker, Susie I. *Enthusiasm: A Study in Semantic Change.* Cambridge, England: Cambridge University Press, 1972.

Tuve, Rosemond. *Elizabethan and Metaphysical Imagery: Renaissance Poetic and Twentieth-Century Critics.* Chicago, Illinois and London, England: University of Chicago Press, 1947.

Tuve, Rosemond. *Allegorical Imagery: Some Mediaeval Books and Their Posterity.* Princeton, New Jersey: Princeton University Press, 1966.

Walker, D. P. *Spiritual and Demonic Magic From Ficino to Campanella.* London, England: Alec Tiranti, 1967 (original edition, 1958).

Walker, D. P. *The Ancient Theology: Studies in Christian Platonism from the Fifteenth to the Eighteenth Century.* Ithaca, New York: Cornell University Press, 1972.

Webber, Joan Malory. *Milton and His Epic Tradition.* Seattle, Washington: University of Washington Press, 1979.

Wetherbee, Winthrop. *Platonism and Poetry in the Twelfth Century: The Literary Influence of the School of Chartres.* Princeton, New Jersey: Princeton University Press, 1972.

Williams, Arnold. *The Characterization of Pilate in the Towneley Plays.* East Lansing, Michigan: Michigan State College Press, 1950.

Wilson, Edmund. *Axel's Castle: A Study in the Imaginative Literature of 1870–1930.* London, England: Collins, 1961 (original edition, 1931).

Wind, Edgar. *Pagan Mysteries in the Renaissance*. London, England: Faber and
  Faber Limited, 1968 (original edition, 1958).
Wittreich, Joseph Anthony, Jr. *Visionary Poetics: Milton's Tradition and His Legacy*.
  San Marino, California: Huntington Library, 1979.
Yates, Frances A. *The Art of Memory*. London, England: Routledge and Kegan
  Paul, 1966.
Yates, Frances A. *Theatre of the World*. Chicago, Illinois: University of Chicago
  Press, 1969.
Yates, Frances A. *The Occult Philosophy in the Elizabethan Age*. London, England
  and Boston, Massachusetts: Routledge and Kegan Paul, 1979.
Yeats, William B. *The Oxford Book of Modern Verse 1892–1935*. Oxford, England:
  Clarendon Press, 1936.

Index